Field Grown Cut Flowers

A Practical Guide and Sourcebook

Commercial Field Grown
Fresh and Dried Cut Flower Production

D1476053

by Alan B. Stevens

Avatar's World ™

Published by:
Avatar's World, 106 E. Hurd Road, Edgerton, WI 53534
800-884-4730 FAX: 608-884-6920 E-Mail: avatar@inwave.com

Field Grown Cut Flowers

A Practical Guide and Sourcebook

Commercial Field Grown
Fresh and Dried Cut Flower Production

by Alan B. Stevens

Edited by Susan Stevens
Cover Design by Concialdi Design
Cover Photo by Ball Seed Company
Graphic Design by Trish Muir Graphic Design
Illustrations by F. Gene Ernst

Library of Congress Catalog Card Number 96-86561

Main entry under title:

Field Grown Cut Flowers

Includes bibliographical references
1. Floriculture 2. Cut flower industry
3. Cut flowers 4. Plants, ornamental
5. Ornamental plant industry 6. Horticulture
ISBN 0-9653065-0-X

Second Edition 1998
First Edition 1997

Copyright © 1998 by Alan B. Stevens
All rights reserved. No part of this book may be reproduced
or transmitted in any form or by any means without written
permission of the author.

DEDICATION

This book is dedicated to the women in my life. All of whom have influenced, shaped, guided, softened, refined and prodded me into whatever I am today. From my grandmother's early training in the proper way to weed a flower bed; Kathleen and Anneee's love and friendship; the joy and beauty of my daughter, Susan; Judith Ann, my heart's most cherished song; an appreciation of country life from my Aunt Dorothy; to the dedication, loyalty and professionalism of my super secretary, Jane, they all have been the special flowers in my life.

This book was partially funded by an Agriculture Development and Diversification Grant awarded to John S. Hurd, owner of Avatar's World from the Wisconsin Department of Agriculture.

"More than anything, I must have flowers,

always, always."

-Claude Monet

TABLE OF CONTENTS

Acknowledgements 1

Preface 2

Introduction 3

Section 1: Marketing
Chapter 1 Marketing 12
Chapter 2 Choosing a Site 31

Section 2: Planting
Chapter 3 What to Grow 37
Chapter 4 When to Plant 55
Chapter 5 How to Plant 58

Section 3: Care As Needed
Chapter 6 Watering 71
Chapter 7 Fertilization 81
Chapter 8 Weed Control 99
Chapter 9 Insect Control 113
Chapter 10 Disease Control 134
Chapter 11 Vertebrate Pest Control 146

Section 4: Harvest
Chapter 12 Harvest 161
Chapter 13 Postharvest Handling 188
Chapter 14 Refrigerated Storage 196
Chapter 15 Preserving 207
Chapter 16 Color Processing 233

Appendix A: Crops 243

Appendix B: Lists, Lists & More Lists 333

Index 379

ACKNOWLEDGEMENTS

The following individuals have contributed to the information presented in various sections of this book. The author would like to acknowledge their assistance and thank them all for their help.

Nancy Anderson
Cooperative Extension Service, North Carolina . . Chapter 8

Robert Bauernfeind
Entomology, Kansas State University . . . . Chapter 9

Rolando Flores
Agricultural and Biosystems Engineering
Iowa State University . . . . Chapter 14

A. Karen Grangetto
International Decoratives Co. Inc., California . . . . Chapters 15, 16

John Hurd
Avatar's World, Wisconsin . . . . Chapter 12

Mark Koch
Robert Koch Industries, Inc. . . . . Chapters 15, 16

James Nechols
Entomology, Kansas State University . . . . Chapter 9

Judy O'Mara
Plant Pathology, Kansas State University . . . . Chapter 10

Ned Tisserat
Plant Pathology, Kansas State University . . . . Chapter 10

John Zehrer
Star Valley Flowers, Wisconsin. . . . . Chapter 8

A special thanks is also due John Dole of Oklahoma State University for his critical review of the manuscript. This book is much improved as the result of his thoughtful suggestions.

The author would also like to thank all the growers who have opened their farms, provided tours and so openly shared information and ideas about growing and marketing.

PREFACE

Agricultural producers looking for ways to enhance their incomes may consider field production of specialty fresh or dried cut flowers. This is an old segment of the floriculture industry currently in revival across the country, with new technology, varieties and market conditions. Growers can profitably serve the national, regional and local markets that already exist for high-quality cut flowers. As an emerging industry, it offers unique opportunities for those who enter in its early stages of development.

This book discusses marketing approaches, basic production factors and management issues for those beginning cut-flower production. Lists of sources for supplies and references for further reading are included as an aid in getting started. The term 'cut flower' in this book refers to all fresh and dried flowers, seed heads and stalks, fruits and vegetables, branches, vines and all plant parts used for floral and decorative purposes.

Portions of the information contained in this book have been previously presented by the author in a series of Kansas State University Cooperative Extension Service publications. The material is presented here in an effort to make it available to those outside the State of Kansas. These sections have been updated and expanded to provide a much greater depth of information than was originally presented.

INTRODUCTION
THE STEVENS LABOR MODEL

Planting:	all activities involved with planning, preparing and planting into the production bed.
Care as Needed:	all activities involved with the actual growing of the plants (product), i.e., watering, fertilizing, weeding, insect and disease control.
Harvest:	all activities involved with harvesting and delivering the product to the customer, i.e., cutting, handling, storage, packing, shipping.

The heart of this book is organized around the Stevens Labor Model. Marketing is discussed in Section 1, because you should plant only what you can sell. Section 2 covers planting, including crop selection, time to plant and how to plant. Section 3 covers caring for the plants, including watering, fertilizer, weed, insect and disease control. Section 4 covers harvest and postharvest handling. Appendix A lists more detailed descriptions of some crops. Appendix B provides a list of additional literature and sources for most anything you might need to buy to grow and market your specialty cut flowers.

Get Out of the Field — Make Time For Lunch.

Old Willy, a 72-year-old grower from Germany, taught me a valuable lesson in my first job in a greenhouse in Chicago. I had asked Willy how long my workday was going to be. "25 hours," he replied. Being the brash young lad that I was, I said, "But

Willy, everyone knows there's only 24 hours in a day." "I know," was the reply. "The extra hour is your lunch hour." Willy's message was clear. If I wanted to have "lunch" (or dinner or sleep or anything else), I would have to manage my time, the crew and all our activities.

Willy had an invaluable lesson for anyone in business: labor management is critical to success. This holds true whether you hire others to work or you intend to do everything yourself. Managing labor is not the exclusive domain of larger companies with many employees. It is even more critical for family farms where the owners do everything, where there are no employees or perhaps only a little part-time help. Old Willy may have found 25 hours in a day, but even he could find no more. If the owners of a family business with no employees fail to manage their own labor wisely, they may soon lack balance in their lives with no time for family or friends or lunch. They run the risk of becoming a slave to their business.

You must step back from the process, get out of the field, wash your hands, manage your business and make time for lunch. Design systems – ways of doing things – to get the job done more efficiently. Achieve in 36 hours what it now takes 40 hours to accomplish. As little as a 10 percent reduction in labor can have a dramatic effect on profits.

Design Systems

Design no-decision systems, ways of doing each task that don't require decisions to be made to do the job. This doesn't mean your workers are unintelligent, only that they shouldn't be required to make decisions to operate the system. Two things happen when workers are required to make decisions: labor cost goes up and quality goes down. It takes time to reach a decision, and therefore any system that requires a decision to be made is less efficient. It is the time spent in indecision, or more correctly in **extended indecision** that wastes time and increases labor costs. In addition, no two people will reach exactly the same decision; each step in a process that requires a decision introduces variables, leading to a nonuniform product. Product variability means quality variability. Quality variability in the perception of a customer is deadly in the marketplace.

Mixing a tank of fertilizer solution to apply through a drip irrigation system is an example of a system that may require many decisions. A given weight of fertilizer must be mixed with a given amount of water. Workers scoop the dry fertilizer from the bag and weigh it on the scale, adding a little or removing a little, back and forth until the exact weight is reached. They also measure the gallons of water required. They must make these measurements each time a new batch of fertilizer is mixed. In a no-decision system, management would measure the fertilizer one time, then find a container that just held that amount of fertilizer. They would mark the solution tank with a line showing how high to fill it with water. In this system, workers don't have to measure the fertilizer or the water each time. Rather, they simply fill the can to the top with fertilizer, brush the excess off, dump it in the solution tank and fill the tank with water to the fill line. A similar system should be developed for everything that needs to be done.

No one knows more about doing a job than the worker who does it. A no-decision system design does not ignore the worker's knowledge, for that know-how is critical in designing the systems to be used. Workers should play a major role in designing systems to do each and every job that needs to be done. Their input will make for better systems, and by being part of the process they will more readily accept and follow the system. No-decision systems cannot be designed for every task required to plant, grow, harvest and market specialty cut flowers. For any task where it is not possible to eliminate the decisions, workers should be trained and retrained constantly. This training should not be done in a formal manner, but simply by the next level supervisor working elbow to elbow with individual workers, gently reminding them of the desired criteria for making the decision. Growers without employees, who do all the work themselves, should simply remind themselves of the desired criteria as they walk out to the field to do the job. This simple recalling of the criteria will result in greater speed in accomplishing the task at hand (eliminating extended indecision) and greatly improve uniformity of the crop.

Activity Chain

Examine all of the activities of your firm. Think of each activity as a link of a chain. A chain is no stronger than its weakest link; a firm can be no stronger than its weakest activity.

Most flower producers are plant people. We concentrate on production. We trust that a high-quality flower is all it takes to be successful. But growing flowers is only part of what we do. If a new person asks what they need to know about specialty cut flowers, they are usually told about watering, fertilizing, weeding, insects, diseases — everything involved with the actual growing of flowers. All of these activities are important in producing a quality cut flower, but they are only part of the production process. **The "Care As Needed" activities represent only a minor portion of the labor required to produce specialty cut flowers.** Watering labor is minimal, especially with drip irrigation. Fertilizer is applied infrequently or through the drip line. With good basic cultural practices, insect and disease control do not require large blocks of time. Mulches and herbicides greatly reduce the labor required for weeding production beds. The activities we think of as growing our product, the "Care as Needed" activities, typically account for only 20 percent to 25 percent of the total labor required for production. Yet these are the activities most growers concentrate on.

Planting accounts for another 20 percent to 25 percent of total direct labor. Planting activities are part of production. They are accomplished before we begin to grow our cut-flower product. How they are done influences the efficiency of the "Care as Needed" activities and the quality of the final product. Poor bed-preparation, inconsistent plant spacing, planting too deep or too shallow and nonuniform distribution of incorporated fertilizer will affect labor usage for the rest of the production cycle.

In many specialty cut-flower firms, labor activities associated with harvest are the most poorly managed. As plant people our focus has been on growing. By harvest time production is over; we are no longer growing anything. But approximately 50 percent of all direct labor is used in harvest activities. **The greatest potential for direct labor cost reduction may be in harvest-related activities.** The area of greatest labor expense is often the area least-managed, at least as far as labor efficiency is concerned. Although we manage bunch size, preservative concentration, cold storage temperatures, packaging and delivery, we often fail to manage the labor used in selecting, bunching, preserving, storing, packaging and delivering our flowers.

Remember the message on no-decision systems: Eliminate extended indecision by eliminating or reducing decisions. The greatest potential for labor savings among harvest activities is in the select-and-cut activity. Selecting and cutting a flower stem requires two basic decisions:

1. To cut or not to cut the stem
   (based on stage of maturity, condition, etc.)

2. Where to cut the stem
   (how many nodes to leave below the cut, stem length, etc.)

Both are complex decisions. The chance for time delay while the worker makes a decision is great for each stem to be cut. If a no-decision system cannot be satisfactorily designed, then labor must be trained and continually retrained to make the required decisions quickly without undo thought. Try to prevent the worker, or yourself, from becoming stuck in extended indecision. In our research on labor usage, we have seen labor reductions of as much as 80 percent from initiating continuous training and from refining the selection activity.

This section has described some basic operations-management concepts for using labor efficiently in the production process. The actual growing of the flower stem (Care as Needed) is only a small part of production, and production is only part of a firm. To be a profitable firm, the whole firm, all activities, must be well-managed. **Make time for lunch.**

make time for lunch !

A Whole-Firm Approach

As stated earlier, a firm can be no better than its weakest activity. Systems need to be developed to accomplish each activity in a most efficient way. Consider the whole firm and the interdependency of all areas of the company. The goal is to reach the lowest possible cost structure for the entire firm while still maintaining quality of product and service. **Do not increase efficiency by decreasing quality; without quality, you may be out of the market.** The following graphic provides a representation of the company's activities.

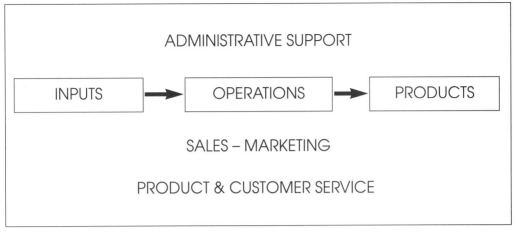

Inputs: all activities involved with having all required inputs available and ready for use when needed.

Operations: all activities involved with the production process (Planting, Care as Needed and Harvest activities).

Products: all activities involved with delivery of product, both goods and services.

The tendency among growers is to concentrate on production because their main interests lie with their crops. Inputs are considered because they are physical objects which we use in production. We also pay attention to our products because they are what we have to sell. The whole firm, all the activities of a company, must be considered in designing systems. As the graphic above displays, the activities of administrative support, sales-marketing and product & customer service all are linked to, and surround, the main line production activities.

Linkages — The All-Important Connection

An Olympic 400-meter relay race team is brought together by recruiting the four fastest 100-meter sprinters in the world. The final race for the gold medal begins. The first runner gains a lead over competing teams. The second runner increases the lead, as does the third. The team is leading by a good margin, but as the last sprinter comes up, the baton is dropped. The runner is left in the dust and the race is lost while the dropped baton is being recovered. The fastest runners in the world don't even place in the race.

A lower cost structure is achieved by designing systems for all activities, but the individual activities are only part of the process. The best designed and executed systems can be no better than the linkages that connect them.

To build solid links between activities, treat the next activity in the chain like a customer. Just as a firm has external customers who purchase its product, it has internal customers — whatever happens to be next in the activity chain. Value is provided to a customer by enhancing the customer's performance or by lowering the customer's costs. Inside a firm, each activity should enhance the performance or lower the cost of the next activity, its internal customer. Design an activity both for efficiency *and* for how it affects the performance and cost of the next activity. **Don't drop the baton.**

Summary

To be a better firm, all activities and linkages must be better managed. To compete in the marketplace, you must use management to achieve the lowest possible cost structure for your firm. Don't grow what you can't sell. If you make less than it costs, you lose money. Labor is everything. Design no-decision systems. Get out of the field. Make time for lunch. Don't drop the baton.

Section 1

MARKETING

Chapter 1 Marketing 12

Chapter 2 Choosing a Site 31

CHAPTER 1

MARKETING

Flowers can be marketed to a flower wholesaler, to a retail florist or directly to the public at a farmers market. Each market has advantages and disadvantages.

Direct to the public is the easiest market to enter. Sorting, handling and packaging are usually minimal, as is the capital investment. A wide variety of species and cultivars may be sold with success. The disadvantage is the volume of sales per customer may limit the income.

Wholesalers will accept large volumes of flowers. However, you will have to package, sort and grade flowers to their specifications, and they may not accept some specialty flowers. They set the price for your flowers. Also, it takes a while for the grower and wholesaler to develop a good working relationship.

Retail florists buy from wholesalers. If you market directly to the florist, you cut out the middleman and can get a higher wholesale price for your flowers. Florists may not be as concerned with packaging as wholesalers, but they will insist on the same high quality. While florists may be more interested in specialty flowers than wholesalers, you will have to deal with several florists to sell the same volume you would to a wholesaler.

> The market or markets you choose to enter must provide sufficient profit margins for you to stay in business.

Direct Sales to the Consumer

The sale of specialty cut flowers directly to the final consumer is the easiest approach to marketing for the beginning grower. The flowers need not be graded, a wider range of quality and maturity is acceptable, and consistent, reliable supply is not as critical. The appearance, the visual impact of the flowers on display and their perceived value are the criteria of this market. Retail sales, directly to the final consumer, is also the most educational of market approaches for the beginning grower. With each sale growers receive feedback from their customers on their flowers and services. A beginning grower will soon learn what people want to buy and in what form they would like it to be offered for sale.

On-Farm Sales

Selling flowers directly from the farm has advantages in transportation, labor utilization and consumer perceptions. A vehicle is not required to transport the flowers to market. Production and marketing can be managed from a single location; the entire spectrum of business activities takes place together on the farm. Customers come to the farm to make their purchases. What flower can be fresher than that purchased from the grower at the farm? Also, production labor activities can be integrated with household and family activities. Parents can be home when children return from school each day.

A major disadvantage of on-farm sales is the necessity of maintaining the farm in a neat and orderly condition at all times. This includes weed control in the production beds. Any marketing advantage gained by on-farm sales can be quickly lost if the customer encounters a disorderly and weedy mess. The higher level of farm maintenance labor incurs a higher cost structure which must be considered in the planning process.

Many of the most successful growers who sell directly to consumers from the farm have made the experience of buying flowers an event in the lives of their customers. They have packaged the buying experience as entertainment for their customers. Special events, elementary school tours and seasonal crop harvests all serve to create customer traffic. Growers who wish to sell directly from the farm should consider providing a reason for customers to make a special trip out to buy flowers.

Roadside Stand

Selling farm produce from roadside stands set up on the farm is a common practice. The stand may be as simple as a temporary table set up in the front yard to sell excess produce from the family garden, to a complete retail operation with permanent buildings, paved parking and full-time, permanent sales staff. A selection of mixed bouquets, buckets of flowers sold by the single stem, and floral arrangements may be offered for sale. Flowers may be the main attraction or may be sold in conjunction with other produce. The location of any retail outlet is a critical factor. Before investing capital and effort into a roadside stand, the quality and quantity of traffic on the road needs to be analyzed. Will enough people traveling down the road stop and buy, or will you need to be able to draw customers from the surrounding area?

Figure 1-1: A Roadside Stand

Pick-Your-Own

A pick-your-own marketing strategy is a variation of the roadside stand approach. It has the strategy of delivering the best and freshest possible product to the consumer. What can be better than a product that consumers selected themselves? What can be fresher than a flower the customer picked?

The physical layout of the production area must be designed to facilitate harvest by the customer. Beds need to be narrow, allowing customers to easily reach the center to pick those flowers we all know grow better there than along the edge. Aisles need to be wider and constructed in such a way to keep the customer out of the mud; they should be planted to grass, heavily mulched, covered with gravel, or paved.

Customers are encouraged to stroll through the production area and cut all the flowers they wish. They are charged by the stem for each one selected. Workers also cut flowers at the end of each day. These are offered for sale the next day to those customers who don't wish to spend the time or effort to cut their own. At first thought, it would seem that harvest labor would be reduced by having customers pick their own flowers, but this is often more than offset by having to repair the damage done to plants and beds.

Off-Farm Sales

Owners of farms that are relatively inaccessible due to poor roads or distance from population centers, or who simply do not wish to have customers coming to the farm at all times will need to explore opportunities to market their products off the farm. Sales can be greatly enhanced by selling off the farm, but capital and labor requirements will also be increased. A vehicle to transport the flowers and display fixtures and labor to load, unload, set up, sell, take down, load and unload on each day will be required.

Roadside Sales

Selling flowers directly from the back of a truck or from temporary stands on street corners and alongside highways is common in many areas. Roadside sales provide growers with the opportunity to sell their product in locations with potentially high customer traffic without making a long-term capital investment in real estate. The best locations have people passing by on their way to shop and traveling at relatively slow speeds or stopping at the corner. Locations where drivers are traveling at higher speeds or are on their way to activities of long duration are less likely to attract many customers. Ideal locations should have space for drivers to safely pull off the road and to park while making their purchases.

A variation of roadside marketing is to approach the owner of a strip shopping mall and negotiate an agreement to use a portion of the parking lot for selling. This may be for every day of the growing season, weekends only or for a few days during harvest of a seasonal crop. Temporary or short-term sales from vacant lots is another possibility. Renting parking space or empty lots provides the owners with extra income from their real estate investment and therefore may be reasonable in cost to the grower.

Growers considering roadside sales should check local ordinances on peddling and sales from temporary stands. Figure 1-2 illustrates how flower marketing can be as simple as selling off the back of your truck.

Figure 1-2: Sales From the Truck

Farmers Markets

Farmers markets are an ideal first market for a new grower of specialty cut flowers. Customers are most forgiving of quality, quantity, availability and display. Prices received are often higher than any other market. It is a market that pays relatively higher prices with lower expectations of the grower. In short it is an excellent place to get started selling specialty cut flowers.

Farmers markets are also an excellent surplus outlet for growers with other primary markets. A Saturday farmers market is a good place to sell surplus production which remains unsold at the end of the week. The flowers offered for sale must be of high quality, but they can and should be slightly more mature than those offered to wholesale markets.

Growers of fruit and vegetables who sell their produce at farmers markets know that their customers are very sensitive to the price of a pound of tomatoes, sweet corn, green beans or peaches. The prices they charge must be in line with others selling the same items at that farmers market, and with prices charged at the local grocery stores. Buyers of fruit and vegetables are sophisticated in the marketplace. Buyers of flowers at farmers markets are not. Who knows how much a bunch of mixed flowers should cost? A bunch from one grower rarely will have the same flowers as a bunch from another grower, making any comparison difficult. If the flowers have visual impact and are of a size to have perceived value at the asking price, people will buy them and not question the price. Customers shopping for salad fixings can still have a salad whether or not they purchase tomatoes. Substitutes are readily available for fruit and vegetables. What substitutes exist for flowers? What product sold at a farmers market is a substitute for flowers?

Flowers can be sold at farmers markets for higher profit margins than food crops. Flower sales at farmers markets range from a hundred dollars to several thousand dollars for the day. Growers selling at certain urban markets have reported gross sales of over $100,000 for a season. The quality of the booth, product and sales staff; the size, quality and composition of the farmers market; and the number and quality of buyers coming to the market all affect the amount of product sold.

Many farmers markets are held in parking lots. No shade and a hot sun baking the asphalt combine to wilt flowers and customers. A covered sales area will help to maintain flower quality and encourage customers to linger a little longer. Figure 1-3 illustrates a simple and unobstructed sales area.

Figure 1-3: A Covered Sales Area

Place some of your product up, off the ground, and put it on display up where customers can smell the flowers. Use three-dimensional space for greater visual impact of your flowers. Decorate your sales area. Make coming to buy your flowers a weekly event in your customers' lives. Note the balloons "supporting" the tent over the sales area in Figure 1-4. Little things can contribute to a festive atmosphere.

Figure 1-4: Creating Visual Impact

Merchandise your flowers. Display them to appeal to your customers. Figure 1-5 shows a variety of container shapes and sizes being used to display both fresh and dried flowers. Figure 1-6 shows dried flowers in bunches and made into a wreath displayed on a simple lattice wall.

Figure 1-5: Display Containers

Figure 1-6: A Lattice Wall Display

Craft Fairs

Craft fairs are an excellent sales opportunity. Very small growers may obtain booth space in only one or two fairs and be able to sell their entire year's production. Others may choose to sell at a fair each week throughout the summer and fall craft fair season. A variety of items are sold at craft fairs, ranging from wreaths, swags and arrangements to picture frames and candles decorated with dried flowers. Merchandising — displaying your creativity — is important when selling at craft fairs. Your display must showcase your artistic talents, or potential customers will think "I can do that" and not buy what you're offering for sale. Small bunches of a single species can also be offered for sale to the I-can-do-it-myselfers, who come to the fair not to buy but to get ideas for their own craft projects. Sales range from a few hundred dollars to a few thousand dollars over a three-day weekend fair. A variation of selling at a craft fair is selling from a booth at the local county fair, or at any gathering of a large number of people strolling around and stopping to look at anything which attracts their attention. Impulse sales predominate, so be sure to have a selection of items priced appropriately.

The amount of direct labor required by each of the marketing options should be considered when deciding on a marketing approach. Selling directly to consumers from off the farm requires an increased amount of labor. Flowers and display fixtures must be loaded onto a truck, driven to where they are going to be sold, unloaded from the truck, the display fixtures set up, flowers placed on display, flowers sold, money handled, unsold flowers loaded back onto the truck, fixtures disassembled and loaded, the truck driven back to the farm and everything unloaded and put away. A lot of labor. Systems should be designed to make all labor required as effective as possible. Fixtures should be designed to be easy to load and unload and for ease of set-up and disassembly. A system should be designed to easily transport flowers to and from the truck and for ease of loading and unloading. Consider how you will do everything that needs to be done to sell from the truck, or at a farmers market, craft fair or wherever sales will take place. Remember to consider the cost of this labor when estimating income from your operation.

Other opportunities exist for selling specialty cut flowers direct to consumers:

Restaurants — Many restaurants place flowers on their tables. Contract to replace them with fresh flowers each week and perhaps an arrangement or large bouquet near the front entrance.

Banks — Fresh flowers at each teller's window and on each customer service desk create a softer banking environment. Approach your own bank about providing the flowers, for after all, they should want to do business with someone who brings their banking business to them.

Hotels/Motels — Hotels and motels offer a couple of opportunities for flower sales. Fresh flowers can be placed on the registration counter, on the receptionist's desk in the administrative offices, and in the lobby at the front entrance. These flowers could be replaced weekly. Another opportunity exists in the guest rooms. Few motels can justify the cost of fresh flowers in guest rooms, but they might consider a small dried flower arrangement placed on the table in each room and replaced annually or semi-annually.

Corporate Gifts — Many companies send gifts to customers, employees and employee spouses. Why not flowers, either fresh, dried or glycerin-preserved? Offer to provide a choice of floral products to meet their gift needs. Custom-design something that is distinctive of their company.

Subscription — Offer a subscription service where you periodically deliver a seasonal selection of flowers to the subscriber's home or office. This may be a weekly, bi-weekly or monthly service. It could also be a special-occasion service where flowers are delivered on a spouse's birthday, wedding anniversary and Valentine's Day. Fresh flowers would be used during the growing season and dried or glycerin-preserved arrangements would be delivered when fresh flowers are not available.

Classified Ads — Dried flowers and glycerin-preserved plant materials can be sold by placing classified advertisements in craft magazines. Craft hobbyists read craft magazines, become excited about creating something featured in the magazine and begin a search for the materials required. Your ad in the classified section, encouraging the reader to buy directly from the grower, may be just what they're looking for.

Value-Added Activities

Opportunities abound for marketing value-added products. A value-added product is one where the basic flower has been processed in some way to add value to it. This may be as simple as placing it in a bouquet, using it in an arrangement of fresh flowers, preserving it as a dried flower or placing it in a unique package. Value-added products can be sold through any of the above outlined marketing strategies.

A few ideas for selling value-added products and services are:

- dried flower bouquets, decorations, wreaths sold at craft fairs

- three to five decorative items sold to a retailer for a special promotion

- dried or glycerin-preserved decorations sold through furniture stores

- dried or glycerin-preserved decorations sold through interior decorators

- a premium decorative piece sold through a mail-order catalog

- design materials sold to consumers at workshops you hold

- preserved arrangements and decorations sold to gift shops

Value can be added through simple accessories such as a weathered board with wooden pegs used to hang a few bunches of dried herbs as in Figure 1-7.

Figure 1-7: A Wooden Hanger With Herbs

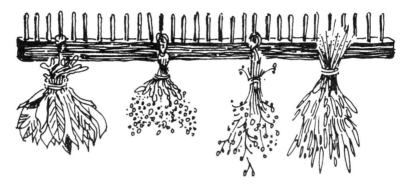

Design talent can be used to add value by creating an arrangement such as shown in Figure 1-8.

Figure 1-8: A Floral Wall Arrangement of Dried Flowers

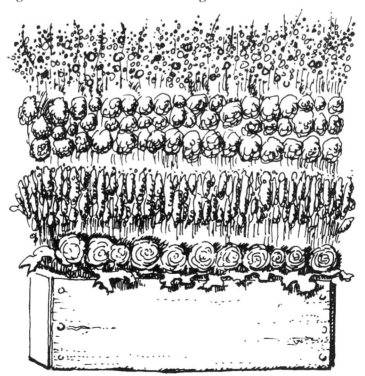

Figure 1-9 illustrates a variety of value-added products created with dried and glycerin-preserved decorative plant materials.

Figure 1-9: A Variety of Dried and Glycerin-Preserved Products

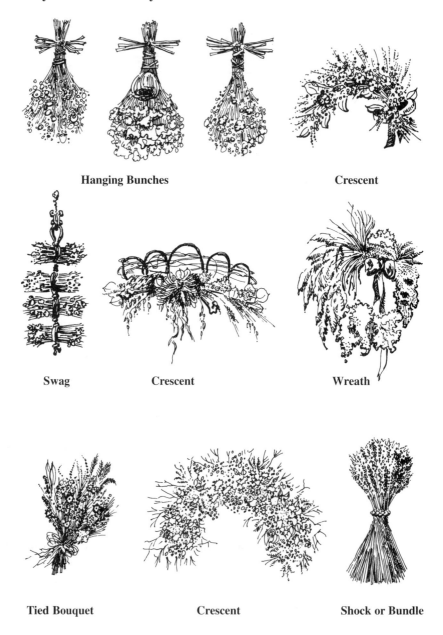

Hanging Bunches   **Crescent**

Swag   **Crescent**   **Wreath**

Tied Bouquet   **Crescent**   **Shock or Bundle**

To market value-added products you will need to convince others that you have the ability to deliver the product. Part of convincing them will be to describe how you will achieve the desired level of production. Systems will need to be developed to manufacture the value-added products. Think of your barn as a factory. Set up a production line. Design a system to do each labor activity. Describe these systems in your business plan and follow them when you get into production. Assembly labor can quickly consume all your potential profits. Don't get so absorbed in the beauty of your creations that you neglect to use all labor as effectively as possible.

National Mail-Order Catalogs

The huge influx of mail-order catalog companies has created opportunities to sell value-added products to a national market-place. Flowers can be grown and value-added products manufactured in rural areas far removed from densely populated cities and still be sold across the country. A consumer will call the catalog company to place an order and charge it to a credit card. The catalog company will notify the grower of the sale, and the grower will then ship the product directly to the consumer, usually by UPS or parcel post. At the end of the month, the catalog company pays the grower for the products sold and shipped during the month. Much of this communication is from computer to computer, speeding the process and reducing errors. Growers attempting to interest a catalog company in displaying their product should study a few previous issues of the catalog to learn the company's market niche and approach to marketing. Products can be designed and samples produced to fit the target market of the catalog company. A quality product alone is not sufficient to interest a catalog company. Growers will also have to convince the company that they have the ability to produce the item in sufficient quantities and to ship in a timely manner. Packaging that provides visual impact and assures the product will arrive in good condition will also be required.

Computer Sales —
World Wide Web & Online Internet Services

The age of direct selling through online computer services has arrived. Like with mail-order, you can sit in your barn in a rural location and sell directly to consumers anywhere in the country (or the world). Customers can access your advertising (home page) on their computer, make a purchase with a credit card and you can ship it via any of the rapid delivery companies in your area. You can do this as an individual company or you might want to subscribe to a commercial online directory, which charges a fee to list you along with a number of other firms offering products in a particular category. Professional assistance in setting up a home page and developing marketing materials is available.

Wholesale Sales

Wholesale Sales to Retailers

Sales to retailers increase the amount sold per customer. Each individual sale becomes less costly. After selling directly to consumers, sales to retailers will generally provide the next highest prices for your flowers. This market approach has greater grading, uniformity and consistency of supply requirements than selling directly to consumers. You and the retailer define what will be acceptable in terms of grading and packaging. Retailers need a reliable source of supply for the products they sell. You must have product available when they need it, because they count on you to deliver the goods.

Potential retailers include:
- Florists

- Grocery Stores

- Craft Stores

- Garden Centers

- Produce Markets

A first step in selling to retailers may be to offer them mixed bouquets. Two sizes, an average sized one and a larger one or one with "premium flowers" is a good way to start. Try approaching retail florists with a mixed bouquet for them to sell to their customers as cash-and-carry weekend bouquets or "Friday Flowers." Point out the labor savings of having the bouquets delivered pre-made instead of using their higher cost floral designers. The bouquets are a good item for you. They require extra labor but they allow you to use whatever species you have in bloom. The contents can be adjusted slightly to help use up items in surplus each week. Once you have begun selling to a retailer and have built a relationship, you can then expand your offerings to bunches of a single-type flower.

Another marketing approach to try is to sell specials. A special is a product(s) which the retailer markets as a promotional item, advertising it as a special for that time period, usually a weekend or holiday. The product is custom designed by the grower to provide value to the consumer and yet be able to be supplied at a cost low enough to be profitable. Specials are often contracted for in advance and crops grown specifically for that use. Many chain store retailers contract with growers for a series of specials to be supplied during a season.

Wholesale Sales to Wholesalers

Selling to wholesale florists is the most demanding as far as grading, uniformity, consistency and packaging. The prices you will receive will be lower than in other markets. A single sales call will sell a lot of product. You'll have fewer but larger accounts. Your cost of labor to sell your products will be less. Most large growers sell a portion if not all of their production to wholesalers. You can't be in competition with your customers, so you may consider selling directly to local consumers or retailers, and selling to distant wholesalers who sell to retailers outside your market area.

A good place to begin the search for wholesale accounts is in the membership directory of the Wholesale Florists Association. You may also explore wholesale craft store suppliers and produce wholesalers.

Brokers

Larger growers often use brokers to sell their crops. The broker is provided with a continuously updated product availability list. The broker then sells the flowers to various accounts and notifies the grower of where to ship the flowers. The broker is paid a commission on the sale. The use of a broker allows a grower to concentrate on production and may provide increased marketing opportunities.

Marketing Cooperatives

The marketing dream of many new specialty cut flower growers is a marketing cooperative. Over and over I hear new growers remark "I like the growing but I really don't like the selling. I wish we could have a cooperative to sell everything for me." Like everything else, cooperatives have their advantages and disadvantages.

A marketing cooperative offers the opportunity for growers to pool their production and serve larger markets with a broader product mix. Member growers can concentrate on production and have quality marketing expertise available through the cooperative. The cooperative can provide storage, handling and shipping services and thereby reduce the capital investment requirement through shared facilities.

The primary disadvantage of a cooperative is the loss of individual control over what you do and how you do many things. Member growers elect a board of directors, who as a committee will set policy and hire and supervise a manager. Crop determination, varietal selection, grading and packaging are all typically dictated by the cooperative. Many cooperatives specify a minimum amount of educational training to become a member and require some additional continuing education to stay a member. This is done in an attempt to ensure some quality control and professionalism among member growers. Marketing cooperatives can be large and formal organizations as described above or small, very informally organized groups of growers who simply agree to sell a portion of their flowers together.

An example of a small informal marketing cooperative is Friendship Gardens in Lawrence, Kansas. Friendship Gardens is four growers who have been friends for a number of years. They individually sell flowers at the local farmers market and directly from each of their farms. In the fall of each year, they combine their products and time to sell at local craft fairs. None of them wants to make enough product to fill an entire booth and none wants to give up every weekend during the fall to stand in a craft fair booth. So they each produce enough to fill a portion of the booth and take turns working. Each one gets paid for their products that sell. Nothing fancy or too formal, just a friendly association that benefits each one. The group also gets together occasionally to hold workshops for hobbyists in the area.

Pricing

How should you price your product? **When setting prices, remember why you are in business — to make money.** Why make less money by setting your price lower than what people are willing to pay? It is extremely difficult to raise prices, so always set your initial price high. If after several weeks you find your flowers are not selling, you can lower your prices slightly. You should never sell out. Do not feel good when you sell out. When you sell out you have made less money than you could have. The only reason you have sold out is because your prices were too low. Set your prices high enough so that you always have a few flowers left over, generally less than five percent of the total flowers you brought to sell. Never compete on price. All that happens is both you and your competitor will make less money. Compete on unique selection, display, quality, service, packaging, knowledge and advice, or anything else that distinguishes you from your competitors. Your costs are relatively the same regardless of the price you charge, so why make less by charging less?

Summary

There exists an almost unlimited number of ways to market specialty cut flowers. The choice of market and approach will depend on the particular resources, talents and desires of each individual company. Owners of specialty cut flower farms whose self image is that of a grower need to remember that growing a crop incurs only expenses. No income is created until the flowers are sold. Marketing is an essential part of any commercial enterprise. The markets chosen must provide sufficient profit margins for a company to cover all costs with a little left over for a return on investment. The cost of labor to market flowers varies between marketing approaches and is often overlooked when business plans are developed. Effective labor systems will need to be developed for all labor activities involved with marketing your flowers.

Once a market and approach have been chosen, the questions of what to grow and how to grow it can be discussed. Crops should be grown to meet the needs of the intended market, with a knowledge of what is desired in the marketplace. Do not simply plant crops that appeal to you and then hope that someone, somewhere, will want to buy them.

••• Produce what you can sell —
Don't produce and then hope to sell •••

CHAPTER 2

CHOOSING A SITE

Most cut flowers prefer a location in full sun throughout the entire day. The field and soil should be well-drained. Wind protection is highly desirable for all plants, as windbreaks reduce water stress on the plant and help prevent floral damage and stem breakage. However, it is important to consider any competitive effect that may occur from the roots of a plant used as a windbreak. The location should also have sufficient cold air drainage to avoid recurring early- or late-season frosts. A source of irrigation water is essential. If animal foraging is a problem, fencing may be required.

Labor efficiency is a critical factor in choosing a site. Flower production requires intense management of all input factors. The site should have ready access for production equipment, as well as room for handling and removal of the harvested product. Make sure that it will be easy to move people, plants and materials into the site before production; that it will be easy to move people, plants and materials within the site during production and harvest; and that it will be easy to move the finished product out to storage and packing areas. The idea is to maximize efficiency of the labor required for all production and marketing functions.

If a pick-your-own marketing strategy is your choice, a site with convenient access is critical. Easy access from public roads to parking areas and from parking to the fields will enhance the consumer's overall shopping experience.

A Checklist

    Field Drainage.
The production field and service area need to have sufficient water drainage for ease of all-season movement of people, materials and equipment.

✔   Quality of the soil: texture and structure.
The textural composition and structure of the soil should facilitate the production of quality crops. Don't complicate the production process by attempting to grow in a poor soil. A slightly sandy loam of good tilth is desirable.

✔   Organic matter content of the soil.
The soil should have some organic matter. It will help maintain the structure of the soil for proper aeration and drainage.

✔   Absence of residual herbicide from previous use.
The field soils should not have any residual herbicide from previous crops. Ask what, if any, herbicides may have been used and when they were applied, to help determine the possible residual effects on your crops.

✔   Absence of toxic materials buried on site.
Environmental laws hold the current property owner responsible to pay for any toxic chemical cleanup required, regardless of whether or not they were involved with the dumping of the toxic substance. Pesticide containers and surplus spray mixes have been known to be buried on agricultural sites and sprayers cleaned and dumped out repeatedly near water sources.

✔   Quality of irrigation water.
It is much easier and far cheaper to buy land with good quality water than to deal with poor water quality and attempt to grow a quality crop. Check for low soluble salts, alkalinity, sodium and nitrate levels.

✔   Availability of utilities and cost of access.
Electric service is essential and natural gas desirable. Lines have to be run to the property, and the greater the distance, the higher the start-up costs will be. Compressors for cold storage facilities can require significant power loads. Make sure you have the proper transformer size to meet your power load requirements. Check

the distance from the nearest transfer station as an indication of how soon power may be restored after outages.

✔ Cold-air drainage.
In areas subject to recurring early- and late-season frosts,
the cold air drainage provided by slopes and elevated production areas may be desirable.

✔ Presence of windbreaks.
Windbreaks are desirable for reducing water stress and
stem breakage. In general, for every foot in height of a
windbreak, fifteen feet of wind protection is provided.
Also realize that there is a competitive effect from the
roots of trees used as a windbreak. In designing the production field, it may be necessary to leave unplanted the
area within the drip line of the trees or to place shade-tol-
erant cut materials there.

✔ Amount of dirtwork required to prepare the site for use.
A "level" site is less expensive to prepare for use than one
with hills and depressions which require cut-and-fill dirtwork with heavy machinery.

✔ Suitability of any buildings on site.
Check foundations and structural integrity of all buildings
you hope to use. Unsound structures will cost money to
tear down and remove the debris.

✔ Availability of workforce: quality and quantity.
Workers are required to get the job done. They need to
have the ability to do the tasks you need completed or the
ability to be trained for those tasks. They also must be
available and willing to work at the times and seasons
you need the work done.

✔ Roadway accessibility.
Direct frontage on a paved road is ideal. The important
consideration is how easily customers, workers, materials
and equipment can get to and from the site in any type of

weather. If you intend to market direct to retail customers, the amount and type of traffic passing along the roadway are important considerations, in addition to accessibility.

✔   Proximity to markets.
The greater the distance from the marketplace, the greater the transportation costs to deliver your products. The distance from the market also relates to the length of time your products will be in transit and subject to stress, which may impact the quality of your delivered product.

✔   Proximity to suppliers.
Closeness to suppliers affects both freight costs and the time span between the placement of the order and delivery of the materials. Longer order-to-delivery times mean you must stock larger quantities of production and maintenance materials in inventory, thereby increasing capital investment and warehouse size.

Choose a site that provides an optimal combination of the above criteria. Figure 2-1 illustrates a cut flower farm where materials are delivered to a storage and equipment area to the rear of the farm. The materials and equipment are used to grow the crops in fields located below the storage and equipment area. The crops are harvested and moved on down to the sales and shipping area at the front of the farm. This linear flow of production activities lends itself to more effective labor utilization.

Figure 2-1: A Cut Flower Farm

Section 2

PLANTING

Chapter 3 What to Grow 37

Chapter 4 When to Plant 55

Chapter 5 How to Plant 58

CHAPTER 3

WHAT TO GROW

The single most important rule to remember when deciding which crops to grow is: Grow what you can sell. Study the marketplace. Grow crops that are in demand and that have a high enough market price to allow you to make a profit. Remember that profit is the result of both price received and the costs required for production.

Have a marketing plan: Know where and in what form you will sell your crop before you plant it. You may readjust your plan in midseason to take advantage of a newfound opportunity, but have a plan before you plant. Flowers are perishable and have a short shelf life. Harvest time is too late to begin thinking about selling them.

The Ideal Crop

An ideal cut-flower crop, either fresh or dried, would have the following characteristics:

- low cost of production, both materials and labor

- high value and unlimited demand

- high production per square foot of bed space

- extended production and marketing season

- long productive life

- ability to sell as fresh material and to sell additional production as a dried or preserved decorative product

- post-harvest vase life of at least seven days

- resistance to diseases and pests of all types

- resistance to heat and drought stress

- long stems (at least 18 inches)

- easy harvest and handling

- aesthetically pleasing and/or fragrant flowers, foliage or stems

No variety of plant material will meet all of these criteria. They are presented here to provide a means of evaluating the relative desirability of producing a crop of a specific plant.

When choosing plants, start with a test plot. Begin small, learn to grow the plant and determine if it is suitable and economically advantageous to produce. Use the limited production as samples to learn the marketability of the potential crop.

Definitions

Annual: A plant that grows, blooms and dies completing a life cycle within a single year. Annuals usually bloom continually during the growing season.

Biennial: A plant that normally requires two years to complete its life cycle. Biennials will grow and produce leaves the first year but produce flowers and seed pods only after undergoing a cold period, usually the second year.

Perennial: A plant that has a life span of more than two years, but generally flowers for only a set period during the season.

These definitions are general in nature and relative to specific locations and climate conditions. For example, snapdragons are an annual in Wisconsin but are perennial in many southern states. Sweet William is considered a biennial even though many of the newer varieties perform as annuals.

Fresh Cut Flowers — Annuals

Ageratum houstonianum . . . Floss Flower; try the variety Blue Horizon. *Ageratum* is desirable for its blue flower.

Ammi majus . . . . False Queen Anne's Lace; a white, lacy filler flower.

Antirrhinum majus . . . . Snapdragon; a tall line-flower. Varieties to try are the Rocket Series and the Potomacs. Snapdragons do poorly in hot weather.

Callistephus chinensis . . . . . China Aster; a wide range of colors are available. Caution: Asters are susceptible to aster yellows disease, a disease transmitted by leafhopper insects.

Caryopteris incana . . . . Blue Spirea; long stems of whorled blue flowers.

Celosia argentea var. *cristata, plumosa,* and *spicata* Cockscomb, Feather or Plume Celosia and Wheat Celosia; the Chief Series is a good red-crested flower type. The Sparkler Series is a feather-type with several colors to try. Wheat Celosia bears slender white or pale pink plumes during summer heat and becomes rose-tinted under the cool night conditions of fall.

Centaurea cyanus . . . . Cornflower, Bachelors' Buttons; frilly buttons of white, pink and blue.

Centaurea americana . . . . . . Cornflower; a lilac-pink, larger-flowered type.

Clarkia amoena . . . . Godetia; try the Grace Series. Prefers cool temperatures.

Consolida ambigua and *Consolida orientalis* Larkspur; Giant Imperial Strain is the standard strain. Might try Blue Cloud. Prefers cool temperatures;

can be planted in the fall for spring flowering.

Cosmos bipinnatus . . . . Lace Cosmos; tall stems with flowers available in a variety of colors. Short postharvest life may limit market acceptability.

Dianthus barbatus . . . . Sweet William; old types are biennials, new types act like true annuals. Try the Pride of Park Avenue Series. Overwinters best in well-drained soil.

Eustoma grandiflorum . . . . . Lisianthus, Sweet Lissies; try the Yodel varieties, Echo Series and the Heidi Series. Can be difficult to grow from seed; most growers will want to plant as plugs.

Gomphrena globosa . . . . Globe Amaranth; try Rubra and Lavender Queen.

Gomphrena haageana . . . . . Globe Amaranth; try Strawberry Fields.

Gypsophila elegans . . . . Annual Baby's Breath; the large, white-flowered form is the most commonly grown. Recommended for fresh use only.

Helianthus annuus . . . . Sunflower; flower colors of yellow to white and shades of mahogany and rust. Try Sunbright and Full Sun — they are regularly branched plants that do not produce pollen. In our trials, pollen production has proven to be a trait objectionable to the consumer. Pollen shed from the vase appears dirty. Bright, clear yellows sell best in the summer, while oranges, bronze and maroons sell better in the fall.

Iberis amara . . . . Rocket Candytuft; fragrant and early bloomer.

Limonium sinuatum . . . . Annual Statice; try the Excellent Series and the Turbo Series. This is a standard item, sold fresh, air-dried or glycerin-preserved. Susceptible to aster yellows disease. Shades of blue, purple and white retain their color when dried. Pastel shades tend to fade upon drying. Yellow-colored varieties tend to have weaker stems. White varieties tend to be the most vigorous overall with substantial stems.

Matthiola incana . . . . Stock; a fragrant spike-type flower best grown during cool season.

Molucella laevis. . . . . Bells of Ireland; apple-green "flowers" (calyces). Sold fresh or dried.

Nigella damascena. . . . . Love-in-a-Mist; delicate flowers for fresh use. Allow additional production to sell its fruit as fresh and dried material.

Physalis alkekengi . . . . Chinese Lantern; grown for its bright orange calyces that surround the fruit, resembling a lantern. Gigantea has the largest size fruit. Can be invasive.

Salvia leucantha . . . . Velvet Sage; purple flower excellent as a dried material.

Scabiosa atropurpurea . . . . . Pincushion Flower; dense, rounded and rich-colored flower heads.

Zinnia elegans . . . . Zinnia; several flower types and sizes available. Never water overhead — subject to leaf diseases. Giant Mammoth, Zenith, State Fair Series and Benary Dahlia Blue-Point are some of the best large-flowering zinnias. Try the Pumila Series, Ruffles and Cut-and-Come-Again for medium-sized flowers. Button-flowered types offer an interesting small-flower form. All forms are sold fresh or dried.

Fresh Cut Flowers — Perennials

Achillea species . . . . Yarrow, Fernleaf Yarrow; try Gold Plate and Coronation Gold. Long stems can be sold fresh or dried. The yellow- and gold-flowered types hold their flower color better when dried than the pastel shades. Foliage odor may be offensive to some people.

Artemisia ludoviciana . . . . . . White Sage; grown for the silver-gray foliage used fresh or dried. Silver King and Silver Queen are standard cultivars.

Asclepias incarnata and *Asclepias tuberosa*
Butterfly Flower; rose-purple and neon orange, respectively. Easy to grow, shippable and long-lasting cut flowers. *A. incarnata* does not overwinter well and might ought to be treated as an annual. *A. tuberosa* has

short stems which may be difficult to market.

Aster novi-belgii and *Aster ericoides*
Aster; hybrids of both species are good cut flowers. Monte Casino is the standard variety grown.

Astilbe hybrids. . . . . Astilbe, False Spirea; requires moist soil in summer. Color range of white, pink, red and lavender.

Chrysanthemum x superbum Shasta Daisy; most popular cutting-propagated variety is T.E. Killin, and seed-propagated, Alaska.

Echinacea purpurea. . . . . . . Purple Cone Flower; sold fresh, or the cone may be dried. Subject to aster yellows disease.

Echinops bannaticus
Echinops exaltatus
Echinops ritro
Echinops sphaerocephalus. . Globe Thistle; rich blue, gray blue, common globe thistle, and pale blue to almost white, respectively. Excellent producer for either fresh or dried markets. Long-lived but should not be transplanted after it has become established.

Eryngium amethystinum and *Eryngium planum*
Eryngo, Sea Holly; easiest of the Eryngo to grow. Excellent fresh or dried.

Gypsophila paniculata . . . . . Perennial Baby's Breath; the standard filler of the floral industry. Used fresh, dried and glycerin-preserved. Perfecta is the standard variety.

Liatris species and hybrids. . Gayfeather, Blazing Star; one of the longest-lasting and finest cut flowers. Well-adapted to a variety of climates and soils. A tall line-flower. Can be sold fresh or dried.

Limonium latifolium, Limonium perezii, Limonium tataricum
Statice; sold fresh and dried.

Paeonia hybrids . . . . Peony; herbaceous types are among the choicest of fresh and dried cut flowers. Extremely long-lived. Short harvest season but can be stored cool and dry for an extended period of time. Plants require three to five years from planting to reach full productive potential. Double-flowered and bomb types are the most popular. Try a small trial planting of a couple of single-flowered varieties.

Phlox paniculata . . . . Summer Phlox; vigorous grower with a wide selection of colors. Subject to powdery mildew.

Physostegia virginiana . . . . . Obedient Plant; tall, upright spike form of purple to pink flowers.

Platycodon grandiflorum . . . Balloon Flower; large bellflower-like blooms follow balloon-like buds.

Salvia farinacea . . . . Blue Salvia, Mealycup Sage; strong grower in extreme heat. Can be used fresh or dried. Try Victoria, Catima and Blue Bedder.

Scabiosa caucasica . . . . Pincushion Flower; a traditional florists' cut flower. Try Fama and Complement.

Solidago species . . . . Goldenrod; the Dutch hybrids should be planted. Note: Goldenrod is not the cause of hayfever.

Fresh Cut Flowers — Bulbs, Corms, Tubers

Allium species . . . . Flowering Onion; most species are good fresh cut flowers. The best species for cutting are: *A. aflatunense, A. caeruleum, A. giganteum* and *A. spaerocephalum.*

Anemone coronaria . . . . Poppy Anemone; grow in cool spring for sale before Mother's Day.

Dahlia hybrids. . . . . Dahlia; plant after all threat of frost as tuberous roots are not cold hardy. Good clear, bright colors.

Gladiolus . . . . Gladioli; standard item for florist and farmers market sales. Try both standard and mini glads. Can be sold fresh or dried. Corms are not cold hardy.

Liatris spicata also species and hybrids
Gayfeather, Blazing Star; one of the longest-lasting and finest cut flowers.

Well-adapted to a variety of climates and soils. A tall line-flower. Can be sold fresh or dried. Also listed above under perennials.

Lilium hybrids . . . . Lily; the Asiatic, Aurelian and Oriental hybrids are the best for commercial cut flower production.

Polianthes tuberosa . . . . Tuberose; flowers are known for their sweet, heavy fragrance produced on an open spike. Bulb is not cold hardy.

Fresh Cut Flowers — Woody Stems

The stems or branches of many woody plants can be cut when dormant, held cool and forced into bloom as fresh flowers for late-winter and early-spring sales, or used for the berry, the beauty of bark or form of twig. Numerous useful species and hybrids exist for most of the following:

Callicarpa . . . . Beautyberry; attractive fruit of unusual color among woody plants. Berries are violet to deep metallic purple in color. Berries mature in the fall.

Celastrus scandens . . . . Bittersweet; vine grown for its clusters of colorful fruit which split open to reveal brilliant red seeds. Sold as fruited branches.

Cercis . . . . Redbud; flower buds are reddish purple and open to a rosy-pink color. Spring blooming.

Chaenomeles . . . . False cypress, Port Orford Cedar; scalelike leaves, flattened fan-shaped branches. Sold fresh and glycerin-preserved.

Cornus. . . . . Dogwood; branches with a rich red or yellow winter bark color.

Eucalyptus. . . . . Eucalyptus; fragrant branches are sold fresh or as glycerin-preserved and color-processed decorative materials.

Forsythia . . . . Forsythia; beautiful, clear, bright yellow flowers along stems for late-winter and early-spring sales.

Gaultheria. . . . . Salal, Lemon Leaf; cut branches sold fresh or glycerin-preserved and color-processed.

Humulus . . . . Common Hop; vigorous vine that produces bracts/flowers with a cone-like appearance.

Hydrangea. . . . . Hydrangea; large clusters of long-lasting flowers in white, pink, red and blue. Most commonly sold as a dried flower.

Ilex . . . . Holly; shiny, waxy evergreen leaves and red berries. Stems are commonly sold as a Christmas holiday decoration.

Mallus . . . . Flowering Crabapple; flowering stems with white to pink to red blooms. Spring flowering tree.

Quercus. . . . . Oak; the leaves of several oak species are commonly glycerin-preserved and color-processed for fall sales.

Salix . . . . Willow; branches of species with twisted, corkscrew-like growth habit with red or yellow bark color.

Spirea . . . . Snowmound, Bridal Wreath Spirea, Red Spirea; white or red flowering branches which bloom in spring.

Syringia . . . . Lilac; fragrant flowers, white to violet to purple in color, blooming in late spring to early summer.

Vitis . . . . Grape; vines are used in a variety of value-added products.

Dried or Glycerin-Preserved Materials — Flowers and Miscellaneous Plant Parts

The following is a list of commonly grown flowers, foliages and plant materials for drying or glycerin preserving.

Achillea species (yarrows)

Ammobium (herb)

Artemisia species (silver king, silver queen and annual sweet annie)

Branches of Plants (myrtle, cedar, willow, dogwood, grape)

Capsicum hybrids (peppers)

Carthamus tinctorius (safflower)

Celosia cristata (cockscomb)

Chrysanthemum parthenium (feverfew)

Consolida regalis (larkspur)

Daucus carota (queen anne's lace)

Echinops species (globe thistle)

Eryngium species (seaholly)

Eucalyptus species

Gomphrena globosa (globe amaranth)

Grass and Grains (wheat, black bearded and durum, rye, oats, rice, buffalo, quaking, barley, canary, flax, hare's tale, milo and sorghum)

Gypsophila perfecta & *Gypsophila paniculata* (baby's breath)

Helichrysum bracteatum (straw flower)

Helipterum manglesii (rhodanthe)

Helipterum manglesii (acroclinum)

Hydrangea

Iberis sempervireas (candytuff)

Lavandula (lavender)

Lepidium (peppergrass)

Limonium latifolia (latifolia)

Limonium caspicum (caspia)

Limonium sinuatum (annual sinuata)

Limonium suworowii (rattail statice)

Limonium tataricum (german statice)

Lunaria (money plant)

Molucella laevis (bells of Ireland)

Nigella damascena (love-in-a-mist, devil-in-the-bush)

Paeonia hybrids (peony)

Papaver somniferum (poppy pods)

Rosa (roses)

Salvia farinacea (blue salvia)

Scabiosa atropurpurea (pincushion flower)

Scabiosa caucasica (pincushion flower)

Tanacetum species (tansy)

Xeranthemum species (common immortelle)

Zea Mays (indian corn, strawberry corn)

Table 3-1 lists rose varieties that dry well. Flower color will become slightly darker when dried. Flowers with any blue in the basic color will darken the most. Pink flowers may develop a slight lavender hue, dark pink flowers may turn purple, and dark red flowers may become black in appearance. The two red varieties in this list have little or no blue tone in their red color. Their red is more toward the light red or orange-red portion of the color spectrum, and therefore they tend to dry closer to a true red in color.

Table 3-1: Rose Varieties for Drying

Variety	Color
Ariana	light pink
Bettina	dark orange to red
Brandy	apricot
Bridal Pink	light pink
Bridal White	white with a slight touch of pink
Brigadoon	coral
Candia	cream and rose bi-color
Carnival	cream and purple bi-color
Fire and Ice	cream with deep red edges
Marina	red
Mercedes	red
Pride n Joy	orange with a slight touch of yellow on reverse side of petal

Variety	Color
Prive	dark pink
Sonia	peach
Supra	yellow
Tropicana	orange

The plants listed above are all being commercially grown and marketed as specialty cut flowers. While the lists comprise only a portion of the flowers currently being grown, they could serve as a starting point in the decision process of determining a product mix. You should consider the generic use of the materials. What qualities are needed in each plant being grown? How will they be marketed? What colors, flower and stem forms are desired? Products in colors from each segment of the color wheel could be desirable. Designer products such as arrangements, wreaths, bouquets and wall decorations all require various flower and stem forms. Designers need flowers and stems to develop line, to serve as focal point and to provide filler. Your product mix should contain flowers to meet these customer needs. Table 3-2 lists a variety of plants by color and functional use.

Table 3-2: Color and Functional Use of a Variety of Plants

Color	Plant	Use
Red	*celosia* - plume	focal, filler
	celosia - cockscomb	focal, filler
	peony	focal
	strawflowers	focal
	strawberry corn	focal
	indian corn	focal
	buddleia	focal
	zinnia	focal, filler
	sumac	filler
Orange	marigold	focal, filler
	chinese lantern	focal, filler

Color	Plant	Use
	bittersweet	line, focal, filler
	sunflower	focal
	mini pumpkin	focal
	indian corn	focal
	strawflower	focal
	zinnia	focal, filler
	gourds	focal
Yellow	yarrow	focal, filler
	gladiolus	line
	sunflower	focal
	marigold	focal, filler
	annual statice	filler
	tansy	filler
	strawflower	focal
	goldenrod (solidago)	focal, filler
	indian corn	focal
	wheat	line, filler
	grasses	line, filler
	rye	line, filler
	zinnia	focal
Green	bells of Ireland	focal, filler
	tree leaves - oak, aspen, hawthorne, sycamore	filler
	ferns (purchase)	filler
	grasses	line, filler
	hare's tail	line, filler
	milo	line
	wheat	line, filler
	barley	line, filler
	flax	line, filler
	peony leaves	filler
	magnolia leaves	filler
	milkweed pods	focal
	rosemary	line, filler

Color	Plant	Use
	nigella	focal, filler
	thyme	filler
Blue	*liatris*	line
	salvia - victoria, indigo, horminum, splendens	line, filler
	larkspur	line, focal
	Canterbury bells	focal, filler
	echinops - globe thistle	focal
	cornflower	focal
	hydrangea	focal
	annual statice	filler
Violet	lavender	line, filler
	buddleia	focal, filler
	larkspur	line, focal
	strawflower	focal
	lilac	focal
	oregano	filler
	globe amaranthe	filler
	annual statice	filler
White	annual statice	filler
	buddleia	focal, filler
	dusty miller	focal, filler
	lamb's ear	focal, filler
	gladiolus	line
	sage - Russian	filler
	salvia	line, filler

Begin with a small trial planting of each crop. Learn how to grow the plant and determine if it can be produced and sold for a profit under your conditions. You should be able to produce a high-quality product before expanding production past the experimental stage. Keep a journal. You may find little information available on many of the plants you wish to grow, and a record of your early experiences will be useful in future seasons. Always remember to have a marketing plan for how you will sell a crop before you plant it.

CHAPTER 4

WHEN TO PLANT

Planting dates depend on your target market and on plant classification — whether it is an annual, biennial or perennial. In general, the peak demand period for the retail florist trade is autumn through spring with highest demand occurring from Valentine's Day to Mother's Day. Field production of fresh cut flowers for this market should be planted for maximum harvest in the spring and fall seasons. Farmers markets typically operate from late spring until frost in the fall. Consistent production throughout this period is desirable.

Annuals

Annuals are planted into the field as soon as the danger of frost is past. Using transplants will bring the crop to flower earlier and may return higher prices early on if you are able to harvest for the Mother's Day market. Sequential plantings may be required to assure a continuous supply of product throughout the market season. Staggered plantings — two to four weeks apart into July — are common for many annuals. Transplants may be used initially to hit the earliest possible market, with later plantings direct-seeded. When choosing cultivars, be careful to select those suited for cut-flower production. Many annuals have been developed for use as landscape bedding plants and are not suitable as commercial cut flowers.

Biennials

Biennials should be planted in the fall to ensure an adequate cold treatment before regrowth starts in the spring. The overwinter cold treatment is required for more uniform flowering. If beds or plants are not ready for planting in the fall, some alternatives exist. Placing the plants into cold storage or spraying them with 500 to 1,000 parts per million of gibberellic acid will substitute for over-wintering the plants in the bed. While these alternatives do promote flowering, production quantity and quality are reduced compared with fall-planted stock.

Biennials tend to bloom in a condensed time period. Staggered planting usually does not result in staggered periods of bloom. Most biennials will bloom at the same time unless subjected to cold storage or gibberellic acid treatments. Some biennials are excellent cut flowers, but because of this concentrated, all-at-once bloom habit, few are grown as commercial crops. Exceptions include Sweet William.

Perennials

Perennials are placed into categories based on the presence or absence of storage organs and whether or not they must be dug in the fall and replanted each spring.

1. Cold-hardy plants that have storage organs and can remain in the ground for several years. If allowed to remain in place over winter, they typically will bloom at the same time each year. Extended bloom periods can be achieved by digging in the fall, placing in 40°F storage, and planting every two to three weeks beginning in mid-spring. Examples in this group are liatris and lilies.

2. Non-hardy plants which have storage organs and must be dug each year. Continuous bloom periods are relatively easy to achieve by staggering the planting dates from spring through mid-summer. The additional labor required to dig, store and replant the plants in this category increases their cost of production. The economics of producing each species should be analyzed before extensive production is undertaken. Examples in this group are anemones, dahlias, gladioli and ranunculi.

3. Cold-hardy plants which have rhizomes or a clump-forming growth habit and may be left undisturbed for a few years before being divided. After the first year, plants in this category tend to bloom together, typically within a week or so of the same time each year. Bloom periods can be extended slightly through cultivar selection. Examples of plants in this group are peony and yarrow.

Table 4-1:
Height and Flowering Periods of a Few Perennials For Field-Grown Cut Flowers

Plant	Approx. Height	Flowering Period
Achillea species		
'Coronation Gold'	2-3 ft.	June-August
Achillea filipendulina		
'Parkers Variety'	3-4 ft.	June-August
'Cloth of Gold'	2-3 ft	June-August
Achillea millefolium		
'Cerise Queen'	1.5-2.5 ft.	June-August
Asclepias tuberosa	2-3 ft.	July-September
Aster ericoides	2-3 ft.	September-October
Aster novae-angliae	1-4 ft.	August-September
Aster novi-belgii	1-4 ft.	August-September
Astilbe x arendsii	1.5-4 ft.	July-August
Delphinium hybrids	3-4 ft.	April-June
Echinacea purpurea	3-4 ft.	June-August
Echinops bannaticus	3-5 ft.	July-August
Eryngium planum	2-4 ft.	July-August
Gypsophila paniculata	2-4 ft.	June-July
Limonium latifolium	2-2.5 ft.	July-August
Limonium perezii	2-2.5 ft.	July-August
Limonium tataricum	2-2.5 ft.	July-August
Lysimachia clethroides	2-2.5 ft.	August-September
Paeonia hybrids	2-3 ft.	May-June
Phlox paniculata	3-4 ft.	July-August
Physostegia virginiana	3-4 ft.	August-September
Platycodon grandiflorus	2-3 ft.	July-August
Solidago hybrids	2-3 ft.	August

CHAPTER 5

HOW TO PLANT

Preparing the Bed

Grow plants in beds raised four to six inches to maximize drainage. Correct poorly drained soil by placing drain lines 10 to 12 inches deep under the beds. Check for the existence of a hard-pan in the soil. A deep-rooted cover crop such as alfalfa may help to break up the hardpan. A well-drained soil environment is essential for maximum root development and to reduce the potential for root rot.

Incorporate organic matter into the beds to a depth of 10 to 12 inches. The addition of organic matter is best if incorporated in the fall, but it can be done anytime before planting if the nitrogen status of the soil is monitored. Remember that for beds planted to perennials, you may not be able to work additional organic matter deep into the soil until the plants are divided or replaced. For these beds, add sufficient organic matter before planting to provide a soil structure with optimum aeration and drainage.

Always have the soil tested for nutrient content before adding any fertilizer to the planting bed. Production decisions made without appropriate information are mere guesses and can be costly. If nitrogen levels are low and large amounts of organic matter have been recently added, an application of 20 to 25 pounds of actual nitrogen per acre should be made prior to planting .

Marketing strategy, plant growth habit and labor efficiency determine the ideal size of a planting bed. If you decide to follow a pick-your-own market strategy, beds should be narrow — about two and a half to three feet wide — so consumers can easily pick their flowers without damaging the crop. Beds should be about 25 feet long, with sodded aisles to give customers quick and clean access to any product they desire. Traditional production beds are three to four feet wide, depending on the growth habit of the crop.

Bed width is set to allow for maximum light penetration to the center of the bed and to facilitate harvesting. The wider a bed is, the better the ratio of production space to aisle space and the greater the return per acre. Tall, dense flower growth habits reduce the amount of light reaching lower leaves in the center of the bed. A worker can efficiently reach only two feet into a bed to make a proper cut and remove the flower without damage to the crop. The greater the distance to the center of the bed that workers must stretch, the less efficient their efforts will be and the greater the cost of labor.

Bed length also is set to maximize the area in production versus the area in aisles. The limiting factor to bed length is labor efficiency. The maximum distance a worker should carry harvested flowers is about 60 to 75 feet. Planting beds should be a maximum of 120 to 150 feet long. Uniform drip irrigation is also easiest for beds less than 200 feet long. For more information on irrigation requirements refer to Chapter 6.

A Plastic Mulch-Covered, Raised-Bed System

A common bed preparation system incorporates a raised bed covered with plastic mulch and watered with drip irrigation. First, a three or four foot wide bed is thrown up. The bed is then firmed with a press plate. The drip irrigation tape is laid and the plastic mulch placed in a single pass of the tractor. The plastic mulch significantly reduces the labor required to control weeds; helps to keep the plant and flowers cleaner by reducing soil splash from rain; and reduces water loss from evaporation. This system was developed for the production of vegetables and adapted for the specialty cut flower industry. The following sections describe the system. The reader might also want to refer to Chapter 8 on weed control for additional information on this system.

Types of Plastic Mulch

Many different kinds of plastic mulch material are available. Widths vary from 36 to 60 inches; thickness varies from ¾ to ½ mil or more. The surface texture of the material may be slick or embossed. Embossed plastic has visible patterns on the surface, which give the plastic a wrinkled appearance. This kind of mulch is generally more resistant to wind fatigue and cracking than slick mulches. Linear, low-density mulches have a slick surface with parallel lines that intersect to form a diamond-shaped pattern. These lines reinforce the mulch and help prevent tears from crossing from one diamond to another. Be sure to use a material of adequate strength. Mulch that becomes brittle and breaks up too early is usually worse than no mulch at all, not to mention the money wasted.

Most agricultural mulch is black. Clear mulch is used in some areas because of its increased soil-warming characteristics, despite the weed control problems. White or aluminum reflective mulch is used where soil cooling is desired, such as in establishing fall crops during the heat of summer.

Research is being conducted on plastic mulch materials that degrade either by sunlight or biological organisms in the soil. Degradable materials need not be removed from the field at the end of the growing season.

Soil Preparation and Fertilization

Plastic mulch is not a substitute for soil preparation. A seed or transplant bed prepared for mulch application should be the same quality as non-mulched fields. The soil should be free of rocks, sticks, hard clods and other materials that could puncture the plastic.

Rows should be laid off on widths compatible with available mulch-laying equipment. The ability to work aisles may be restricted depending on the height of the bed and the amount of mulch used for anchorage. Weed control in the aisles should be provided for with either chemicals or mechanical cultivation.

Machinery is available to accomplish all operations associated with use of plastic mulch. At a minimum, a furrow must be opened with a lister for fertilizer application and a ridge must be raised with a bedder or disc hillers and shaped to accept the plastic. Equipment is available to accomplish both in one operation. When finished, the bed should be four to six inches high, about 30 to 42 inches wide (depending on mulch width) and have about a ½ to 2-inch slope from center to edge.

Plastic mulch should never be applied to excessively dry or wet soil. Dry soil settles and allows mulch to loosen after wetting, while wet soil does not seal the mulch well, making it subject to blowing off the bed.

An acceptable procedure is to apply fertilizer and raise ridges with disc hillers to settle the bed before mulch application. The top of the ridges can be knocked off with a bed shaper (Figure 5-1). If the bed has thoroughly settled, it can be shaped using a pre-shaped device mounted on a tool bar ahead of a mulch layer.

Figure 5-1: A Bed Shaper

Mulch Application

Plastic mulch is most efficient when used in conjunction with drip irrigation. A drip tube should be applied on the soil surface under the mulch or buried two to three inches beneath the soil surface. Either way, the tube must be installed before the mulch. Rodents may damage tubes if not buried. If buried, the drip tube should be installed with the emitter holes oriented upward and without excessive stretching. For spring planting, the mulch should be applied at least seven days ahead of planting to allow time for soil warming. Soil fumigation can also be accomplished during mulch application. Fumigation is a specialized operation; make plans well ahead of time to allow for equipment readiness as well as necessary waiting periods between treatment and planting. Confer with your county Extension agent for fumigation recommendations.

It is important to apply the mulch properly to get the most benefit. The plastic should be in continuous contact with the soil, and the bed should be uniform with no dish shapes to hold the mulch off the soil. Space between the soil and the mulch interferes with heat transfer and prevents the soil from warming as quickly and thoroughly. It allows the plastic to whip in the wind, which can start tears. Spaces also allow movement of the mulch against the stems of transplants, which can cause abrasion of stems and death of the plant.

The mulch should be applied with a properly adjusted machine containing the components shown in Figure 5-2.

Figure 5-2 Plastic Mulch Installation Equipment

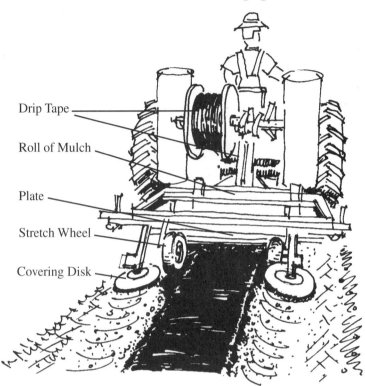

Drip Tape

Roll of Mulch

Plate

Stretch Wheel

Covering Disk

The edges of the mulch should be secured with a generous amount of soil. However, do not apply more soil than is needed, as this makes the mulch more difficult to remove. Stretch wheels should be adjusted to stretch the mulch edge securely into the anchoring furrow for covering.

The soil should roll smoothly from the covering discs onto the edge of the plastic. Ideally the furrow openers will prepare a rounded opening, the stretch wheels will securely hold the plastic in the furrow, and the covering discs will return to the furrow all soil removed by the openers. This should result in a lip of plastic filled with soil. Mulch applied properly will not blow off the row and requires minimum effort to remove.

For crops grown in single rows, install the drip tube approximately three inches off the center of the row. For crops grown in two rows per bed, install the drip tube in the center of the bed. This keeps the tube from being damaged during the transplanting or seeding operation. Beds planted to three or four rows will require a second length of drip tube. Production in hot, dry climates may also require additional drip tubes.

If equipment dimensions prevent working the aisles after installing the mulch, apply herbicide to the aisles before laying the mulch. It is generally best to leave adequate space between beds to allow aisles to be worked with a rototiller or small tractor.

Planting

Planting through plastic mulch can be accomplished either manually or mechanically, depending on the size of your operation. Transplanters can be constructed or purchased at prices ranging from $1,200 to $1,500. Depending on the type and capabilities of the machine, planting space can vary from 12 to 60 inches in a row. The simplest planter is a water wheel planter, which punches a hole through the mulch and fills it with a water and starter solution. Two workers ride the machine and set a plant into each hole of water. The water settles the soil around the plant's roots as it percolates into the ground. Other types of transplanters receive the plant into a pocket, punch a hole in the plastic, set the plant in the hole, press the soil around the plant and deliver water and starter solution onto each plant.

Modifications are available to allow use of some transplanters for delivering a plug mix into the planting hole. A plug mix consists of potting soil and seed mixed in a ratio that provides an average of three to five seeds in each one-fourth cup of mix. The planter deposits a measured amount of the mix into each planting hole. The practice is effective on many crops including zinnias and sunflowers. A list of equipment suppliers is included in the last section of this book.

With some organization, hand transplanting and seeding can be accomplished efficiently. A crew of at least four is generally needed. Tractor-mounted or hand devices can be built to mark and punch holes for hand planting. Measuring devices can be as simple as a long pole painted with stripes at the desired plant spacing. Another method is to place a stem supporting mesh on the bed and merely plant into each or every other square of the mesh.

In general, transplants should be planted shallow, with the roots placed just below the soil surface. Planting too deep reduces oxygen exchange between the newly developing root system and the atmosphere, thereby slowing growth. Too deep planting encourages the development of root and stem rots. Firm the soil around the transplants to remove large pockets of air, but not so much so as to pack the soil. Water all plants as soon after planting as possible. Delaying watering may severely reduce overall production. Figure 5-3 illustrates a plastic mulch bed being planted manually.

Figure 5-3: Transplanting Into a Plastic Mulch Covered Bed

Black Plastic Mulch

Planting

Figure 5-4: Bed at Time of First Cutting

Harvest

Plant Density

A closely spaced crop of annual flowers will usually produce more flowers over the growing season than a crop at wider spacing. The essential criteria in cut flower production is the number of flowers produced per square foot of bed space and not the number of flowers per plant. In general, the closer the spacing of annuals, the more flowers produced. A six- to eight-inch spacing within the row and ten to twelve inches between rows is ideal for many annual flowers. This will vary depending on the growth habit of each species and on the specific environment of the planting site. Spacing of up to 12 x 18 inches may be needed for plants such as *cosmos*.

Perennials left in place each year have the potential to crowd each other to an extent that may reduce overall production in succeeding years. Plants that may be divided every three years, such as yarrow, may be planted closer than plants like peonies that may be divided every 20 years or more. In general, plant perennials about one foot apart, within and between rows. Plant peonies three feet apart in a single row or staggered in a double row, with a three-foot spacing within each row and two feet between rows. Plant density will vary depending on growth habit of individual species and the growing conditions.

It should be noted that closer spacings produce more flowers per square foot of bed, but also reduce air circulation within the bed. Poor air circulation increases the likelihood of foliar and stem diseases. If powdery mildew or leafspot fungus is a common problem on a species you intend to produce, then a slightly wider spacing may be appropriate.

Crop Support

Some cut flowers may need support to ensure a high percentage of straight stems. The simplest support method is to place a bamboo stick beside the stem and to twist-tie them together as shown in Figure 5-5. The primary disadvantage of individual staking is the labor involved.

Figure 5-5: Bamboo Stake Support System

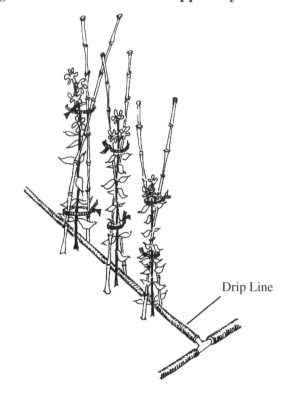

Drip Line

A plastic or nylon material in rolls of either a four- or six-inch mesh is a popular supporting material. It is laid out horizontally and suspended above the bed by steel fence posts placed along the edges of the bed. The plastic mesh can be raised as the crop grows taller, or additional layers can be added. The following series of figures displays the use of a plastic mesh support system.

Figure 5-6: Plastic Mesh Support System

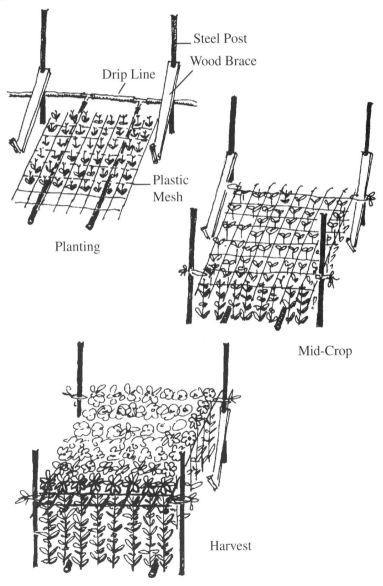

Steel Post
Wood Brace
Drip Line
Plastic Mesh
Planting
Mid-Crop
Harvest

Figure 5-7: A Detail Drawing of a Plastic Mesh Support System

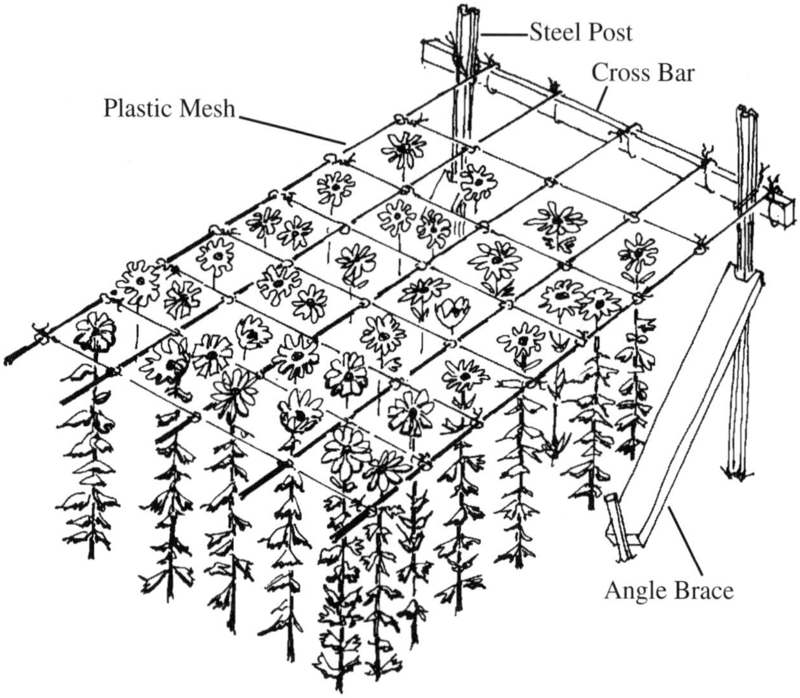

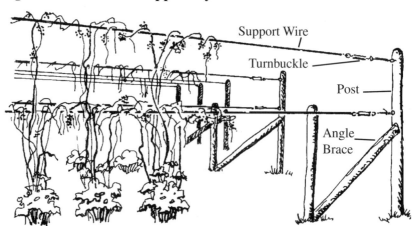

Woody perennial vines such as bittersweet require stronger and higher support. A trellis system as used in grape vineyards works well. Other methods exist and any method which produces the desired result with low cost and minimal labor is acceptable.

Figure 5-8: A Trellis Support System

Section 3

CARE AS NEEDED

Chapter 6   Watering 71

Chapter 7   Fertilization 81

Chapter 8   Weed Control. 99

Chapter 9   Insect Control 113

Chapter 10 Disease Control 134

Chapter 11 Vertebrate Pest Control. 146

How to Grow Specialty Cut Flowers

Specialty cut flowers are a high-dollar crop. Their value may be measured in dollars per square foot, not dollars per acre. Withholding or delaying application of any input, which reduces flower production or quality, is false economy.

CHAPTER 6

WATERING

Specialty cut flowers grown in the field, for fresh or dried markets, will require more total water than many other field crops. To maintain floral quality and peak production, the plants must be watered frequently, or occasionally daily with some soil types. A water source of sufficient volume and quality should be readily available to the production area. Growers should not attempt to produce cut flowers without supplemental watering. Natural rainfall is often neither sufficient nor reliable. Without supplemental watering, production may not be economically realistic.

The activity of watering your flower crop is a subsystem of your production system. How you apply water to your crop will affect not only the number of flowers harvested and their quality, but also the amount (cost) of labor required to accomplish the watering activity. Your watering system may be as simple as a garden hose laid on the ground with the water allowed to flow down the row or as technically complex as a fully automated, soil moisture-sensing, irrigation system. Whatever level of technology you choose, your watering system must be designed to enhance the productivity of the entire production system at the lowest cost while maintaining product quality. Labor is a cost which must be considered in designing and operating the system. This is particularly important for a small family farm where the only source of labor are members of the family. Remember the 25-hour day. The system used must be integrated with your planting and fertilizing systems.

Irrigation should be scheduled based on the soil moisture status in the root zone. Proper irrigation management provides sufficient but not excessive water to the crop. Water stress will reduce production and quality of a crop, while consistently saturated soil will reduce growth and promote the development of root rot. The amount and frequency of water required will vary with the weather and stage of maturity of the crop.

Overhead watering is not recommended. It may physically damage the flowers, cause spotting on the petals, splash soil onto the foliage and promote the spread of disease. Trickle or drip irrigation is recommended. It has the advantage of placing the water on the ground where it is needed and not on the flowers or foliage. Very little water is wasted because little water spreads to the soil between crop rows. Wind does not affect this kind of irrigation because the water is applied at or below the ground surface. A well-designed and maintained trickle irrigation system is capable of a field application efficiency of 90 percent.

The basic principle in designing an irrigation system for cut flowers is to place the water uniformly around each plant. Spacing of irrigation lines is dependent on soil type and structure. Coarse, open soils require closer spacing than dense, fine soils. The irrigation system plan should be developed by a competent designer, with the grower having a thorough understanding of the system and its operation. Many irrigation suppliers offer design services when materials are purchased from them.

Irrigation Components

Trickle irrigation systems can be arranged in a variety of ways. The arrangement of components in Figure 6-1 represents a typical layout. The goal is to create a system that applies water uniformly to each plant. Changes in elevation and pressure loss within the pipes will affect the discharge of individual emitters, but there should be no more than a 10 percent variation between the emitters with the highest and lowest output. Pipes and tubing should be sized correctly. Laterals should run across slope, following contour lines or running slightly downhill. Areas of a field at different elevations should operate as separate sub-units with separate pressure regulators.

Figure 6-1: Typical Trickle Irrigation System

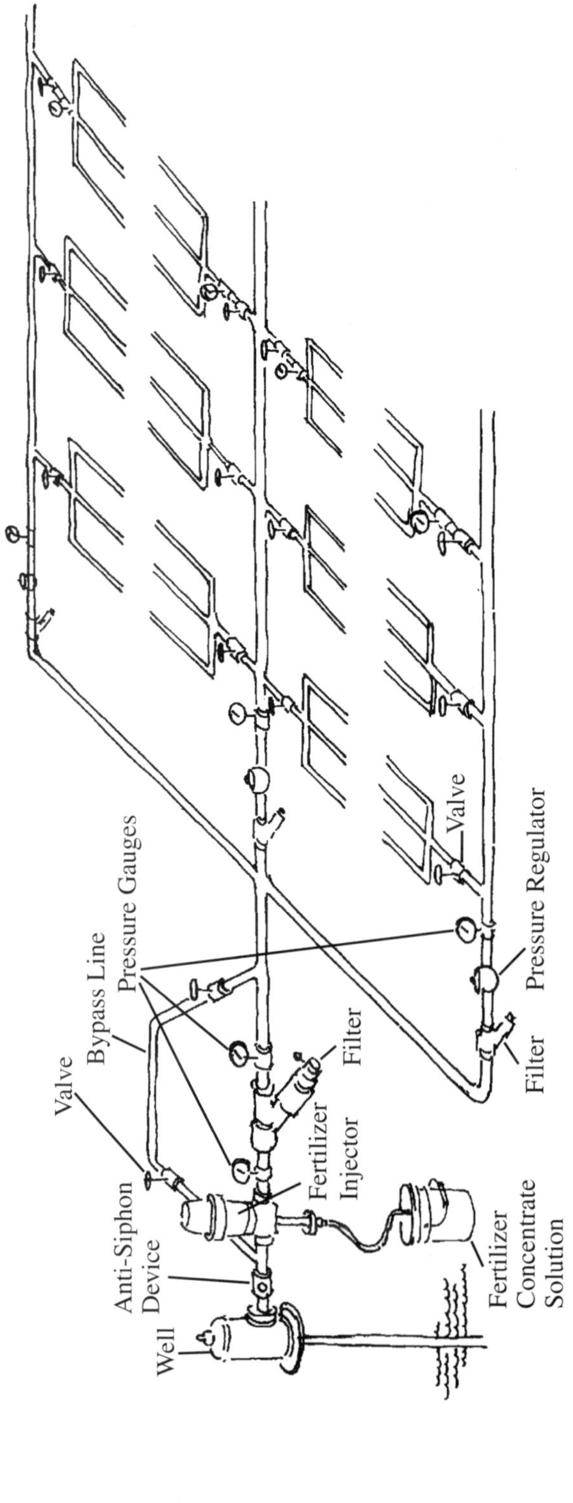

Valve

Pressure Regulator

Filter

Valve

Bypass Line

Pressure Gauges

Filter

Fertilizer Injector

Anti-Siphon Device

Fertilizer Concentrate Solution

Well

Trickle irrigation laterals can be divided into two categories: line-source emitters and point-source emitters. Line-source emitters are used when plants are closely spaced within a row, with the rows spaced further apart. For flowers, the preferred emitting device is tubing with closely spaced perforations. The volume of soil irrigated by each perforation overlaps with that of the perforations next to it, resulting in a long, narrow block of irrigated soil that surrounds the roots of the entire crop row.

The typical line-source emitter is bi-wall tubing, which has two pipe chambers. The larger, inner chamber is for water flow along the row length. The smaller, outer tube is connected to the inner chamber by widely spaced, relatively large openings. The outer tube is perforated with small openings, typically spaced three to six inches apart, through which the water is emitted to the crop. The dual-chamber design reduces the effect of pressure loss in the tubing, providing a more uniform rate of discharge along the tube length. Typical operating pressures for drip tubing depends on the operating pressure of the tubing, the perforation spacing and the field slope. The length of the tubing must be limited to keep water application uniform.

The rate of water application from drip tubing depends on the spacing of perforations and the operating pressure. Most tubing with six-inch perforation spacings discharge approximately one gallon per minute (gpm) per 100 feet of tubing length at normal operating pressure. Tubing with 12-inch spaced perforations typically discharges ½ gpm per 100 feet of length. The perforation spacing that you should use depends on the soil type. On coarse-textured soils, water moves downward with little horizontal spread. The perforations in the drip tubing must be relatively close together to ensure a uniform line of water exists along the row length to promote even crop growth. On finer-textured soils, the capillary action of the small soil pores permits greater horizontal movement of the water. Water from each perforation could spread to cover two to three feet of row length on fine-textured soil.

Recent developments in tubing manufacturing have led to the production of drip tubing with turbulent flow properties in the outer chamber. These devices are generally better than drip tubing with mechanical- or laser-drilled openings. Turbulent drip tapes have larger openings at the same rate of discharge, which makes them less susceptible to blockages. They also have better pressure-compensating qualities, which permits their use on longer rows and irregular slopes. Turbulent flow drip tubing is more expensive than conventional drip tubing, but in many applications is worth the added expense.

Point-source emitters are used when widely spaced point sources of water are needed, as in the case of woody shrubs and trees where the plants are spaced several feet apart in each direction. In this type of system, one or more emitting devices are attached to a pipeline near the base of the plant, irrigating a bulb of soil surrounding the root mass of the plant.

Emitting devices for widely spaced plants are normally attached to polyethylene (PE) tubing. Most deliver either ½ gallon per hour (gph), 1 gph or 2 gph at their design operating pressure. The maximum length of run for a single lateral depends on the emitter discharge rate, emitter spacing, tubing diameter and field slope.

With shrubs and trees, locate emitters so they provide balanced root development. While a single, small-capacity emitter may be sufficient during the early years of plant development, a higher flow rate will be needed as the shrub or tree matures. Divide this large flow between several emitters, spaced around the base of the plant within the canopy dripline. The dripline is simply the line marking the extent of the plant's canopy coverage on the ground surface.

Pressure Regulators

Because trickle irrigation systems operate at relatively low pressures, even small variations in pressure can have a significant effect on how uniformly the system applies water to the crop. For this reason, pressure regulators are often used, especially on fields where the elevation varies considerably. For every 2.3 feet of elevation fall, the water pressure in a pipe will increase one pound per square inch (psi). For every 2.3 feet of elevation rise, the pressure decreases 1 psi. So, if a field has a variation of 10 feet in elevation from the highest to the lowest point, the emitters at the lowest point will be operating at a pressure more than 4 psi greater than the highest emitter. In a system that may have a design operating pressure of only 8 psi, that is an extremely large variation.

Variations in pressure due to elevation change can be handled by using pressure regulators, or pressure compensating emitters. Regulators are devices that maintain an outlet pressure that is virtually constant as long as they are driven by an input pressure higher than their output pressure. There are two common types of regulators used in trickle systems: adjustable regulators, on which the output pressure is set by the irrigator, and preset regulators, which have a fixed output pressure to match the pressure requirements of the emitting devices. Preset regulators are generally less expensive than adjustable regulators.

Fields with elevation variations must be broken into sections with only slight variations of elevation within each section. A pressure regulator would be placed at the inlet to each section, and the delivery system pressurized to maintain enough pressure to the regulator in the section with the highest elevation. All sections with lower elevations would have their increased pressure reduced by the regulators, resulting in a reasonably uniform application of water.

Pressure-compensating emitters are emitting devices that maintain virtually constant discharge as long as their operating pressure stays within a certain range. Most pressure-compensating emitters maintain an acceptable uniformity of discharge in the operating range of 10 psi to 30 psi. Pressure-compensating emitters require no pressure regulator but are substantially more expensive than ordinary emitters.

Water Quality and Filtration

Water quality and filtration are probably the most serious concerns in drip irrigation. To discharge very low flow rates, the diameter of the emitter openings must be very small. This results in the emitters being blocked by even the smallest contaminants in the water supply. Of special concern are suspended solids, such as silt and sand, minerals that precipitate out of solution, such as iron or calcium, and algae that may grow in the water. Virtually every drip irrigation system must include a filtration system to prevent plugging of the emitters. A system with poor-quality water and poor filtration simply will not function reliably enough to warrant the maintenance needed to keep it in operation.

Suspended solids will normally be less of a problem when ground water is used for irrigation than when surface water is used. Emitters are usually rated by the manufacturer as to the degree of filtration needed to prevent plugging. This is usually expressed as a screen mesh number, or as the diameter of the largest particle capable of passing through a filter.

Filters may be constructed of stainless steel or plastic screens, which are reusable and require periodic cleaning. You may also use disposable fiber cartridges. For water with a heavy load of large contaminants, you may use a separator that uses centrifugal force to remove most of the particles. Water with large amounts of fine silt and clay in suspension will normally require filtration with a media filter. Media filters use graded layers of fine sand to remove sediment. They are effective filters capable of handling very large flow rates but are relatively expensive to buy and maintain.

The precipitation of minerals in irrigation water is usually a problem only with groundwater. Dissolved minerals may come out of solution with a change of pH or temperature or when aeration occurs. If calcium is the problem, inject acid into the water to lower the pH to prevent precipitates from forming. Sometimes there is not sufficient calcium to precipitate out of solution, but enough to form a "lime" crust over the openings of emitters after the system is shut off and the components dry. If this situation causes frequent blockage of emitters, inject acid into the system for the final few minutes of operation before shutdown. The choice of sulfuric or phosphoric acid, and the rate to inject it will depend on your specific water analysis and fertilization program. Many national companies which sell soluble fertilizers offer soil and water testing services and will make recommendations to growers using their products. Another source of information and recommendations may be your local county extension agent. If iron is the problem, oxidize the iron by chlorination or aeration and then filter the water. Injection of chemicals such as fertilizers or pesticides into the water may cause precipitation of minerals. Any filtration should take place after chemical injection has been done.

Growth of algae within the irrigation system is seldom a problem because most algae require sunlight to grow, and almost all parts of the system are made of opaque materials. However, when white PVC plastic pipe is exposed, enough light to support algae growth may penetrate the pipe. Painting the pipe with either silver or black paint will correct the problem. Surface water often contains algae and may introduce it into the water supply. Pumping unfiltered water from an algae-laden source will result in frequent blockage problems. Treat ponds with algae problems by adding copper sulfate to reduce the filtration load. Occasionally a bacterial slime may develop in systems where the water has considerable organic matter. Routine use of a 2 ppm chlorine rinse at the end of each irrigation set will normally prevent slime development. If a slime problem does develop, clean the system with a 30 ppm chlorine treatment.

The use of high-quality water and an adequate filtration system cannot be over-emphasized. Using poor-quality irrigation water in a trickle irrigation system can result in so many maintenance problems related to emitter plugging, that any labor savings you would expect relative to other irrigation methods will be eliminated. Maintaining the filtration system, chemically treating the water if necessary and frequently flushing the system will help prevent these problems.

System Capacity

The hours of operation needed to meet your irrigation requirement depends on the flow rate of the emitting device, the irrigation interval and the rate of water use by the crop. In no case should the system be designed to operate more than 18 hours per day. The time off gives time for drainage of the crop root zone, time for system maintenance and time for catch up in case of system breakdown.

When computing the daily water requirement, the calculations are based only on the area of the field that is actually covered by vegetation. This is possible because only the vegetated area is irrigated with trickle irrigation systems. For example, if flowers are planted in beds that are five feet wide, but the vegetation is only three feet wide, 100 feet of row length would have an area of 300 square feet, not 500 square feet. It is assumed that the unvegetated area uses no water and is not irrigated.

Summary

Trickle irrigation can be an extremely versatile production tool in horticultural enterprises. It can stretch a limited water supply to cover up to 25 percent more acreage than a typical sprinkler system. It can reduce the incidence of many fungal diseases by reducing humidity and keeping foliage dry. It allows automation of the irrigation system, reducing labor requirements. It delays the onset of salinity problems when irrigation water of poor quality must be used.

Trickle irrigation requires careful water treatment to prevent emitter blockage problems. Frequent inspection of the system is necessary to ensure it is functioning properly. Improper design and component sizing can result in a system with poor uniformity of application and a much lower than expected application efficiency.

A properly designed and installed trickle system will normally be substantially more expensive than a sprinkler system initially. However, the lower operating cost and higher efficiency of the trickle system can justify the added expense very quickly in many crop situations.

CHAPTER 7

FERTILIZATION

Fertilization is a subsystem of your production system. It must be designed in such a way so as to enhance the productivity of the entire system at the lowest possible cost while still maintaining product quality. The system you use for fertilizing a crop must be integrated with your planting and watering systems. A fertilization system has two components: the material used to supply the desired nutrients and the method used to deliver the nutrients to the plant.

What Fertilizer Material Should You Apply?

Test the Soil

Before initiating any fertilizer program, always test the soil and water for nutrient content and pH. You must know what nutrients are deficient in your soil before you can decide what must be added. Adding nutrients which are unneeded is not only costly in material and labor expense but may lead to a toxic build-up or contribute to ground water pollution. Extremes of acidity or alkalinity (low or high pH) may place the nutrients in a form unavailable to the plants. A soil test is the place to start in developing your fertilization system. Your local county extension agriculture agent should be able to tell you how to collect soil and water samples and send them off to be tested.

Nutrition

Table 7.1 lists low, medium and high nutrient content from soil tests for use in determining the amount of each nutrient to be added in your fertilization program.

Table 7-1: Nutrient Levels for Fertilizer Additions Based on Soil Test Results

Nitrogen	0-25 ppm	Low
	26-50 ppm	Medium
	51-80 ppm	High
Phosphorus	0-50 lb/acre	Low
	51-200 lb/acre	Medium
	201+ lb/acre	High
Potassium	0-250 lb/acre	Low
	251-500 lb/acre	Medium
	501+ lb/acre	High

A standard agricultural soil test includes only phosphorus and potassium, which are relatively immobile in the soil and remain in place until used by the plant. A test is required each year to determine if a deficiency exists and the amount of fertilizer required to raise the level of each nutrient to that required for the crop being planted. A crop's requirement for phosphorus and potassium can be provided in a single application or in successive light applications.

An evaluation of the level of nitrogen is not included in most standard soil tests and must be requested when the soil sample is sent in. Nitrogen is relatively mobile in the soil — it is absorbed by the crop, it may be leached out of the root zone by irrigation water or rain, or it may escape into the atmosphere. Because of these losses, nitrogen will normally need to be added to each crop. Lighter, more frequent applications of nitrogen will provide for more uniform and consistent crop growth with less potential loss to the surrounding environment.

A note of caution. Text and home gardening books typically recommend nitrogen (N), phosphorus (P) and potassium (K) be added as fertilizer in a 1-1-1 or a 1-2-2 ratio. Most fertilizers packaged for flowers will be in a similar ratio. This is the correct general ratio of the requirement of each nutrient for the production of flowers. However, this does not mean that fertilizer should be added in this ratio. It means that the nutrients should be available to the plant in this ratio. Depending on soil test results, the nutrients may need to be added in a different ratio. Often phosphorus and potassium are present in sufficient quantities and only nitrogen may need to be added. Adding P and K when they are not needed is very costly in material and labor expense and will increase their levels in the soil each year. It is not uncommon for soil tests to come back with the amount of P and K off the scale of the average test. If your results show a "+" after the "lbs/acre" value, it means the level of that nutrient is greater than the ability of the test to measure. You may not need to add any P or K for several crops. Based on soil test results, try to find a fertilizer in a ratio as close to what you actually need for the crop under the existing nutrient status of your soil.

pH

The pH of a soil is a measure of its acidity or alkalinity. Extremes of either acidity or alkalinity may make nutrients unavailable to plants. Micronutrient availability is particularly affected. The optimum pH range for most decorative plant materials lies somewhere between 5.5 and 7.5. The optimal range will vary in both width of the range and in upper and lower limits depending on the particular crop. The pH of a soil may vary because of the parent rock material from which the soil came, cropping sequence, previous fertilizer use, irrigation water quality, or other factors.

Table 7-2 lists materials to add in order to correct soil pH.

Table 7-2: Soil pH Corrective Materials To Increase Soil pH

Effective Calcium Carbonate (from soil test)	Lime Required lbs per 1,000 sq.ft.
5,000	110
3,000	90
2,000	70
1,000	30
500	10

Dolomitic limestone containing both calcium and magnesium is preferred over calcium-only materials.

To Decrease Soil pH

pH value (from soil test)	Amount of Sulfur – lbs. per 1,000 sq.ft.		
	Sandy Soil	**Loam Soil**	**Clay Soil**
7.0	.5-.75	.75-1	1-1.5
7.5	1-1.5	1.5-2	2-3
8.0	2-3	3-4	4-5
8.5	4-5	5-6	6-7
9.0	7-8	7-8	7-8

A conductivity meter, also known as a sol-u-bridge, is a way to monitor changes in total soil fertilizer levels. This instrument is a handy indicator of the total amount of fertilizer in your soil. It provides a measure of the amount of mineral salts and fertilizer present in the soil by measuring the resistance to flow of electrical current through a soil and water suspension. A significant change in readings over time indicates that you may need to add fertilizer or leach excess salts from the soil. Table 7-3 lists soluble salt conductivity readings for field soils and the recommended action.

The electro-conductivity (EC) of your irrigation water should also be monitored. Water high in soluble salts can cause undesirably high levels of salt in the soil and severe production problems, leading to crop loss. Irrigation and fertilization practices must be adjusted when irrigating with water that contains medium to high levels of salt. With higher levels of soluble salt in the irrigation water, drainage from the production beds becomes critical. Table 7-4 lists EC readings and water quality ratings for irrigation water.

Table 7-3: Soluble Salt Electrical Conductivity Readings - (field soils expressed as mmhos/cm)

Saturated (1:1) Paste Extract	2:1 Water to Soil Suspension	5:1 Water to Soil Suspension	Meaning	Recommended Action
< 1	< 0.15	< 0.1	very low	add fertilizer
1-2	0.15-0.5	0.1-0.3	low - OK	may need fertilizer
2-3	0.5-1.0	0.3-0.8	satisfactory	maintain at level
3-4	1.0-1.8	0.8-1.0	high	may need to leach
4-6	1.8-2.25	1.0-1.5 +	very high	leach heavily

mmhos = millimhos = 2 teaspoons NaCl in 5 gallons of water.

Table 7-4:
Electro-Conductivity Readings and Water Quality
Ratings for Irrigation Water

mmhos	Relative Salt Content	Water Quality Rating
< 0.25	Low	Excellent
0.25-0.75	Medium	Good
0.75-1.50	Medium to High	Fair
1.50-2.00	High	Permissible
2.00 +	Excessive	Unsatisfactory

Fertilizer Selection

The fertilizer to be used to supply the required nutrients for a highly productive crop depends on the existing levels of nutrients in the soil, the soil pH, and the soluble salt content of the irrigation water and the soil. There are many different sources and formulations of fertilizer available. Some are more or less soluble in water or the soil solution and, therefore, either immediately available to the plant or more slowly available for absorption and use. Other fertilizers must be decomposed or have a coating which must be dissolved or broken down in some manner before they are available for plant use. Soluble fertilizers are available in granular, powder or liquid form. They are relatively inexpensive. Slow-release or controlled-release fertilizers are typically granular in form and formulated to last from three to nine months. Their relative cost of materials is high but this may be partially offset by a reduced cost of application labor and decreased nutrient waste.

The greatly reduced rate of nutrient release from slow-release fertilizers reduces the risk of crop injury from over-fertilization. Mechanisms which control the rate of nutrient release include:

A. Low-Solubility. The rate of release is determined by soil microbial activity, temperature, moisture level and soil pH. An example fertilizer is Urea Formaldehyde.

B. Sulfur-Coated. The rate of release is determined by soil moisture content and particle size and to a lesser extent by soil temperature and pH. An example fertilizer is sulfur-coated urea.

C. Resin-Coated. The rate of release is determined by soil temperature and fluctuations in soil moisture content. An example fertilizer is any of the various formulations of Osmocote.

Table 7.5 lists nutrient composition, salt index, pH reaction and water solubility of several common inorganic fertilizers.

Table 7-5: Inorganic Fertilizers

Chemical	N	Analysis (%) P²O⁵	K²O	CaO	S	Salt Index	Acidity / Basicity	Water Solubility
ammonium nitrate	33.5	-	-	-	-	105	A	high
calcium nitrate	17	-	-	3.6	-	53	B	high
ammonium sulfate	20.5	-	-	-	24	69	A	medium
urea	46.6	-	-	-	-	75	A	high
superphosphate	-	20	-	23	9	8	N	very low
triple superphosphate	-	45	-	20	2	10	N	very low
potassium nitrate	13.8	-	46.6	-	-	74	B	high
potassium sulfate	-	-	54	-	18.4	46	N	medium
magnesium sulfate	-	-	-	-	13	44	N	high
sulfate of potash-mag	-	-	21.9	-	22	43	N	medium
gypsum	-	-	-	30	16	8	N	very low

Salt index is a measure of the effect of fertilizers on the concentration of the soil solution compared to an equal weight of sodium nitrate, which is assigned a value of 100.

Acidity/Basicity: A = acid reaction, B = basic reaction, N = neutral.

N = Nitrogen, P²O⁵ = phosphorus, K²O = potassium, CaO = calcium, S = sulphur

Organic fertilizers are commonly used to provide nutrients to crops of decorative plant materials. Their composition can be quite variable. The type and amount of bedding mixed with manure, and salt levels of other components can vary greatly. The rate of nutrient release, and therefore application rate, depends on soil microbial activity, temperature, moisture, pH, soil soluble salt content and the degree of decomposition of the organic material when applied to the crop. Several commonly used organic fertilizers are listed in Table 7-6. It should be noted that most manures are very low in nutritive value and are used primarily for their effect on soil structure.

Table 7-6: Organic Fertilizers

| Material | Analysis | | | Rate lbs / 1,000 sq.ft. | Comments |
	N	P^2O^5	K^2O		
dried blood	12	1.5	0.53	0 - 40	rapidly available, short term
bat guano	6	9	3	30 - 40	nutrition in a 2-3-1 ratio
kelp or seaweed	1	0.5	9	50	potassium source
raw bone meal	4	20	-	50	very slowly soluble
steamed bone meal	2	27	-	50	phosphorus is soluble
cotton seed	6	2.5	2	30 - 40	acid reaction
wood ashes	-	2	6	50	very alkaline
Manures *					
cattle	0.5	0.3	0.5		All manures are generally
chicken	1	0.50	.8		low in nutrients and should
horse	0.6	0.3	0.6		primarily be used to
sheep	0.9	0.5	0.8		improve soil structure.
swine	0.6	0.5	1		

* application rate of manures depends on the state of decomposition, salt level and bedding material contained in the manure.

When Should Fertilizer Be Applied?

Timing of fertilizer application should coincide with the nutritional needs of the crop. Fertilizer should be applied slightly ahead of need so that it is available on demand for growth and development of the crop. Lead time will vary with the solubility and nature of the fertilizer. Highly soluble fertilizers may be applied on demand to the crop. Fertilizers which must be transformed (organic materials) will need to be applied well in advance of crop requirements. Timing of application is also dependent on the type of plant material being grown, be it annual, herbaceous perennial or woody perennial shrub or tree.

Annuals

For annual crops harvested throughout the growing season, lighter and more frequent application of nitrogen may be necessary to reduce the nonproductive cycle between flushes of bloom. Nitrogen availability is a limiting factor of optimum production. When a stem is cut, a number of leaves — sites of photosynthesis — are also removed which reduces the plant's capacity to produce more growth. New vegetative growth must occur, in the form of new branches, before a new flower will be produced. Nitrogen is required to feed this vegetative growth. Remember that increased stem length is extra value. Nitrogen levels should be sufficiently high, but not excessive, to keep the plant rapidly growing.

Perennials

Some perennials have a single flush of vegetative growth followed by flower bud development and subsequent harvest. No further above-ground vegetative growth may occur during the remainder of the growing season. No additional stems or leaves will be produced after bloom, so the requirement for nitrogen is reduced. The leaves, which remain after harvest, carry on photosynthesis and store excess carbohydrates in portions of the plant that over winter so they are available to fuel next spring's growth.

Other perennials form a rosette of foliage in the fall which then elongates and flowers the next year.

Fertilizer should be applied so that it is available for early spring growth. Many growers provide a late fall application of fertilizer (after dormancy) to feed the roots and provide a residual pool of nutrients in the soil for late winter or early spring vegetative growth. A second application may then be applied at the emergence of new growth through the soil surface. Peonies are an example of a crop often fertilized in this manner.

Woodies

Timing of fertilizer application for woody shrubs and trees is primarily a matter of when not to fertilize. Fertilizer application should cease early enough in the summer to allow plant growth to slow and harden off before a fall freeze. After the plants are dormant, fertilizer can be applied to provide a residual pool of nutrients in the soil for early spring growth. Increased branch length is valuable in the market. A consistent supply of nutrients, early to mid growing season, will yield stronger, steadier growth and longer branches than a single spring application of fertilizer.

How Should Nutrients be Applied?

The choice of nutrient delivery systems depends on the level of nutrient management the grower is willing to supply, on the availability and delivery system of irrigation water, and on the amount of capital available for investment. Crop fertilization is not a process in and of itself. It is accomplished in conjunction with planting and watering systems. Fertilizer may be incorporated into the planting bed or dissolved in the irrigation water.

Row Application

In this method of fertilizer application, a small trench is dug two to three inches deep on either side of the plant row before planting. A measured amount of the desired fertilizer is placed in each trench and then covered over. Plant in the row between trenches immediately following placement of the fertilizer. This application method can be labor-intensive at a time of great pressure to get the crops planted. It also affords little control over the rate at which the fertilizer is available for plant growth; more fertilizer is available at planting, with a diminished supply as the crop grows. However, row application has the advantage of placing the fertilizer in close proximity to the root zone of the plants. This is particularly important with phosphorus due to its relative immobility in the soil.

Broadcast Fertilization

Fertilizer is spread uniformly over the surface of the area in production. If applied before planting, it is incorporated into the soil immediately prior to planting. Post-plant application of phosphorus to the soil surface may have reduced value as the phosphorus may not move into the root zone of the crop. Care must be taken with any post-plant application to keep the fertilizer granules off the foliage. A completely pelletized fertilizer should be used with this application method. A mixture of fertilizers may not provide satisfactory results because particles of different sizes and weights in the mixture will disperse in varying patterns from the dispersal mechanism. Non-uniform application of the various nutrients will occur and can result in variable growth of the crop. Using this method may also result in fertilizer application in non-productive areas, thereby wasting fertilizer and encouraging weed growth.

Sidedress Application

Nitrogen fertilizer, applied before planting, often leaches or washes out of the crop root zone. This is most common in sandy soils or in periods of heavy or frequent rainfall. To help correct this problem, fertilizer can be sidedressed by placing it alongside the row of growing plants. Sidedressing is usually done when the first flowers of an annual crop begin to bloom or when the crop exhibits nitrogen deficiency symptoms of yellowing foliage. The fertilizer may be placed in a band or narrowly broadcast alongside the crop row. Care should be taken to keep the fertilizer off the crop foliage. This method provides an additional "peak" level of nutrients which then begins to diminish as the crop continues to grow. Frequent, light sidedress applications of fertilizer will provide for more consistent nutrient levels, but add significant labor costs.

Slow-release fertilizers can minimize the variations in nutrient supply that are evident with common fertilizers applied dry to the soil. The higher cost of these fertilizers may be offset by reduced labor costs due to fewer applications.

Fertigation

Materials

Adding fertilizer to the irrigation water is an effective delivery system both in terms of labor utilization and control of crop growth. The fertilizer used must be completely soluble in water and must not form any precipitate in the tank or irrigation lines. Table 7.7 lists solubilities of a few common fertilizers used in fertigation. In addition to the commonly available fertilizers listed in Table 7-7, there are several fertilizers specially formulated for use in fertigation systems. All are highly soluble, complete fertilizers. Among these are various formulations of Peters brand fertilizers from The Scotts Company and those from Plant Marvel Laboratories, Inc.

Table 7-7: Fertilizer Solubilities

Material	Solubility lbs. / 100 gal. cold water
ammonium nitrate	984
calcium nitrate	851
potassium nitrate	108
urea	651
diammonium phosphate	358

Equipment

Fertigation requires an irrigation system. It can be as simple as a garden hose or as complex as an integrated drip system. It may use city water, well water or water pumped from a farm pond. The irrigation system available will influence the design of the fertigation system.

Fertilizer can be mixed with water to its final concentration in a large tank. It can then be pumped out and applied directly to the plants as the crop is watered. A very large tank is required or you will have to continually stop watering to mix more fertilizer solution.

Injectors

The problems of very large tank sizes or constant stops to mix more fertilizer solution can be overcome by the use of an injector. This device injects precise amounts of a concentrated fertilizer solution into the irrigation water line. The simplest type of injector uses the suction of a venturi bypass. Water passing through a restriction and across an opening creates a suction that draws fertilizer concentrate up a tube and into the water stream. The "hozon" siphon proportioner is an example of a widely used venturi bypass injector. Its primary advantage is its low cost (less than ten dollars). Its greatest disadvantage is its small capacity. It can only handle a water volume equivalent to that of a single garden hose. A further disadvantage is that the flow of water through the proportioner must remain at a high rate or the amount of fertilizer added to the water may become quite variable. The hozon has a proportioning ratio of one part fertilizer concentrate to fifteen parts irrigation water. It can be a useful, low-cost means of adding supplemental nutrients to a crop.

Water-driven piston or diaphragm pumps pull a measured volume of concentrated fertilizer solution from a tank and inject it into the irrigation line. These injectors are available in a range of proportioning ratios, or the amount of water the fertilizer concentrate is blended into. Common fixed proportioning ratios are 1:100 and 1:200. Several other proportioners are available with variable ratios from 1:50 to 1:1,000. Injector pumps, with their higher ratio proportioning, allow the use of relatively small tanks of fertilizer concentrate to add nutrients to large areas of production, without stopping to remix the fertilizer solution. Models are also available in a wide range of flow rates to accommodate almost any water system.

Anti-Siphon Device

All fertigation systems, connected in any way to potable water should have an anti-siphon device or backflow preventer included in the system. These devices are used to prevent any fertilizer remaining in the irrigation line from being siphoned back into the water system and contaminating potable water. The simplest form of anti-siphon device is a vacuum breaker. Figure 7.1 illustrates how a vacuum breaker functions. Under normal water flow conditions, the check valve is open and the fertigation water flows through the line. When the irrigation is finished and normal water flow is turned off, the pressure in the line will drop. At a predetermined low pressure level, the check valve in the vacuum breaker will close and allow air into the device and line, eliminating negative pressure and any backflow of fertilizer water. Most states have laws requiring anti-siphon devices to be installed on all irrigation systems.

Figure 7-1: How A Vacuum Breaker Functions

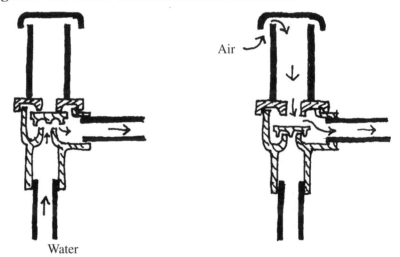

Air

Water

Normal open position   Closed position when
during irrigation   not irrigating

Filters

A screen should always be placed on the end of the draw tube used to pull fertilizer concentrate from the tank to the injector. A filter should be installed after the point of fertilizer injection into the irrigation line to prevent undissolved particles from plugging emitters in the drip lines. Figure 7-2 illustrates a typical arrangement of fertigation system components.

Figure 7-2: A Typical Arrangement of Fertigation System Components

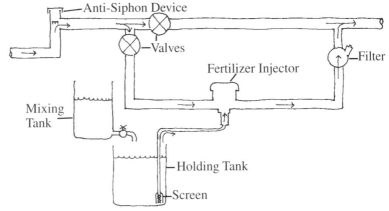

Mixing/Settling Tank

Many growers strive to contain fertilizer costs by using less expensive fertilizers, which are often less soluble. These fertilizers should be mixed in a tank and left overnight to permit settling of undissolved solids, which occasionally occur. The concentrated fertilizer solution is then transferred to a holding tank supplying the injector. This tank sequence helps prevent undissolved solids from damaging the proportioner or plugging the irrigation system.

Checking the Fertigation System

The fertigation system should be routinely monitored and checked for accuracy of fertilizer concentration. The easiest method is to check the blended fertilizer and water solution as it is applied to the crop. A sol-u-bridge is used to measure the electrical conductivity of the fertigation water. First calibrate the meter using a standard solution. Using the meter, measure the conductivity of the irrigation water before any fertilizer is injected into it. Then test the fertigation water as it comes out of the line (after the injector) and subtract the raw water reading from the combined reading. Routine monitoring of this fertilizer index will alert you to problems of improper mixing of the concentrate solution or of a malfunctioning injector.

Integrated Fertilizer and Irrigation Management

The application of fertilizer and water to the soil creates a potential for pollution. Leaching of nutrients down through the soil can pollute ground water, and surface runoff can carry fertilizers into streams and lakes. John Dole and Janet Cole at Oklahoma State University are developing a comprehensive approach to runoff control. Their Integrated Fertilizer and Irrigation Management (IFIM) system is similar to IPM, the integrated pest management system designed to reduce the amount of pesticides being used. Through careful application of water, choice of fertilizers and timing of application, the system should reduce the risk of pollution. Apply only the amount of fertilizer and water required to keep your crop actively growing. Do not apply either one to excess.

Summary

Plants need food to grow and produce flowers. How and in what form the nutrients are furnished to your crop will have a big impact on productivity, quality and labor requirements. A fertilizer delivery system must be designed to deliver the required nutrients to the crop when needed and in a form available for plant growth while requiring a minimum of labor. The system used to fertilize your crops must be integrated with your planting and watering systems. Consider the amount of labor required to conduct each of the activities in your fertilizer delivery system. Fertigation enables the grower to use the same system to deliver both water and nutrients to the crop.

Fertigation is rarely used as the only method of providing nutrients to a crop. Phosphorus may be expensive in a highly soluble form. A common practice is to use superphosphate or triple superphosphate as a pre-plant application and then apply nitrogen and potassium through the fertigation system. Another approach is to apply a slow-release form of fertilizer pre-plant and then provide supplemental nutrients through the fertigation system. A disadvantage of fertigation is that in periods of constant rainfall, when you are not irrigating, you cannot fertilize. If you are using plastic mulch, you will need to water even when it rains and so fertilizer may always be applied through fertigation. Once a production bed is covered with plastic mulch, fertigation may be the only method of providing nutrients.

In designing a system to supply nutrients to your crops, you must link it with all other subsystems so that the entire production system is enhanced at the lowest possible total cost while maintaining quality.

CHAPTER 8

WEED CONTROL

Weeds must be controlled in the field production of cut flowers, as competition with weeds reduces the quantity and quality of floral production. A bed full of weeds also increases the time required to harvest, raising labor costs. Many growers consider weed control to be their greatest care-as-needed problem. Many a sore back and blistered hand attest to the magnitude of the problem of weed control. Several methods are available to control weeds, including hand weeding, mechanical cultivation, herbicides and a variety of organic and inorganic mulches. An ineffective weed control system reduces yields, lowers quality and greatly increases the amount of labor required in most other activities. The appearance of the farm and production beds is critical to any on-the-farm approach to marketing. Weed control, or lack thereof, impacts all activities from production to marketing and therefore is critical to the success of any specialty cut flower enterprise. In designing a weed-control subsystem, consider the effectiveness of the activity; on controlling weeds both immediate and long term; how well it is integrated, linked with all other activities; and the labor requirements to perform the activity.

Hand-Weeding

A hoe and hand-weeding are sure methods for control, but availability and cost of labor may be prohibitive in all but the smallest production situations. A variety of shapes and sizes of hoes exist; from broad, flat rectangular-shaped heads; to narrowly pointed, triangular heads; to stirrup-type hoes which use a push-pull motion to cut weeds just below the soil surface. Most types are available with either long or short handles. The two-finger hand-pull method of weed control is labor intensive but may be a desirable approach to within-the-row removal of weeds growing against young plants or within newly planted or shallow-rooted perennials.

Mechanical Cultivation

Mechanical cultivation is a common method of weed control. A walk-behind rototiller or tractor-mounted cultivator is used between rows to cultivate the soil and thereby cut the weeds below the soil surface. Row spacing must be planned to facilitate the width of the rototiller, allowing it to pass between the rows without coming close enough to severely damage crop roots. When using tractor-mounted cultivation, row spacing must accommodate the wheel spacing of the tractor. Crop height as compared to tractor and implement height are also factors to consider. All weed control cultivation of tall-growing crops must be accomplished before the crop reaches the height of the tractor axle or the tool bar of the implement.

Flame Weeding

Flame weeding kills plants by searing (not burning) plant tissue. A hand-held or tractor-mounted propane burner is used to pass a flame quickly over the weeds. The sudden intense heat inflicted on the plant tissues causes cell contents to rapidly expand and rupture cell walls, killing or severely damaging the weeds. Young weeds are most susceptible to flaming as are broad-leaved plants. Grasses are more difficult to control with flaming because of the protective sheath around their growing point and possible presence of underground rhizomes. Flame weeding in mature crops is difficult and requires intense concentration and considerable skill. Inconsistent tractor speed, uneven ground, differing stages of weed maturity, and sudden changes in wind speed or direction all combine to increase the risk of damaging the crop. Flaming can be an effective non-chemical means of controlling weeds but it must be carefully and intelligently done.

Herbicides

Increasing concern about pesticide residues contaminating the environment makes it especially important to select and use herbicides as effectively as possible. Herbicides should not constitute the only method used to control weeds. They should be used in conjunction with cultural and mechanical means of weed control. The following discussion of environmental concerns and safety guidelines and regulations applies not only to herbicides but also to all pesticides.

Protect Groundwater

The basic environmental concern with herbicide use is that of groundwater contamination and the potential for entry into sources of drinking water. Because the problem occurs underground, out of sight, it is difficult to recognize when groundwater is being contaminated. The following practices can reduce the potential for herbicides to contaminate either surface or groundwater.

Soil Characteristics

Know the potential for the herbicide to leach through your soil. Sandy soils and those with high percolation rates allow pesticides to pass through readily. Pesticides which are highly soluble and those which do not become readily adsorbed onto the soil are most likely to leach. Areas with shallow water tables are also at higher risk of contamination.

Irrigation Practices

Applying irrigation water at high rates can cause surface runoff or an increased rate of leaching down through the soil. Herbicide applications should be delayed when heavy rain is suspected to minimize the contamination potential.

Drift

Do not spray when the wind speed is greater than ten miles per hour. Avoid unnecessarily fine droplet sizes or spray pressures higher than required. Avoid any condition which may contribute to spray drift.

Label Directions

Follow label directions exactly as stated. Mix to carefully measured concentrations and never add a little extra, just to be sure. Follow the directions about timing and placement of the herbicide. Calibrate the application equipment carefully and often to avoid over- or under-application of the chemical.

Mixing

Position the spray tank or applicator on an impervious surface such as a concrete pad when mixing or filling with chemicals. Design a mixing system that greatly reduces the risk of spills. If you must mix or fill in the field, change the location each time to avoid concentrating chemicals from spillage. Mix only the amount of chemical to be used. Triple rinse all containers and empty rinse water into a spray tank and use it for treating the site.

Disposal

Take empty pesticide containers and any chemicals left over at season's end to your county hazardous waste disposal unit. Do not burn or bury chemical containers either on site or in a landfill.

Always store and mix herbicides away from water sources such as wells, springs, ponds and streams.

Protect Yourself and Your Workers

Always wear protective clothing and equipment when handling any pesticide. Full-coverage protective clothing, chemical-resistant gloves, eye protection, boots, head protection and a respirator approved for the chemical to be used should be worn when handling, mixing, applying and cleaning up from the use of pesticides.

Worker Protection Standard

Federal law requires you to provide training and notification to workers to prevent accidental or occupational exposure to pesticides. Your local county Extension agent or your state Department of Agriculture can supply you with information on the specific requirements of the law and may have training programs and materials available for your use.

- Any person who handles or uses pesticides needs to be trained and periodically retrained in appropriate safety measures.

- You must conduct a worker Right-to-Know training program for all your employees on the potential hazards of exposure to the chemicals you use.

- Label instructions on Restricted Entry Intervals (REI) must be followed. You may be required to notify workers, either orally or by posting warning signs or both, that pesticides have been applied. Workers will be required to be kept out of the treated area for the entire REI.

Record Keeping

Anyone who applies restricted use pesticides (RUP) must keep records and retain them for two years. These records include:

- The brand name or product name and the EPA registration number of each RUP applied.

- The total amount of the chemical used.

- The location of the application.

- The size of the area treated.

- The crop the chemical was applied to.

- The date of the application.

- The name and certification number of the applicator.

Contact your county extension office or State Department of Agriculture for an update of record-keeping requirements.

Emergency Planning and Community Right to Know

Laws require notification of your State Emergency Response Commission, the Local Emergency Planning Committee and the local fire department if extremely hazardous materials are stored. The name and telephone number of a knowledgeable contact person must also be provided. A list of EPA established Extremely Hazardous Substances and their threshold quantities should be available from your state Department of Natural Resources or a similar agency. Any spill must be reported to the listed agencies.

The above discussion on pesticide handling and reporting applies to all pesticide use, including the insecticides discussed in Chapter 9 and fungicides in Chapter 10.

Herbicide Classification

Herbicides are grouped into several classifications. Knowledge of the classification of a herbicide is essential to the development of an effective chemical weed-control system. Herbicides are commonly classified as follows:

- Pre-emergent vs. post-emergent
  A pre-emergent herbicide's mode of action is to kill the germinating weed seed. It is generally not effective on mature weeds. A post-emergent herbicide kills weeds after they have sprouted. It is more effective on young plants than on fully mature weeds.

- Contact vs. systemic
  A contact herbicide kills all green plant tissue it comes into contact with. A systemic herbicide is one which must be absorbed into the plant either through the roots or leaf surface and kills the weed plant by disrupting one or more of its life processes.

- Soil-applied (incorporated or surface) vs. foliar-applied
  A soil-applied herbicide either must be absorbed into the plant roots to be effective or act on a germinating seed in the soil. A foliar-applied herbicide either acts directly on leaf and stem tissue or must be absorbed into them to become effective. It generally has no effect when applied to the soil.

- Selective vs. non-selective
  A selective herbicide is effective in controlling only a specific type of plant such as monocotyledonous or dicotyledonous plants. Examples of selectivity in herbicides would be killing weeds in your home lawn without killing the grass or a bean farmer killing the annual grasses in the field without killing the bean crop. A non-selective herbicide kills all plants in the treated area.

Herbicide Selection

Select a herbicide that is labeled for use on the target weed(s) in your crop. Be sure it has an appropriate mode of action and application method for the conditions you face. Due to limited production of many species, only a few herbicides are labeled for use on specialty cut flowers. Table 8-1 lists several herbicides which at one time have been labeled for use on one or more species of flowers. Other herbicides may also be labeled for use on flowers, and new chemicals enter the marketplace each year. The table represents a starting point in a search for a herbicide effective on your soil type, against your particular weed pests and for your specific crop.

Table 8-1:
Herbicides Which Have Been Registered For Use On Flowers*

Crop	Herbicide
Achillea millefolium, Yarrow	Dacthal, Fusilade, Treflan, Acclaim
Ageratum houstonianum, Ageratum	Dacthal
Antirrhinum spp., Snapdragon	Dacthal, Fusilade, Treflan, Metoclachor, Poast, Acclaim
Artemisia albula, Silver King	Fusilade
Astilbe x arendsii, Astilbe	Fusilade, Acclaim
Calendula officinlis, Calendula	Betasan, Treflan
Centaurea cyanus, Bachelor's Button	Betasan, Treflan, Acclaim
Chrysanthemum x superbum, Shasta Daisy	Fusilade, Betasan, Treflan, Poast, Acclaim
Consolida ambigua, Larkspur	Dacthal
Cosmos bipinnatus, Cosmos	Dacthal, Acclaim
Dahlia spp., *Dahlia*	Dacthal, Betasan, Treflan, Poast

Crop	Herbicide
Delphinium elatum, Delphinium	Dacthal, Metoclachor
Dicentra eximia, Bleeding Heart	Dacthal, Poast, Acclaim
Gladiolus spp., Gladiola	Dacthal, Fusilade, Betasan, Treflan, Metoclachor, Poast, Acclaim
Gypsophila elegans, Baby's Breath	Dacthal, Treflan, Acclaim
Helianthus spp., Sunflower	Dacthal, Treflan
Helichrysum bracteatum, Strawflowers	Dacthal
Iris spp., Iris	Dacthal, Metoclachor, Poast, Acclaim
Lavandula spp., Lavender	Poast
Lilium spp., Lily	Dacthal, Metoclachor, Acclaim
Limonium latifolium, German Statice	Poast
Limonium sinuatum, Annual Statice	Fusilade, Metoclachor, Acclaim
Matthiola incana, Stock	Betasan
Paeonia hybrids, Peony	Dacthal
Phlox spp., Phlox	Treflan, Acclaim
Ranunculus spp., *Ranunculus*	Betasan
Rudbeckia hirta, Black-eyed Susan	Metoclachor, Acclaim
Rudbeckia nitida, Cone Flower	Dacthal, Acclaim
Scabiosa caucasica, Pincushion Flower	Treflan
Senecio spp., Dusty Miller	Fusilade, Treflan, Metoclachor, Poast
Tagetes spp., Marigold	Dacthal, Fusilade, Betasan, Treflan, Metoclachor, Poast

Crop	Herbicide
Veronica spp., Speedwell	Treflan
Zinnia spp., *Zinnia*	Dacthal, Fusilade, Betasan, Treflan, Metoclachor, Poast, Acclaim

*Contact your county extension agent for an update on herbicides labeled for flower production. Registration of chemicals and their approved uses change periodically. Always read labels carefully, check to be sure the chemical is registered for your intended use and follow all label directions carefully.

Organic Mulches

Organic mulches reduce weed competition, improve water retention and reduce temperature fluctuations within the soil. Organic mulches include straw, hay, peanut shells, leaf mold, compost, sawdust, wood chips and shavings, and animal manures. These mulches slowly decompose and increase organic matter in the soil. Organic mulch, properly used, can provide all the benefits of any mulch with the possible exception of early season warming. Finer-textured organic mulches like sawdust, grass clippings or newspapers provide an insulating layer which results in a soil temperature approximately two to three degrees cooler than unmulched soil. Coarse-textured organic mulches such as straw provide soil temperatures about five to six degrees cooler. Natural mulch materials are often not available in adequate quantities for commercial operations or must be hauled a distance to the field at increased cost. Natural materials are not easily spread on growing crops, require considerable hand labor and must be reapplied each year. Expense and logistical problems have generally restricted the commercial use of organic mulch to small-acreage growers. The cost-to-benefit ratio of using organic mulches requires greater depth of analysis than simply their effect on weed control. Their effects on improving soil structure must also be factored into the analysis.

Inorganic Mulches

Inorganic mulches such as plastic have several advantages:

Earliness

Plastic mulch can be used effectively to modify soil temperature. Black or clear mulch absorbs the sun's heat and warms the soil. White or aluminum mulch reflects sunlight and keeps the soil cool. Black mulch applied to the bed before planting will warm the soil and promote faster growth in early season, generally leading to earlier harvest. A first harvest acceleration of seven to 14 days is not uncommon, depending on weather conditions. Clear mulch warms the soil more than black and usually provides even earlier harvest.

Soil Moisture Regulation

Plastic mulch helps prevent soil water loss by evaporation during dry periods and sheds excessive water away from the root zone during periods of excessive rain fall. Like most other mulches, it provides a more uniform, consistent moisture content.

Weed Control

The type of mulch selected can affect weed control. Black plastic mulch prevents light from reaching the soil surface, which prevents most weeds from growing. Intact plastic controls essentially all annual weeds and some perennial weeds such as Johnson-grass. Nutsedge is not effectively controlled by plastic mulch. Clear mulch does not prevent weeds from growing and may in fact make their growth more vigorous due to the improved growing environment beneath the plastic.

Reduced Fertilizer Leaching

As excessive rainfall is shed from the root zone, fertilizer loss through leaching is reduced. This is particularly true in sandy soils. This allows the grower to place more fertilizer in the row before planting the crop.

Improved Quality

Plastic mulch restricts soil splash onto foliage and flowers from rain and irrigation, thereby enhancing appearance.

Reduced Soil Compaction

Soil under the mulch remains loose and friable. Aeration and soil microbial activity are enhanced.

Reduced Root Pruning

The mulch strip effectively prevents cultivation equipment from injuring crop roots. Cultivation or chemical weed control can still be used between the rows.

Improved Plant Growth

A combination of the above results in more vigorous, healthier plants that may be more resistant to pest injury.

The major disadvantage with plastic mulches is their disposal after removal from the bed. Recycling facilities are not widely available. Some photodegradable plastic mulches are available. First-time users often find removal a frustrating experience until individual techniques are developed. Machines are available to lift the plastic, but the bulk of the labor is done by hand. Approximately eight hours of labor are required to remove plastic from one acre.

Plastic mulch costs about $275 to $300 per acre, including installation and removal. Most of this is an up front cost which must be born for the duration of the crop. Some additional equipment is also required. At a minimum, a plastic mulch-laying machine must be purchased or constructed. Equipment must also be available to prepare and shape the planting bed for mulch application. Transplanting or seeding equipment capable of planting through the plastic should be purchased. Detailed and illustrated information on the installation of plastic mulch is provided in Chapter 5.

Woven Polypropylene Mat

Woven mat or landscape weed barrier fabric is a desirable material for weed control. It has advantages over plastic film and organic mulches. The weave allows water to pass through the fabric and into the soil and also permits gas exchange between the soil environment and the atmosphere. Woven weed barriers have an effective life of several years, thereby eliminating the labor required to place and remove plastic film each year. This annual labor savings may help to offset the initial higher capital cost of the woven material. Woven materials are thicker and tougher than plastic sheet mulches and therefore planting holes are more difficult to cut. Paul Sansone of Here and Now Flower Farm near Portland, Oregon, has developed a hole-cutting system where he uses a hot branding iron to burn a hole through the mat. The system not only cuts a hole, but the heat of the iron also melts the ends of the plastic strands together and helps prevent any unraveling of the woven material.

Removal

Remove plastic as soon as possible after use. Do not allow the plastic to become overgrown with weeds before removing it. Do not attempt to plow or disc under a non-degradable plastic mulch, or you will deal with the residue problem for years. Disposal of used plastic mulch is a significant problem for the industry. Degradable mulches will likely reduce or eliminate the disposal problem in the future.

Summary

Controlling weeds is essential not only in reducing crop competition for water, nutrients and light but also as an integral part of insect and disease control systems and in controlling labor usage during harvest. Searching through weedy production beds for harvestable flowers does not lend itself to efficient labor utilization. Weed control is best accomplished when weeds are small and actively growing; they are easiest to kill and remove at this stage, before they flower and produce new seeds.

Plastic mulch does not eliminate the need for good cultural practices. On the contrary, more intensive management is needed to ensure use of the mulch to its greatest advantage. If the mulch loosens after installation and flaps in the wind, apply a shovel of soil in the middle of the plastic at regular intervals down the row to prevent the mulch from blowing off the row or damaging transplants. Establish and follow a good integrated pest-control program. Crops should be observed regularly for insect build-up under the plastic around plant openings. Chapter 9 discusses insect control. Effective control of weeds will simplify controlling insect pests. Since a plastic mulch covers the soil, it reduces water evaporation from the soil surface. If irrigation is not closely monitored the soil may remain saturated over increased periods of time and lead to problems with root rot pathogens. Chapter 10 discusses disease control.

Follow good irrigation practices. Drip irrigation is the method of choice when using plastic mulches for weed control. Drip irrigation is discussed extensively in Chapter 6. Furrow irrigation along the edge of the plastic can be used, but with less success. Soil conditions must be suitable to furrow irrigation. While sprinkler irrigation may be better than no irrigation at all, it is generally of only marginal value. Use tensiometers to determine proper watering frequencies and amount for the drip system. Fertilization can be accomplished by injecting water-soluble fertilizer through the drip system. This type of fertigation system is discussed in Chapter 7. Use good judgement and soil tests to assess the nutrition status of the plants and act accordingly.

As the above discussion illustrates, the care-as-needed production subsystems of watering, fertilizing, weed control, insect control and disease control are all linked together. How one system is accomplished affects the operation and effectiveness of all the other systems. They are an interlocked chain of activities. The strength or performance of the chain depends not only on the strength of each activity but also on the strength of the connecting linkages, the effectiveness of their interrelationships.

Design a weed control system to enhance the performance or lower the cost of all other activities.

Weed control is critical. If not accomplished to a high degree, it will destroy the effectiveness of all the other care-as-needed activities, tremendously increase harvest labor costs, reduce production and decrease quality. In other words, weed control has a large impact on profitability.

CHAPTER 9

INSECT CONTROL

Good cultural practices are the best insect control available. A healthy, actively growing plant is more resilient to insect attack. The ideal approach is a preventative program. Keep production areas clean of plant debris and weeds. Control insects early, when they are first detected; do not wait until a serious infestation occurs. Less control is needed for a few insects in a small area than would be required for the entire crop. Aphids, leafhoppers, spider mites, thrips, grasshoppers and various caterpillars are the most common insects encountered in the production field. An assortment of moth larvae and beetles which naturally feed on grains, cereals, and other dry plant products are the major insect pests of preserved decorative plant materials and flowers in storage.

A system must be developed to control insect pests throughout the entire chain of activities which comprises your company. Each group of activities has its own insect pests and requirements for a system to deal with those specific pests. For example, cutworms may cut seedlings and newly planted transplants off at the soil surface just after planting, thereby increasing the cost of seed or transplants, raising labor costs to replant, and potentially delaying harvest beyond the higher price, early-season markets. Failure to control leafhoppers in the early stages of production may result in the loss of a major portion of the crop due to disease spread. Grasshoppers and caterpillars consume large quantities of leaves and petals, reducing photosynthetic area for plant growth and making the stems unsaleable. Damage from thrips may also render a flower unsaleable. Failure to control insects that attack products in storage is the most costly of all losses from insect pests because by the time products are placed into a warehouse, all production and harvesting costs have been incurred. Also, the potential exists for insect-infested products to be unknowingly shipped from the warehouse to customers and cause a very serious negative reaction in the marketplace. For a cut flower company to be profitable, it must develop and follow an effective system and subsystems to deal with insect pests in each activity, from planting through final distribution of the product.

Integrated Pest Management

Integrated pest management (IPM) is the process of using different methods of controlling insects in an integrated approach. The main goal is to reach an acceptable level of insect control with minimal use of chemical pesticides and as little labor as possible, all at the lowest possible cost while maintaining crop productivity, product quality and marketability.

Insect Monitoring

Monitoring insect species and keeping records of insect numbers and location are integral parts of an IPM program. Place yellow-colored cards coated with a sticky material among your flower crops to capture insect pests such as aphids, leafhoppers and thrips. Check the cards at regular intervals to determine which pests are present. The number of each insect pest species trapped on the card provides a measure of the effectiveness of your insect control system. If the number of a particular pest increases from period to period, either your control program is not adequate or there has been a migration of the insect into your production area. Either way, you must adjust your control measures quickly to reduce the potential damage to your crops.

Monitoring of natural enemies also is important if biological controls are to be used. The presence of naturally occurring insect predators or parasites will affect control strategies.

Identifying Insects

Many insects look similar to the untrained eye but are very different in their biology, habits and controls. Biological controls or chemical selection and placement, cultural tactics and frequency of treatment hinge on proper identification. A grower must also be able to distinguish pests from beneficials, including pollinators and natural enemies.

Unless the insect actually flies up into your face, you will probably first detect it through the damage it causes to your flower crop. By examining the damage, you can partially identify the insect and then choose an appropriate control. Insects damage flowers in several ways, depending on the anatomy of their mouthparts. Most conspicuous are those that chew holes in flowers and leaves, such as caterpillars, slugs and beetles. Less apparent, but perhaps more damaging, are insects that suck plant juices, such as aphids, spider mites, thrips and leafhoppers. Finally, some insects, such as aphids, thrips and leafhoppers, transmit diseases from infected to uninfected plants.

Chewing Mouthparts

Insects with chewing mouthparts cut or tear, and then eat, bits of plant tissue. They attack starting from the edges of leaves and flowers, leaving a ragged margin. In other cases, the insect may not be able to chew completely through the leaf surface, which then acquires a lacy appearance. This is most common with small insects or insects in their immature, early feeding phase. Some insects prefer the tender, interveinal tissue, leaving only a skeleton of veins after attack.

A common control of chewing insects is placing chemicals that work as stomach poisons on the leaf, stem and flower surfaces. The effect on appearance and potential for residues remaining after harvest must be considered when selecting the most appropriate insecticide.

Piercing-sucking Mouthparts

Insects with piercing-sucking mouthparts pierce the plant surface with needle-like structures called stylets. The insect pumps sap or cellular fluid through a straw-like structure to its stomach. At the same time, the insect pumps saliva into the plant to facilitate food withdrawal. The saliva may cause a toxic reaction in the plant or transmit a virus or mycoplasm-like organism to the plant.

The damage produced by piercing-sucking insects varies from species to species. Some species produce small spots where the plant or flower was punctured. Larger sucking insects can produce circular spots on leaf surfaces that may turn brown and become brittle. The toxic saliva of some insects causes twisted, curled or deformed plant or flower growth.

Because insects with piercing-sucking mouthparts do not consume any of the plant surface tissue, stomach poisons placed on leaves or flowers are not very effective controls. The best controls are systemics, which enter the plant tissue and can be picked up by the insect as it feeds on plant sap or internal fluids. Contact insecticides, which are absorbed through the insect's body, may also control insects with piercing-sucking mouthparts. Contact insecticides need to be located where the insect is likely to make direct contact with the chemical residue or sprayed directly onto the insect. Insecticidal soaps must be applied directly to the insect because they have no residual effects. Leafhoppers and mites, both difficult to control, are examples of pests which have piercing-sucking mouthparts.

Rasping-sucking Mouthparts
Rasping-sucking mouthparts have characteristics of both chewing and piercing-sucking mouthparts. The stylet acts as a cutting device that breaks open leaf tissue. The insect then eats the sap and cellular fluid that is released from the damaged plant tissue.

Damage caused by rasping-sucking insects appears as sunken, irregular areas of plant tissue that is yellow-green to silver or bronze. Flowers appear streaked or mottled with areas of no-color. New growth may be deformed and buds may fail to open. Thrips, an insect with rasping-sucking mouthparts, may also transmit diseases such as tomato spotted wilt virus.

Systemic and contact insecticides are effective on insects with rasping-sucking mouthparts. Because some species prefer to feed in tight spaces, multiple applications may be necessary. Insecticides placed on leaf surfaces, which work primarily as stomach poisons, are less effective because the insects feed primarily on released plant fluids.

Controls

Cultural Controls

Good cultural practices are the initial step in an integrated insect control system. Weed control is essential. Weeds within production areas harbor insects and obstruct optimal penetration and coverage of insecticidal sprays. Weeds in surrounding areas are a primary source of insect reinfestation. A buffer zone around production areas should be kept either mowed or cultivated to reduce the potential for insect movement onto crops.

Proper sanitation practices will reduce insect populations. Removing plant debris from production areas reduces the reinfestation potential from insect eggs deposited on the plant materials. Dormant season removal of the dead portion of perennial crops can help reduce the population of over-wintering insects. The use of insect-resistant varieties coupled with crop rotation can reduce the incidence and magnitude of insect pest infestations.

Biological and Biorational Controls

Biological controls using parasitoids, predators or pathogens can help keep insect levels in balance. Biological control systems release, manage or manipulate natural enemies to reduce the effects of pest insects on production and salability of crops. They are especially useful when the grower specializes in only a few crops. Some biologicals tend to be specific to one insect on a crop. It is easier to biologically manage one insect on one crop than it is to manage several insects on a variety of crops.

Microbial Insecticides

Microbial insecticides are formulated with bacteria, viruses, protozoa or the toxins produced by these organisms. Each product has individual differences specific to its use, but there are several general advantages and disadvantages to this group of microbial insect controls.

Advantages of Microbial Insecticides
- The active ingredients (organisms) used are essentially nontoxic to any but the target insect. This includes humans, wildlife or any other organism not closely related to the target pest.

- Most microbial insecticides do not adversely affect beneficial insects in the treated area.

- They can be applied close to harvest times since their residues are not hazardous to humans or animals.

- Some of the pathogenic organisms may become established within the target pest population and provide some control of future generations of the pest.

Disadvantages of Microbial Insecticides
- Their specifity of action on a single targeted pest will require additional treatments to control any other pests present on the crop.

- Several types of microbial insecticides are subject to degradation from exposure to heat, ultraviolet radiation or drying out. They must be properly stored and carefully applied.

- Because many of these controls are very specific as to a targeted pest, they are sold in very limited markets. They can be expensive to purchase and not widely available.

Nematodes
Nematoades are multicellular roundworms which are nearly microscopic in size. They infect a wide range of insects including numerous beetles, fly larvae and caterpillars. They are most effective when applied to control insects in moist soil or protected environments. Their viability and persistence in the soil varies with soil moisture, temperature and other organisms present. Because of their decline under low soil moisture conditions, nematodes may only be effective within irrigated production systems.

Commercial availability of nematodes is increasing and their cost may begin to decrease, but applying nematodes to large production acreages may still be cost prohibitive. A grower in Kansas has related success with applying the nematodes to transplants before planting into the field. He felt that the "nematode inoculated" transplants allowed the treatment of large areas with economical quantities of nematodes. No controlled studies have been done to substantiate this method of application.

The beneficial nematodes described above should not be confused with other species of nematodes which can themselves damage plants through feeding on the roots or lower foliage.

Table 9-1:
Microbial Insecticides and Nematodes and Their Hosts

Product	Pathogen	Hosts
Bactur, Biobit, Dipel Thuricide, Tribactur	*Bacillus thuringiensis* var. kurstaki (BT)	caterpillars (larvae of moths and butterflies)
Bactimos, Gnatrol Teknar, Vectobac	*Bacillus thuringiensis* var. israelensis (BT)	larvae of mosquitoes, flies, and fungus gnats
Trident II	*Bacillus thuringiensis* var. tenebrionis	larvae of Colorado potato beetle
Doom, Milky Spore Disease, Safer Grub Killer	*Bacillus popilliae* and *Bacillus lentimorbus*	grubs (larvae) of Japanese beetle
NOLO Bait, Grasshopper Attack	*Nosema locustae*	grasshoppers
Biosafe, BioVector, Scanmask	*Steinernema carpocapsae* *Steinernema* spp. *Heterorhabditis* spp.	larvae of many soil-dwelling insects

Microbial and nematode insecticides can be effective controls of many insect pests. Their pest specificity and general nontoxicity make them desirable alternatives to chemical controls. These biological controls are likely to become increasingly important tools in insect management systems.

Beneficial Insects and Mites

The natural enemies of insect pests can be divided into two categories: predators and parasitoids. Predatory insects are free-living; they tend to move with the availability of a food supply and consume many insect prey over the course of their development. Some predators are predaceous only in their immature stage of development, while others are predaceous in both their immature and adult stages. Predatory insects also vary in their range of prey; some may consume only very specific insect pests while others may feed on a broad range of pest species. Some examples of common predators are lady beetles, lacewings, spiders, praying mantis and mites.

The term parasitoid means parasite-like. True parasites are usually much smaller than their host organism, and usually weaken but don't kill their host. In comparison, parasitoids may be as large as their host, and they always kill their host insect. Parasitoids usually kill by laying their eggs in or on the host insect. When the eggs hatch, the emerging larvae feed and slowly consume the body fluids and tissues of the host. Most parasitoids are host-specific, laying their eggs on or into only a single species of insect pest and often attacking only a specific stage in the life cycle of the target insect pest. Common parasitoids include certain species of flies, beetles and very small wasps.

Table 9-2 lists some of the predators and parasitoids of a few common insect pests that often damage floral crops. Many of the beneficial insects or mites listed are available from commercial insectories.

Table 9-2: Natural Enemies of Selected Insect Pests

Pest	Natural Enemy	Classification
Aphids	*Aphidius matricariae*	parasitic wasp
	Aphidoletes aphidimyza	predatory fly
	Hippodamia convergens	predatory lady beetle
	Chrysoperia carnea	predatory lacewing
Fungus gnats	*Steinernema feltiae*	parasitic nematode
Spider mites	*Amblyseius californicus*	predatory mite
	Phytoseiulus longipes	predatory mite
	Phytoseiulus persimilis	predatory mite
Thrips	*Amblyseius cucumeris*	predatory mite
	Amblyseius iroquois	predatory mite
	Amblyseius mekenziei	predatory mite

Certain plants have been reported to serve the function of insectary plants, that is they attract and harbor beneficial insects. Table 9-3 lists some common insectary plants and the beneficial insects which are apparently attracted to them.

Table 9-3: Insectary Plants

Plant	Common Name	Attracted Beneficial Insects
Achillea millefolium	common yarrow	Syrphid Flies and parasitoids
Achillea ptarmica	sneezewort	Syrphid Flies and parasitoids
Achillea taygeata	yarrow	Syrphid Flies
Brassica hirta	crop mustard	Predatory Hemiptera
Brassica campestris	wild mustard	Hymenopteran parasitoid
Chenopodium album	lambsquarter	Hymenopteran parasitoids
Chrysanthemum coccineum	painted daisy	Hemipteran predators
Coriandrum sativum	coriander	Hymenopteran parasitoids

Plant	Common Name	Attracted Beneficial Insects
Cotoneaster spp.	cotoneaster	Insect predators and parasitoids
Daucus carota	wild carrot	Insect predators and parasitoids
Eriogonum spp.	wild buckwheat	Syrphid predators and Tachinid parasitoids
Eryngium alpinum	sea holly	Hymenopteran parasitoids
Fagopyrum	annual buckwheat	Syrphid predators and *esculentum* Tachinid parasitoids
Foeniculum vulgare	common fennel	Hymenopteran predators and parasitoids
Helichrysum angustifolium	whiteleaf	Insect predators and parasitoids
Lantana camara	lantana	Lady beetle larvae
Liatris pycnostachya	blazing star	Hemipteran predators and Hymen parasitoids
Ligustrum spp.	privet	Insect predators and parasitoids
Mentha spicata	spearmint	Predatory wasps
Monarda spp.	bee balm	Insect predators and parasitoids
Phacelia spp.	phacelia	Hymen and Trichogramma & Aphytus parasitoids
Polygonum aviculare	knotweed	Predatory beetles
Polygonum aubertii	silver lace vine	Insect predators and parasitoids
Ranunculus repens	buttercup	Hymenopteran parasitoids

Plant	Common Name	Attracted Beneficial Insects
Rhamnus californica	coffeeberry	Hymenopteran parasitoid and predatory beetles
Rumex acetosella	common sorrel	Hymenopteran parasitoids
Salix spp.	willow	Insect predators and parasitoids
Santolina chamaecyparissus	lavender cotton	Predatory beetle larvae in litter
Scabiosa caucasica	scabious	Syrphid flies and Hemipteran predators
Sesbania exaltata	hemp sesbania	Insect predators and parasitoids
Solidago canadensis	goldenrod	Predatory beetles
Spergula arvensis	corn spurry	Syrphid flies
Tamarix spp.	tamarisk	Insect predators and parasitoids
Tanecetum spp.	tansy	Lady beetle larvae and Hymenopteran parasitoid
Taraxacum officinale	dandelion	Insect predators and parasitoids
Trachymene caerulea	blue lace	Hymenopteran parasitoids

The economic use of beneficial insects and mites requires a two-fold approach: conservation and augmentation. A great number of beneficial insect species exists naturally and helps to regulate the population of pests. Conserving and encouraging the populations of these beneficials is an important part of any biological control system. The following practices help to conserve and encourage naturally occurring beneficial insects as well as populations of purchased and released beneficials.

- Learn to identify both pests and beneficial insects. The ability to distinguish between pests and beneficials is the first step in determining if control measures are required. Local county Extension agents can help in identifying insects. There are also insect field guides which are useful for identification purposes.

- Minimize the number of insecticide applications. Most insecticides kill both pests and beneficial insects. Applying insecticides only when pest populations exceed economic threshold levels will minimize the potential for unnecessarily reducing the number of beneficial insects.

- Use selective insecticides whenever possible and use all insecticides selectively. Many microbial insecticides are toxic to specific pests and are not directly harmful to most beneficial insects. Other microbials have varying degrees of selectivity. Insecticides which act as stomach poisons when ingested along with treated foliage typically will not affect predators or parasitoids.

- Maintain areas of vegetation surrounding production sites. Many naturally occurring beneficials require the protection of vegetation to overwinter and survive. These areas supply prey when crops have been clear cut in harvesting and provide some degree of weather protection. Many naturally occurring populations of beneficial insects will migrate back and forth from woodlots, fencerows and noncrop areas to cultivated fields depending on the density of the food supply (pests) in each area.

There are two approaches to augment beneficial insects in naturally occurring populations in an effort to control pests. The first approach is to inoculate an area with relatively low numbers of a beneficial species. As the food supply of pests increases, the number of beneficials will also increase and provide control. This control lags behind the pest damage for the time required for the beneficials to reproduce in response to the increasing food supply of pests. The population of beneficials will also decline rapidly and may extinguish as the pest insects are consumed and diminish in number. This approach requires a balance to be maintained in the numbers of beneficials and pests. The grower will also have to be willing to accept that some level of crop damage will always exist because a population of pests must remain to serve as a food supply for the beneficials. A management system using this approach must control the two populations carefully to minimize the base level of crop damage, and the conservation practices discussed earlier must be an integral part of the system.

The second approach to augmentation is to inundate the crop with a very large number of beneficials. This management strategy is to overwhelm and rapidly reduce insect pest populations. This is perhaps the easier of the approaches for the grower to manage. The integration of conservation practices for population maintenance is less critical when the inundation approach is taken. However, the economic viability of this approach is limited by the cost of purchasing, transporting and releasing beneficials, and by the commercial availability of effective beneficials in sufficient numbers to control the target pest.

An effective biological insect pest management system will integrate a combination of inoculative or inundative releases of beneficials closely aligned with conservation practices in an actively monitored and controlled system.

> All growers should integrate effective nonchemical control measures into their insect pestmanagement systems whenever possible.

Chemical Control

All chemicals should be applied intelligently and at the lowest possible effective rate. Learn the life cycles of all insects involved in the culture of your crops. Know which stage of each insect's life cycle is susceptible to which chemical spray, and spray only when control is possible.

Choice of insecticide is a critical part of effective control. Chemicals range from broad-spectrum to highly selective. Some chemicals perform well on one insect but not on another. Even chemicals with broad labeling are not equally effective on all the pests on the label.

Insecticidal Soaps and Botanical Insecticides

Insecticidal soaps are soaps which have been selected for their insecticidal properties. Botanical insecticides are naturally occurring insecticides which have been derived from plants. They both have advantages and disadvantages which should be considered before use.

Advantages of Insecticidal Soaps and Botanical Insecticides

• Botanical insecticides and insecticidal soaps degrade rapidly. They break down quickly when exposed to sunlight, air and moisture. Their short life results in reduced risk to nontarget insects and little persistence in the environment.

• Soaps and botanicals stop insect feeding very quickly, although actual death of the insect pest may require an extended period of time.

Disadvantages of Insecticidal Soaps and Botanical Insecticides

• The rapid degradation of botanicals can also be a disadvantage in that more frequent insecticide applications and careful timing of each application will be required.

• Botanicals are not as widely available as synthetic pesticides and tend to be more expensive.

• The potency of some botanicals may vary from one batch to another.

A common insecticidal soap is Safer Insecticidal Soap. Some common botanical insecticides are Neem, Sabadilla, Pyrethrins, Ryania, Rotenone and Nicotene.

Botanical insecticides and insecticidal soaps have a definite place in any insect pest control system. Their short life and rapid knockdown capabilities make them particularly useful in treating new "hot spots" of insects in a crop. They will be an integral part of an organic grower's insect control system.

It must be stated that all botanical insecticides are not safer than synthetic insecticides just because they are organic or "natural." For example, Nicotine is extremely toxic to mammals either by dermal exposure or inhalation. Rotenone is comparable in acute toxicity to the commonly used synthetic insecticides malathion or diazinon. Handle all pesticides carefully regardless of their origin.

Refined Light Oil Sprays

Sprays of highly refined light oils can be applied to non-flowering plants to control many insect pests. These light oil sprays act by smothering the insect. To achieve control they must completely cover the insect, so proper application is important. They are considered to be low in toxicity to humans. A risk of plant damage exists when oil sprays are applied under high temperature conditions.

Table 9-4 lists chemicals which at some time were available for use in controlling insect pests on flowers. Variations in spray coverage also affect the effectiveness of a control. To properly use contact insecticides, you need to know where the insect is found on the plant.

Table 9-4: Materials Which Have Been Labeled[1] for Control of Insects Associated with Flowers.

Pest	Chemical
Aphids	Orthene
	Insecticidal Soap
	malathion
	diazinon

Pest	Chemical
Thrips	Orthene
Aster leafhoppers (as a vector of aster yellows)	malathion Sevin Mavrik Orthene
Spider mites	Kelthane Insecticidal Soap Pentac
Caterpillars	Thuricide Dipel Mavrik Sevin Orthene
Slugs	Mesurol bait metaldehyde bait

[1]Due to changing laws and registrations, all materials may not be currently registered for use. Always read the label carefully and check to be sure the chemical is labeled for your intended use. Follow all directions on the label carefully. No endorsement is intended, nor is discrimination of similar products not listed.

Registration and Rates

Use and labeling varies from state to state and from crop to crop. Growers must follow labels and rates approved in their state for their crop. It is illegal to use pesticides in any manner that is inconsistent with the label. Always check for phytotoxicity by testing chemicals on a few plants of each variety before treating the entire crop.

Phytotoxicity

Phytotoxicity is damage to plants caused by chemicals. Extensive information about phytoxicity is not readily available because of the wide range of possible interactions between various plants and chemicals. Because of this variability, it is important for growers to use the information on labels, in publications and from other growers only as a general guide when applying chemicals. Growers should do small-scale tests the first time a chemical is used on a particular crop to avoid extensive damage to the whole crop. Growers should also know the general principles of phytotoxicity to avoid major problems.

Symptoms

Phytotoxicity may appear as marginal burn, chlorosis, necrosis, spotting, distortion or abnormal growth. Marginal burn is usually associated with systemic insecticides, which can become concentrated in the outer leaf margin if they are applied at high rates.

Pesticide Formulation

In general, emulsifiable concentrates burn plants more than wettable and soluble powders and flowables. Pesticides formulated as emulsifiable concentrates contain an oil-based active ingredient that requires the addition of an organic solvent and emulsifying agent so it can mix with water. These agents are often responsible for the plant damage. Adding a wetting agent (surfactant) to a spray may increase the chance that the spray will cause plant damage. If a wetting agent is necessary, do a small-scale test. Tank mixing two or more chemicals may result in plant injury even if each chemical alone causes no damage. Tank mixes should also be tested.

Frequency of Application

Mixing instructions on chemical labels are determined by the amount of chemical necessary to provide adequate control with the least phytotoxicity. Do not increase the rate of a chemical above the label recommendation. Multiple treatments may also contribute to phytotoxicity as some chemicals persist longer than others. Repeat applications may eventually increase the amount of active ingredient on the leaf surface to a level toxic to plant tissue.

Pesticide Safety

All pesticides are classified as poisons, although there are considerable variations in the degree of toxicity to warm-blooded animals. Poisoning with pesticides can occur through the mouth and nose or through skin contact. It usually requires less pesticide to be fatal when ingested through the mouth, although the greatest hazard in the use of pesticides is more closely associated with skin contamination. Pesticides should be applied only by trained and experienced personnel who follow all label precautions. All notice, posting and re-entry regulations must be followed at all times.

Personal Safety
A respirator, rubber gloves and goggles should be worn when working with insecticides or any concentrated sprays or dusts. Additional personal protection may be required depending on the pesticide, method of application and environmental conditions. Clothing worn while applying pesticides should be changed immediately following completion of the pesticide application and carefully, separately laundered to remove any pesticides which may have been absorbed.

The worker protection standards, training requirements, reporting and governmental regulations outlined in Chapter 8 for herbicides apply to all pesticide use and should be reviewed as you consider your insect pest control measures. You must follow all federal, state and local rules and regulations for pesticide use, storage, record keeping and reporting when using insecticides.

Pesticide and Container Disposal
Planning and anticipating needs can reduce disposal problems. Purchase only the amount of pesticide needed for each pest or season. Protect pesticides from damage and contamination so they remain viable. Handle containers in a way to protect their labels, keeping them legible. Store pesticides in a cool location out of the sun, out of reach of children or pets, and in their original containers. Use up old pesticides before they are no longer effective; use older products first.

Dispose of small quantities of waste pesticide and pesticide containers according to label directions. Do not contaminate water or create a hazard to people or property, fish or wildlife. Surplus pesticides and containers should be taken to your county's hazardous waste disposal site.

Control of Insect Pests on Stored Dried and Glycerin-Preserved Decorative Products

Controlling insects on stored products is of critical economic importance. All the input costs of purchasing, planting, growing, harvesting, processing and packaging have been incurred by the time products are put into storage. Loss of product at this stage is very expensive, so controlling insect pests in storage facilities should be considered as very cost-effective product insurance. The primary insect pests that feed on stored products are moths and beetles. Table 9-5 lists the 10 most common insect pests of stored floral products.

Table 9-5: Common Insect Pests of Stored Floral Products

Insect	Common Name	Size
Attagenus unicolor [Brahm]	black carpet beetle	length 0.15-0.2"
Anthrenus scrophulariae [Linnaeus]	carpet beetle	length 0.12-0.15"
Ephestia elutella [Hubner]	tobacco moth	wing spread 0.8"
Lasioderma serricorne [Fabricius]	cigarette beetle	length 0.1"
Plodia interpunctella [Hubner	Indian mealmoth	wing spread 0.8"
Sitophilus oryzae [Linnaeus]	rice weevil	length 0.08-0.12"
Sitotroga cerealella [Oliver]	Angoumois grain moth	wing spread 0.5"
Tinea pellionella [Linneaus]	casemaking clothes moth	wing spread 0.5"
Tineola biselliella [Hummel]	webbing clothes moth	wing spread 0.5"
Trogoderma variabile [Ballion]	warehouse beetle	length 0.12"

Control Measures

The control of insect pests on stored floral products is a three-element system. Sanitation, rotation and fumigation must be integrated into an effective pest management system. Sanitation of the warehouse facility is the initial step in controlling storage pests. Dried materials tend to break or shatter easily, littering warehouse shelves and floor and creating a food supply for the insect pests. The smallest amount of debris from plant materials, seeds or grain can support large populations of pests.

All windows and openings should be screened with fine mesh screen, and cracks and crevices should be sealed to exclude insects.

Inventories of stored products should be rotated regularly. Product should be used or sold and shipped in the order it came into the warehouse. The less time products are in the warehouse, the lower the risk of pest infestation and damage.

Fumigation of plant materials is a very effective method of eliminating insect pests. Whenever possible all plant materials should be fumigated before being placed into storage. Any sanitation or exclusion measure is rendered useless if infested materials are placed into storage. Fumigation is not a cure-all system. While it is very effective in destroying any pest present at the time of treatment, fumigation has no residual effect against reinfestation. Materials in storage must be continually monitored and inspected for pests or damage and appropriate control measures taken.

Fumigation and sanitary storage can be used as a marketing tool to differentiate one firm from its competitors who do not follow these pest management practices. What retailer or consumer wants the risk of loss from purchasing infested materials?

Summary

An effective insect pest control system will use an integrated approach consisting of monitoring, proper cultural practices and microbial and biological controls together with the intelligent and reasoned use of chemicals.

Routine and continuous inspection of all areas for insect pests (and diseases) by everyone in all phases of all activities of a company is critical to the effectiveness of any pest management system. It is not the grower's job to inspect for insects, nor the owner's nor the person who does the spraying. It is everyone's job. Every employee, manager or owner must constantly inspect and be insect pest-aware at all times. Insect inspection does not happen only in the production field. Harvesting, grading and packing crews should also be constantly watching for pests or presence of damage. Careful inspection of dried or glycerin-preserved products at the time of packaging will help prevent infesting warehousing facilities or shipping infested product to customers. Early detection of pest populations makes for easier and more effective control with minimal chemical usage.

Effective weed control will reduce sites for insect infestation; provide for stronger, more insect-resistant plants; and provide open space for more effective application of insecticides. Adequate watering and appropriate application of fertilizer produces healthier, more insect-resistant plants. Designing warehouse facilities to restrict entry of insects will reduce the necessity to treat stored products.

The extent to which insect pests are a problem and the labor and material expense incurred to control them is dependant on the effectiveness of many other subsystems. It is foolish to invest time and money into planting and growing a crop only to lose it to insect pests. An integral part of the process of designing any system must be a consideration of its impact or linkage with insect control.

CHAPTER 10

DISEASE CONTROL

An effective disease control system is essential to profitability. A disease may not always kill an infected plant, but it will weaken the plant, decreasing production and quality. Fewer flowers to sell can easily result in less income.

The best approach to disease control is a preventive program. Manage the crop. Don't neglect it. Provide a managed, healthy environment conducive to healthy plant growth. Apply water and nutrients in amounts and at times to meet specific needs of the crop. Purchase and plant only disease-free plant materials. Practice good sanitation; keep the field free of weeds and plant debris. Adjust planting density for each species to allow sufficient air circulation within the bed. Control insects to reduce the potential for spreading disease organisms. Rogue out diseased plants and remove them from the production area. In general, do not place any undue stress on the crop. A weakened plant is more susceptible to disease.

Problem Recognition

To treat a problem, you must first know that it exists. Learn to observe the normal "order of nature." Develop a sense of when something is wrong. Learn to sense a change in your crop. Early detection is paramount to effective disease management. Growers who carefully and continuously observe their crops' growth, watching for change in the plants or growing environment, will find disease control to be a much easier process. Early recognition of a problem will allow for the treatment of a few plants before the disease is able to spread throughout the crop. Fewer plants affected means less loss of productivity and less labor or chemicals required to treat the problem.

A decrease in plant growth or a decline in appearance can be caused by many factors other than a disease. Often a disease is a secondary problem, one that occurs after another, primary problem has weakened the plant. Stress from poor nutrition, improper soil pH, poor drainage, excess soluble salts, herbicide drift, water stress and insect pest damage all can affect the growth and appearance of a plant. The grower must sift through a variety of symptoms and explore the possibility for the existence of more than a single problem. Correct diagnosis of the problem is necessary before an appropriate choice of cultural and environmental control measures can be made. Incorrectly diagnosing a problem, or focusing on a secondary problem, may result in an ineffective control, wasted labor and chemicals needlessly applied to the environment. The services of soil and disease diagnostic laboratories may be required for final diagnosis. The land-grant university in most states has soil testing and plant disease diagnostic services available to growers. Contact your local county Extension agent for information and assistance in using these services. University diagnostic services may also make recommendations for effective controls. A personal visit to your state university plant disease diagnostic lab and meeting the diagnostician can be an excellent investment in your disease management system.

Common Diseases

Plant diseases may be caused by a number of different pathogens: bacteria, fungi, viruses or mycoplasma-like organisms. Bacteria are microbes of a single cell in size. Common diseases caused by bacteria are crown gall *(Agrobacterium);* soft rot of cuttings, corms and bulbs *(Erwinia);* bacterial wilt *(Pseudomonas);* and bacterial leaf spot *(Xanthomonas).* Bacterial diseases are difficult to control when established. Regulating conditions in the production environment and early detection are key elements in controlling the incidence and effect of bacterial diseases. Avoid planting soft cuttings or corms into cold, wet soils. To reduce spread of the disease, avoid splashing water around infected plants. A drip irrigation system is a definite aid in reducing the spread of diseases.

Fungi are filamentous organisms lacking chlorophyll and therefore must grow on or in another plant or dead organic matter. They are usually microscopic in size. Fungi are more prevalent in damp, humid microclimates. Fungi cause a wide variety of diseases that are economically damaging to flower crops. Common examples of diseases caused by fungi organisms are powdery mildews; root, stem and crown rots (*Phytophthora, Pythium, Rhizoctonia* and *Tielaviopsis*); rusts (*Puccinia* and others); Botrytis blight (*Botrytis*); leafspots, blights and cankers (*Alternaria, Septoria, Leptosphaeria* and *Phomopsis*); and wilts (*Fusarium* and *Verticillium*). Cultural practices, resistant varieties and screening all new plant materials for disease before planting are the first line of defense against fungal diseases. A variety of fungicides exist for use on fungal diseases in floral crops. Many fungicides are effective only on specific fungal pathogens. Few general coverage fungicides exist. An excellent resource on currently labeled fungicides and controls for diseases on commercial field-grown specialty cut flowers is available. *The North Central Regional Extension Publication # 491, Control of Diseases on Commercial Outdoor Flowers*, a 152-page publication, is available for a small charge from either of the following sources.

Michigan State University
Room 10-B Agriculture Hall
East Lansing, MI 48824-1039
phone: (517) 355-0240

University of Wisconsin
Ag Bulletins, Rm. 245
30 N. Murray St.
Madison, WI 53715-2609
phone: (608) 262-3346

Viruses are complex groups of molecules that act like living organisms only when in living plant or animal cells. They are much smaller than bacteria and may be seen only with an electron microscope. They impose a change in the host plant's genetic information system and alter its metabolism to produce more viral particles and proliferate the disease. Common disease symptoms caused by viruses are mosaics, ringspots, streaks, stunts and spotted wilts. Viral particles are spread by the transfer of infected plant material (vegetative propagation) and by feeding insects. Crops which are vegetatively propagated from cuttings, divisions, tubers, corms or bulbs should be purchased from known suppliers of disease-free plants and screened for disease symptoms before planting. Insect pests such as aphids, leafhoppers, whiteflies and thrips are known to spread viral diseases. A system of monitoring crops for the presence of any of these insects and subsequent treatment of the pests should be an integral part of a disease-control system.

Phytoplasmas (mycoplasmas) are free-living organisms intermediate in size between bacteria and viruses. They are the smallest and simplest organisms that can be grown in a laboratory free of living tissue. Phytoplasmic organisms cause a variety of disorders such as distortion, discoloration, stunting and tissue proliferation. A common phytoplasma-like disease and perhaps the most destructive of specialty cut flower crops is aster yellows. Aster yellows is commonly spread by migrating leafhopper insects. A system to monitor crops for the presence of leafhoppers is essential in controlling phytoplasma-like diseases.

Controlling Plant Diseases

Three conditions must be present for plant disease development. Removing any of the conditions will prevent a disease from developing in your crop. Disease control systems are designed to restrict or eliminate each of these three conditions from occurring. Figure 10-1 represents the three requisite conditions as the disease triangle.

Figure 10-1 The Disease Triangle

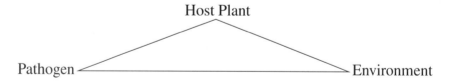

1. A viable, disease-producing pathogen must be present.

2. The host plant must be susceptible.

3. The environment must be favorable for infection.

The following procedures will aid growers in eliminating or restricting the conditions which must be present for disease development.

- Purchasing and screening for disease-free plants at planting, controlling insect vectors, sanitation, and the use of fungicides are all parts of a system to eliminate or restrict the presence of a viable pathogenic organism in the production field.

- Paying attention to every cultural detail at all times — site selection, managing the crop and keeping the plants actively growing with proper nutrition and care — will reduce the susceptibility of the crop to disease pathogens. Disease-resistant varieties should be purchased and planted whenever available.

- While growers cannot control rainfall, sunny or cloudy skies or the wind, they can control irrigation, soil factors and plant density, which may reduce the stress on the crop from the weather.

An understanding of each of the three elements which make up the disease triangle and the factors that regulate their influence on disease development will greatly enhance the design and implementation of a disease control system. However, a grower cannot control everything. Whenever a large number of a single plant species is under intense production, the likelihood of a disease organism being present is increased. When large numbers of a host plant are grown in the presence of pathogenic organisms, the only other requirement for development is environmental conditions conducive to infection. Each pathogen has specific temperature and humidity requirements under which they will grow actively on a susceptible host. When these conditions are present, the disease turns on; when conditions change and are no longer favorable, the disease turns off. The weather is never "normal" for the average is only the middle of the extremes, and it is the extremes of weather that actually happen. Knowledge of specific diseases and control measures is critical to productivity and quality.

Damping-Off

A common problem of germinating seed and seedlings is a disease called damping-off. It is a soil-borne disease caused by several different fungi including *Pythium, Rhizoctonia* and *Fusarium.* The fungi attack germinating seed before emergence through the soil surface and young seedlings after emergence. Infected seedlings seem to rot at the soil line, topple over and die. Seedlings in trays in greenhouses and those direct-seeded into the field are both affected by damping-off.

Damping-off can be controlled by a combination of cultural practices:

• Plant only high-quality seed free of cracks or other injuries. Seed may be pretreated with a fungicide.

• Drench seed bed with a fungicide at time of planting

• Avoid water-logged soils and cool temperatures for germination

• Disinfect any tools used in planting with a 10 percent bleach solution

Leafspots

Leafspots are infections on leaves which are caused primarily by fungi or bacteria. Even minor leafspotting can render a stem unsaleable due to its diseased appearance. Severe leafspotting can cause premature defoliation and a significant reduction in plant vigor. Many leafspot organisms survive on infected plant debris. Removing debris from production areas will reduce the inoculum available for infection. Several leafspot organisms require moisture to penetrate the leaf surface. Providing good air circulation and avoiding production practices which place water on the leaves will reduce infection rates. Mulches can be helpful in reducing the amount of inoculum splashed from the soil onto healthy leaves.

Fungicide sprays are commonly used to control leafspot diseases. They are most effective when applied before or as soon as the disease appears.

Powdery Mildew

Powdery mildew is a fungal disease common to many species of cut flowers. Affected plants develop a white, powdery growth on the surface of the leaves. Strands of the fungus penetrate the leaf surface and absorb nutrients. A severe infection can cause premature defoliation and significantly reduce plant vigor. The white powdery appearance on the foliage will render it unsaleable. Unlike many leafspot fungi, powdery mildew does not require a moist leaf surface for spore germination and penetration of the leaf surface. While the disease can occur at any time, it is most common in late summer and fall. Powdery mildew is most severe on plants growing in shady, humid locations with poor air circulation. For effective control of powdery mildew, fungicides must be applied before or as soon as symptoms appear.

Tomato Spotted Wilt Virus

Tomato spotted wilt virus (TSWV) can be a problem on transplants and plugs for field-grown floral crops. The viral disease has no cure. Infected plants must be rogued out of the field to prevent spread of the disease to surrounding areas. The wide host range of TSWV make it difficult to eliminate from all crop or weed hosts growing on properties near the production site.

A typical symptom of the disease is chlorotic ring patterns on the foliage, which may become necrotic. Eventually the leaf may die. Other plants may become stunted or deformed. Many of the more sensitive species may develop lesions on stems, petioles and veins accompanied by a wilting condition at the tip of the plant. These lesions may appear as brown to black streaks or as shiny black sunken channels.

Tomato spotted wilt virus is introduced into the production field by planting materials infested with the virus, or by transmission from plant to plant by the insect vector, thrips. Control TSWV by purchasing and planting only materials ordered from suppliers known to sell stock free of TSWV. Also, control and eliminate all infestations of the thrips insect. The western flower thrips is considered to be the primary species responsible for spreading TSWV in floral crops. Other species of thrips spread TSWV, but the western flower thrips is the more difficult to control.

Controlling tomato spotted wilt virus centers on eliminating sources of the disease and on limiting the spread of the disease within the production site. If you suspect TSWV in your crops or in new plants, plugs or divisions shipped in for transplanting to the field, contact your county Extension agent and request to send a sample to your land grant university's plant disease diagnostic lab for confirmation.

Impatiens Necrotic Spot Virus

Impatiens necrotic spot virus (INSV) can also be a problem in transplants. Like TSWV, it has no cure. Its symptoms may vary dramatically between species, giving the appearance of more than one disease. It is most commonly introduced into the production field by planting infected transplants. INSV is spread between plants and across fields by thrips. Controls are the same as for TSWV.

Aster Yellows

Aster yellows disease is a major problem in field production of many species of flowering plants. Annual statice (*Limonium sinuatum*) and purple cone flower (*Echinacea purpurea*) are two crops that are particularly sensitive to the disease. Entire crops of annual statice have been lost to aster yellows. Aster yellows disease has a very broad host range including more than 200 plant species.

Symptoms of aster yellows begin as a loss of color in the leaf veins, spreading to a general chlorosis of the entire leaf. This chlorotic effect typically occurs on new foliage and may be exhibited on only a portion of the plant, with the rest of the plant appearing normal. One symptom indicative of aster yellows is adventitious shoot proliferation. This often appears as abnormal new shoot growth out of the flower with a bushy or witch's broom effect in place of a normal flower. Plant leaves may be smaller, narrower and yellow-green in color. As the disease advances, the lower foliage may become red to bronze in color and the plant becomes stunted. Statice plants typically die from the disease, while purple cone flower plants become severely chlorotic, stunted and deformed.

Aster yellows disease is transmitted from plant to plant by the aster leafhopper insect (*Macrosteles quarilineatus* Forbes). Leafhoppers appear as little, light-colored, gnat-sized bugs. The highest infectivity rates are considered to be from leafhoppers migrating north from southern states. The migrating aster leafhopper insects that affect crops in the centraland northern plain states begin their development on wheat plants. As the wheat crops mature, they move on to less mature wheat crops farther north or seek alternate host plants, such as floral crops, on which to feed and complete their development. The greatest concentration of northward migrating leafhoppers arrives in Kansas about mid to late April.

Entomologists at the University of Wisconsin in Madison have developed an Aster Yellows Index. This index is based on the number of leafhopper insects gathered in a sweep of a field and on the percent of the insects found to be infected with the disease. Vegetable producers in Wisconsin base their decision whether or not to spray for leafhoppers on this index. Flower growers in northern states might use this index as part of their system for controlling leafhoppers and aster yellows disease.

An effective management system for aster yellows disease will follow an integrated approach. It's essential to establish an insect monitoring system that is continuously checked for an increase in the number of leafhoppers present, in order to detect a migration. The crops must also be monitored for presence of the disease so infected plants may be rogued out to prevent spreading the disease. Avoid planting annuals and perennials together so that perennials infested the previous year do not act as a reservoir for the aster yellows organism. A system must also be developed to control the aster leafhopper insect. Such a system might entail maintaining a systemic insecticide within the plant at all times, and spray applications of an insecticide when the monitoring system detects an increase in leafhopper populations. Remember that there is no cure for aster yellows; the only possible control is prevention. Table 10-1 lists some of the more common plants that are susceptible to aster yellows.

Table 10-1: A Partial List of Plants That Have Been Reported to be Susceptible to Aster Yellows.

Plant	Common Name
Allium cepa	onion
Amaranthus retroflexus	rough pigweed
Anethium graveolens	dill
Asclepias nivea	common milkweed
Avena sativa	oats
Brassica campestris	common yellow mustard
Calendula officinalis	pot marigold
Catharanthus roseus	periwinkle
Centaurea cyanus	cornflower, bachelor's button
Chrysanthemum frutescens	Marguerite daisy
Coreopsis lanceolata	tickseed
Cosmos bipinnatus	cosmos
Cucurbita pepo	pumpkin
Daucus carota	carrot
Dianthus barbatus	sweet William
Dianthus caryophyllus	carnation
Delphinium x cultorum	hybrid larkspur
Echinacea pupurea	purple cone flower
Eschscholzia californica	California poppy
Gaillardia pulchella	annual blanket flower
Gladiolus x hortulanus	gladiolus
Gypsophila paniculata	baby's breath
Helianthus annuus	common sunflower
Helichrysum bracteatum	strawflower
Limonium sinuatum	annual statice
Nigella damascena	love-in-a-mist

Plant	Common Name
Phlox drummondii	annual phlox
Portulaca oleracea	purslane
Rudbeckia hirta	black-eyed Susan
Salvia azurea	azure sage
Scabiosa atropurpurea	pincushion flower
Spinacia oleracea	spinach
Tagetes erecta	African marigold
Tagetes patula	French marigold
Trifolium repens	white clover
Tropaeolum majus	garden nasturtium
Zinnia elegans	zinnia

Nematodes

Nematodes are microscopic, eel-like worms that normally live in the soil. A large number of species are not harmful to plants. Harmful nematodes use a needle-like mouthpart (stylet) to extract nutrients from roots and other plant parts, causing significant damage. Plants damaged by nematodes appear stunted. Roots attacked by nematodes exhibit galling, excessive branching, decay or a stubbiness. Once established, nematodes are difficult to control. Crop rotation, good sanitation practices and soil fumigation can help reduce the damage caused by nematodes.

Summary

It should be apparent from the discussion in both Chapters 9 and 10 that insect and disease control systems must be fully integrated throughout the Care-as-Needed activities and the activities of Planting. Quality management of watering and fertilization activities provides healthy crops whose plants are less susceptible to insects and disease. Controlling weeds strengthens the crop due to less competition. It also allows for better air circulation thereby reducing the potential for foliar diseases, and removes shelter for insect pests and sites of potential disease re-inoculation. The planting system activities of screening transplants for disease or insects before planting, and spacing plants for improved air circulation are integral parts of insect and disease control. Care in bed preparation and careful placement of plants into the soil at the proper depth makes the crop less susceptible to stress and therefore less susceptible to insects and disease.

Any system developed for a subactivity must be fully integrated with every other system or the firm as a whole will be less productive. The best designed activity subsystems are of little value unless the linkages that connect them are carefully integrated. Design each activity, each system so as to enhance the performance or lower the cost of the other activities. Remember the relay race — don't drop the baton.

CHAPTER 11

VERTEBRATE PEST CONTROL

The conflict between mankind and wild animals on the battlefield of cultivated cropland has existed for centuries. Our cultivated land with its succulent crops is prime habitat and feeding grounds for a broad range of vertebrate animals. Many animals, from mice to deer, find our ground softer for burrow construction or our crops a more tasty food source than surrounding, non-cultivated areas. Systems must be developed to reduce or eliminate the damage caused by animals. Animal damage not only causes losses in yields and quality but also increases the cost of labor to repair or clean up the affected areas.

Gophers

Gophers are burrowing rodents about nine to 12 inches long, weighing approximately seven to 14 ounces. They spend most of their lives below ground as solitary animals except during breeding and while raising young. Their breeding season occurs in late winter and early spring with the half-grown young gophers beginning to disperse from the natal burrow in June.

Gophers construct burrow systems by digging with their claws and incisor teeth. The loosened soil is pushed out of the burrow and deposited in fan-shaped mounds 12 to 18 inches wide and four to six inches high. The burrows are about three inches in diameter and the system may be linear to highly branched in pattern, containing up to 200 yards of tunnels with several mounds. Six to eight gophers per acre is considered a high density.

Gophers feed on roots encountered when constructing burrows, on vegetation they pull down into the tunnel from below and on vegetation growing above ground near burrow entrances. Green and succulent portions of above-ground vegetation are their preferred food in spring and summer. In areas with snow cover, winter-time feeding may include many trees and shrubs, clipped just above ground.

Economic Damage

Gophers have been found to reduce the productivity of alfalfa fields and native grasslands by 20 percent to 50 percent. No studies have been done on their effect on reducing productivity of cut flower fields, but in areas where they are present most growers find them to be a significant problem.

Not only do their feeding habits directly damage crops, but their burrows also create problems. The mounds of excavated soil and collapsed tunnels create uneven surfaces within production areas, which may damage equipment, increase the potential for worker injury and result in serious soil erosion. Gophers may do additional damage to production areas by cutting underground utility cables, irrigation system wiring and water pipes.

Legal Status

Check with state and federal wildlife agencies for existing laws protecting gophers.

At this writing the author is unaware of any laws protecting gophers in agricultural cropland.

Control Measures
Cultural

Control of forbes and alfalfa (the large roots of which are a favorite food of gophers) in shelterbelts and fields adjacent to production areas will reduce area gopher populations. Planting buffer strips of annual grains around fields can help minimize immigration of gophers by providing a zone of unsuitable habitat. In areas where large quantities of water are available and fields are level, flood irrigation will help control gophers. The water-saturated soil prevents diffusion of gasses in and out of the burrow system, and the mud sticks to the gophers' fur and claws, creating an undesirable environment.

Trapping

Trapping is an effective way to rid a field of gophers. Body gripping/piercing traps, available from most hardware or farm supply stores, work well for catching gophers. Figure 11-1 illustrates a commonly available gopher trap.

Figure 11-1: A Macabee Gopher Trap

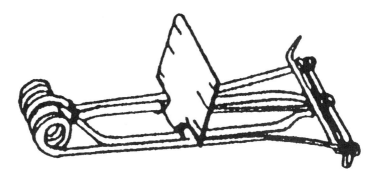

Gophers are generally easiest to trap in the spring and fall when they are actively constructing burrows and building mounds. Traps should be set near the freshest mounds, which are an indicator of gopher activity in that section of the burrow. The actual location of the lateral tunnel below the mound can often be determined by the presence of a circular depression or plug to one side of the mound with the pile of soil forming a fan shape away from the plug. The lateral tunnel will extend down and away from this plug for approximately 12 to 18 inches before reaching the main tunnel as illustrated in Figure 11-2.

Figure 11-2: A Gopher Tunnel and Mound

Use a long handled spade and expose the lateral tunnel by removing a section of soil from the area of the mound containing the plug. Attach the trap to the handle of an empty gallon paint can by means of a two-foot long, 12- or 14-gauge wire. Place the trap about eight to 10 inches down into the tunnel. Cover the tunnel opening with a clump of sod so the gopher does not attempt to close the system and in the process buries the trap without getting caught. The trap is wired to the paint can so the trapped gopher does not run off with the trap, carrying it deep into the system before dying and making it difficult to recover. The trap could also be tied to a stake driven into the ground near the mound, although this system requires more labor and an additional tool. Labor is required to drive the stake in and then to pull or dig it out to move it to the next trapping site. Wood stakes also have a tendency to split and require periodic replacement. The trapper is also required to carry a hammer along to drive in the stake. The paint can is easily portable and provides a means, complete with handle, of carrying or storing the trap between settings.

Traps should be checked twice a day by carefully pulling on the wire and checking for a resistance to pull or a wiggle. Gophers usually visit traps within a few hours after they have been set. If after two days a gopher has not been caught, move the trap.

Baiting

Toxicants formulated on a grain such as milo, barley or wheat can be used as baits to control gophers. Care in handling and placement must be exercised as these baits can also be toxic to wildlife and pets. Underground baiting presents minimal hazards to non-targeted animals but any of the toxic grain spilled on the surface can pose a hazard to pets, birds or any wildlife in the area. Use only baits with toxicants registered for use in your state for controlling gophers. Some may be labeled as restricted use pesticides and only available for use by those with appropriate licenses.

Bait can be placed into the burrow system by digging holes and scattering the bait within the exposed tunnel by hand or by the use of a bait probe dispenser. The system using a bait probe dispenser requires considerably less labor.

Working out 12 to 18 inches from the plug in the freshest soil mound, the probe is inserted into the ground in a searching pattern until a spot of decreased resistance is felt and the tunnel thereby located. A button is then pushed on the bait probe and a measured amount of bait is dropped into the tunnel through the hollow probe. The probe hole is then covered with a small piece of sod. A disadvantage of using bait to control gophers is that you are unable to tell when you have killed a gopher. Your only indication of effectiveness is the subsequent absence of fresh mounds in the treated area.

Fumigants

Gas or smoke cartridges and tanks of compressed gasses are used to disperse toxic substances into the burrow system in an effort to kill gophers. The basic theory is that the vapors will penetrate throughout the entire burrow system and kill the gophers wherever they may be. In practice, their effectiveness may be limited by the gophers ability to sense the poisonous gas and plug off that section of tunnel. Fumigant effectiveness is also reduced in dry soils by diffusion of the gas into the soil and potentially reducing the concentration of gas below toxic levels. Fumigants are pesticides and as such are regulated. State pesticide registrations vary, so check with your local county Extension office or wildlife control specialist for information on what is legal to use in your state.

Other

A grower in Oregon has a unique and apparently very effective means of controlling gophers in his fields. He fills the burrow system with gas, but not for use as a fumigant. He has a hollow probe attached to a tank of bottled gas. The probe is inserted into the gophers' tunnel, and a valve is opened to allow the gas to flow into and fill the burrow system. At the push of a button, a spark arcs across an igniter on the end of the probe within the tunnel. The gas is ignited, it explodes, the ground rumbles, and the gopher is instantly killed.

Moles

Moles are small mammals which live in underground burrows located just below the soil surface. Moles have an elongated head, a short neck and strong legs with paddle-like forefeet and prominent toenails. Their head shape and forefeet enable them to dig tunnels as if they were swimming through the soil.

Moles prefer loose, sandy soil and avoid heavy clay soils. Their activity shows up as ridges of upheaved soil created by their burrowing just below the soil surface as they forage for food. Moles actively feed day and night throughout the year on insects, earthworms and white grubs.

Moles rarely eat bulbs or any vegetative material while burrowing but may physically disturb plants in their tunneling activity. Small plants may be dislodged and plant roots exposed to drying. By continuously searching out and eating white grubs, moles could be of greater benefit than harm.

Control Measures
Baiting
Moles do not normally consume grain so attempts to poison them with toxicant-treated grains as bait are rarely effective.

Repellents
The placement of mothballs, moth flakes, broken glass, razor blades, rose thorns, bleach, lye or human hair within the burrow system are common home remedies to get rid of moles. The theory is the materials will either kill the mole or cause them to leave. There is little to no information to support any of these claims of control.

Trapping
Trapping is the most successful method of controlling moles. Mole traps capitalize on the mole's natural habits. They are set without entering anything into the burrow and are sprung by the mole following its natural instinct to reopen a closed passageway. After a burrow is located, a portion of it is collapsed. The trap is then set over this tunnel obstruction. When the mole tunnels

through to reopen the passageway, a broad trigger-pan will spring the trap as the mole upheaves the collapsed portion of the surface burrow.

Before beginning a mole control program, the extent of any damage they cause should be weighed against the potential benefit of their reducing the numbers of soil insects present in the production beds.

Mice

Field or house mice are small rodents with large ears, small black eyes and long tails. Adult mice are about five to seven inches long, including their three to four inch tail. They feed primarily on cereal grains but will eat almost anything. They are a major cause of damage to stored dried flowers, grasses and grains.

Control Measures

The effective control of mice encompasses three areas: sanitation, construction and population reduction. Sanitation and construction are preventative measures designed to reduce the opportunities for mice populations to become established. Once a population of mice has become established, some form of population reduction must be instituted.

Sanitation

Eliminate nesting sites. Large populations of mice cannot occur where there are few places to rest, hide or build nests to raise young. Sanitation is not a cure-all method. All possible nesting sites cannot be eliminated, but the attempt must be an integral part of any mouse-control system.

Construction

Construct or remodel buildings to eliminate sites of entry for mice. Eliminate openings larger than ¼ inch through which mice can enter a building. Seal all cracks, particularly those around entering water pipes, vents and utilities. Make sure doors, windows and screens fit tightly. Cover edges of wood around openings with metal to prevent gnawing. Remember mice can fit through the tiniest of openings.

Population Reduction

Rodenticides

Rodenticides or toxic baits for mice are available in two forms: single-dose and multiple-dose. Single-dose baits are the most toxic and kill the mice the first time they eat the bait. They provide quick knockdown of a mouse population. Single-dose baits are preferred in situations where competing food sources make it difficult to get mice to take a bait for several days in succession. The higher concentration of toxic ingredients in single-dose baits can make it difficult to get mice to accept the bait. Bait acceptance can be increased by prebaiting or feeding unpoisoned bait for a few days prior to offering the rodenticide.

If the mice do not take the prebait, do not offer the toxic bait, but change the material offered or try placing it in another location. Single-dose baits are very toxic and should be treated with caution. Do not leave single-dose baits exposed for more than three to four days. Collect and destroy any uneaten bait.

Multiple-dose baits are less toxic than single-dose baits. The active ingredients in multiple-dose baits function as anticoagulants which cause death by internal bleeding. Because the toxic substance is applied to the bait at very low levels, the bait shyness common with single-dose baits normally does not occur. For the anticoagulant bait to work the mice must feed on it for several days. Fresh bait must be available to the mice for as long as feeding occurs.

All rodenticides are poisons which can kill larger animals. Place them so that only mice can access them. They pose a hazard to pets, livestock and other nontarget animals. Follow all label directions for storage, use and disposal.

Trapping

Trapping is an effective method for controlling mice. It is often the preferred system for several reasons:

- Trapping does not introduce toxic substances or endanger either people or nontargeted animals.

- It is easier to monitor the success of the system because you know when you have killed a mouse.

- The dead mice can be disposed of in a sanitary manner, eliminating the odors and disease potential of decaying mice killed by rodenticides.

Traps should be set close to walls, in dark corners, and in places where mice are active. Peanut butter, creamy or chunky style, is an easy-to-use bait that is very attractive to mice. Inexpensive wood-based snap traps are available from most hardware and grocery stores. They are easy to use and very effective in catching mice. A disadvantage they have is that they can only catch one mouse at a time. They must be emptied and reset before more mice can be trapped. This is a labor intensive process that can take weeks to reduce a population of mice. Multiple-capture live traps are also available from hardware and feed stores. They can capture several mice without being reset.

Buck Godwin of Alberta Supernaturals in Olds, Alberta, Canada, has invented a most wonderful mouse trap. Even though he lives in the woods, growers of dried materials should beat a path to his door and build one or more of his traps for their own use. Figure 11-3 illustrates Buck's trap and provides several views to make building your own trap an easy process. The basic trap consists of a five-gallon plastic bucket with a 1" by 2" board mounted inside, flush with the top. About a third of the way down from the top of the bucket is a very stiff wire, such as a welding rod, that serves as an axle for an extra-large (28 oz.) juice can. The top of the can should be about one and a quarter inch below the bottom of the board. In the bottom of the bucket is a 50/50 mixture of water and antifreeze, to a depth of about four inches. A lath or narrow board is leaned against the bucket and is held in place with a finishing nail driven through it and into a pre-drilled hole in the 1" by 2" board. The mouse uses the lath as a ladder to climb up to the top of the bucket, walks out on the 1" by 2", senses the peanut butter spread around the sides of the juice can, jumps down onto the can to eat and slips off the spinning can into the antifreeze where it quickly dies.

The trap can easily handle a dozen mice before it needs to be emptied. With the antifreeze solution it can be placed in an unheated barn where dried flowers are being stored over winter and not freeze up. It is a simple, low-cost, highly effective system for controlling mice which is particularly useful in agricultural structures. Users of this trap should be cautioned that the antifreeze solution is toxic and pets should be prevented from drinking out of the bucket. A loose cap of chicken wire placed over the bucket will keep the cats out.

Figure 11-3: The Buck Godwin Mouse Trap

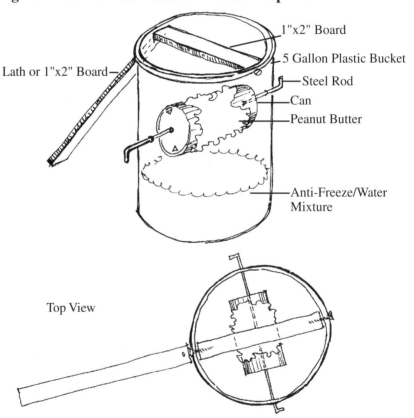

1"x2" Board

5 Gallon Plastic Bucket

Lath or 1"x2" Board

Steel Rod

Can

Peanut Butter

Anti-Freeze/Water Mixture

Top View

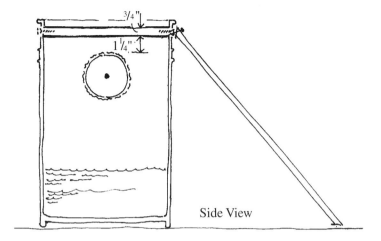

Side View

Deer

Deer cause damage to specialty cut flower crops in three basic ways:

• From feeding directly on the plants

• From rubbing their antlers on trees and shrubs

• From crushing plants and breaking branches as they move through production areas

Methods to control deer include: repellents and scare devices, high fences and electrically charged wires and regulated hunting.

Repellents

There are two kinds of repellents — contact and area. Contact repellents are applied directly to the plants and are most effective on dormant trees and shrubs. Their taste repels the deer. Apply the contact repellent by brushing or spraying it directly on the terminal growth of large mature plants, and over entire small or immature plants. Contact repellents should not be applied to any plant part that will be harvested for sale. Odors may linger and be objectionable to customers.

Area repellents repel deer with very strong odors and must be placed near the plants you want to protect. Large acreages can be protected by placing repellents relatively close together in a perimeter line around the field.

Several deer repellents are available commercially. One, Thiram, is a fungicide which is used as a contact repellent due to its taste. It should be mixed with an adhesive to enhance its weathering ability. Thiram will also protect trees from damage by rabbits and mice. Home remedies such as rotten eggs and tankage (putrefied meat scraps) have been used with mixed results.

Scare Devices

Firing guns, using gas exploders, sirens, strobe lights or lighting fireworks will scare deer away and provide temporary relief, but they are not long term solutions to the problem of deer damage. To maximize the effectiveness of these devices, they should be set to function at irregular intervals and their location within the field should be changed every few days. Otherwise, the deer will soon become accustomed to their presence and loose their fear.

Dogs left free to roam the property have proven to be effective for several growers. On small acreages where neighbors are close or roads have higher traffic, you may not be able to allow dogs to run free. The use of an invisible fence (buried wire around perimeter which signals a device on the dogs collar) is being tested in orchards in Missouri.

Fencing

Permanent, high, woven-wire fences are the ideal deer barrier, requiring little maintenance, but they have a high initial cost. Temporary electric fences provide inexpensive protection from deer during periods without snow. They are easy to put up and use readily available materials. Fencing options between these two extremes include: the offset or double fence, vertical deer fences of multiple electric wires up to the effective height, and the slanted seven-wire deer fence. The offset and the slanted fences both use electric wires in a three-dimensional nature to help discourage deer from jumping over them. Deer, like mice, are partial to peanut butter. If you find deer are merely jumping over your fence, you might smear peanut butter on the wires or on foil strips hanging from the wires. When the deer approach to smell the peanut butter, a shock to the nose will make them more wary of the fence. Plans for constructing these deer fences are available from state wildlife control offices, county Extension offices and retail fence suppliers.

Hunting

The control methods of repellents, scare devices and fencing all attempt to keep deer out of production areas. But they do nothing to address the issue of reducing the population of deer causing the damage. A deer hunting program should be an integral part of any deer control system. To control deer damage, a system which will promote a harvest of adult female deer must be developed. A buck can breed many does in a single season. Hunting for trophy bucks does little to control a deer herd because it doesn't affect the reproductive capacity of the deer population. Landowners, in conjunction with state game agencies, control hunting on their land. Hunters can be family or friends. A deer damage control system that doesn't include population reduction is handicapped.

The key to success in controlling deer is to take action quickly at the first sign of damage, for it is very difficult to change a deer's behavior pattern once established. Use an integrated approach — an effective deer control system will utilize repellents, scare devices, electric fencing and hunting.

Summary

The activities of wild animals can create serious economic problems for growers in crop damage and extra labor. To deal effectively with animal pests, growers are using a variety of homemade and very creative systems. The key to working smarter, not harder, is to design control systems to do each of the little things with a minimum of effort. A poorly designed trapping or bait system can quickly consume many hours of labor. Systems to control wild animals are regulated by a variety of federal and state governmental agencies, including Agriculture, Fish & Game, and Environmental regulators. When designing animal control systems, be sure to check carefully all governmental regulations that my affect which methods you are able to use.

Section 4

HARVEST

```
┌──────────────┐      ┌──────────┐      ┌──────────────┐
│   PLANTING   │ ───▶ │   CARE   │ ───▶ │   HARVEST    │
│              │      │    AS    │      │              │
└──────────────┘      │  NEEDED  │      └──────────────┘
                      └──────────┘
```

Chapter 12 Harvest 161

Chapter 13 Postharvest 188

Chapter 14 Refrigerated Storage 196

Chapter 15 Preserving 207

Chapter 16 Color Processing 233

CHAPTER 12

HARVEST

The quality of the flowering stems is the best it will ever be at the time of harvest. When a stem is cut, it begins to die. The task of the grower and harvest crew, from harvest on, is to slow the decline of the flowering stem. A quality product is essential for a grower to survive in the marketplace. All harvest systems must be designed to slow the decline of the flowering stem and provide the retailer and consumer with the longest vaselife possible. Any activity that accelerates the decline should be avoided or modified to minimize the effects on quality.

Harvest Labor

The harvest section of the Stevens Labor Model is defined as all activities involved from the moment the flower is ready to harvest until it is shipped to the customer. There are several subsystems involved in the harvest process.

Harvest

— Selection
— Cutting
— Transport
— Storage
— Grading
— Packaging
— Shipping

The labor model for effective labor utilization requires systems to be designed for each activity. Each system should be designed so as to not require workers to make decisions. "No decision" systems are a key element in minimizing the labor required for a task. It takes time to make a decision — the more time spent in indecision, the greater the labor cost for the activity. The manager (grower) should think, listen to workers, observe the process and then design a system, a way of doing the activity, that does not require workers to make any decisions. Eliminate or reduce the potential for extended indecision. Remember that labor is the single highest cost of producing specialty cut flowers. System development and effectively using labor is critical to profitability, especially for the one-person company. There are only 24 hours in a day. If you spend your time inefficiently, then there will be less time for other things like lunch.

The activities in the harvest portion of the labor model have been shown to comprise 45 percent to 60 percent of the total labor required to produce specialty cut flowers. Of all the harvest activities, the systems of selection and cutting are the most critical in labor management. Both of these labor activities require workers to constantly make decisions. I know of no system that has been developed that has effectively removed all decisions from these activities.

Selection Labor

In selecting a flowering stem to harvest, each stem with a flower must be considered and two questions answered. Is this flower at the correct stage of maturity for harvest? Is this flower and stem of sufficient quality to justify harvesting? It takes time to answer both questions for every flowering stem in the production bed. The longer a worker takes to answer both questions, the longer it will take to select each flowering stem to harvest. Time is money. Figure 12-1 illustrates the selection decision.

Figure 12-1: Which Flowering Stem Should Be Cut Today?

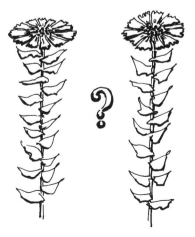

Cutting Labor

Once the decision to cut a particular flowering stem has been made, then the decision of where on the stem to cut must be reached. The length of the stem attached to the flower has value, but so does the length of the stem left attached to the plant. The longer the stem cut with the flower, the higher its value. Longer flowering stems provide increased salability, and likely increased income. The shorter the flowering stem is cut, the more stem remains attached to the plant. The longer the remaining stem, the greater the number of leaves left for photosynthesis, thereby increasing the productive capacity of the plant to produce more flowers. Do I cut here for a longer flowering stem, or do I cut here to maintain the productivity of the plant? In plants being produced in rows, it is also beneficial to cut the stem just above a node located on the side of the stem pointed toward a void or toward the outside of the plant. New growth will be strongest from this node and its growth directed outward, keeping the center of the plant open for better light penetration and improved air circulation for disease control. Again, it takes time to select the best point at which to cut the stem. Indecision time, time spent thinking, is costly time. Figure 12-2 illustrates the decision of where to cut the stem.

Figure 12-2: Where Should This Flowering Stem Be Cut?

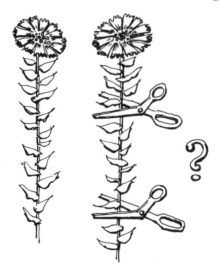

Designing Systems That Require Worker Decisions

The Stevens Labor Model says to develop "no decisions" systems, ways of doing a labor activity that do not require the worker to make a decision. The activities of stem selection and cutting require more than one decision to be made in each activity. How does the labor model address this situation? The first tenant of the Stevens Labor Model is to design "no decision" systems. The second tenant of the labor model is whenever it is not possible to develop a "no decision" system, then develop a system that manages the "time in indecision." It is the time spent trying to reach a decision, the "indecision time," which is most ineffective.

First develop a system for selecting which flowering stems to cut. Establish the selection criteria. Teach the harvest workers the selection criteria. How you teach the selection criteria is critical to reducing the "indecision time." **Do not teach the harvest workers what an ideal or perfect flowering stem looks like. Teach them what an unacceptable stem looks like.** There should be far fewer unacceptable stems in the production bed and therefore fewer decisions to be made. Train them to quickly recognize faults. The selection system then simply becomes: Harvest everything without a fault. Indecision time has been minimized and labor is most effective. This system also tends to yield more harvestable flowers, increasing income. More flowering stems are acceptable when compared to faults or measures of poor quality than when compared to perfection, for few flowers will be truly perfect.

The same principle holds true for the cutting system. Establish the criteria for where to cut. Teach the harvest workers the cutting site criteria. Again, how the criteria is taught is critical to reducing the "indecision time." **Do not teach the harvest workers how long to cut the flowering stem. Teach them how long to leave the plant stem.** What is the minimum stem length you must leave attached to the plant to maintain its health and vigor (productivity)? The cutting system simply becomes: Cut to leave so many inches. Indecision time has been minimized and labor is most effective.

Do not stop training the harvest crew. The greater the time lapse between the training and the activity, the greater the time harvest workers spend in extended indecision. Harvest labor rapidly becomes ineffective and labor cost for harvesting flowers will increase dramatically. **You must train and retrain constantly for all systems that require workers to make a decision.** This does not mean you must call a meeting, bring all workers together in a room and prepare and present a formal training program. The system should involve the next level supervisor, the foreman, working elbow to elbow with each harvest worker for a minute or two each time a crop is harvested. The supervisor subtly and by example reminds each worker what is not acceptable and how much stem to leave on the plant. The supervisor then moves on to other workers.

Many growers I have worked with on lowering labor costs pride themselves on how long many of their workers have been working for their company. I ask about worker training. Growers reply, "All workers have been trained to pick quality flowers." When asked about how and when this training is accomplished, the growers response is typically the same. "All new employees are thoroughly trained in flower quality before they can be on the harvest crew." And then what is your training program? "None, all my employees know what a quality flower is." What is your average employee turnover rate? "It is very low, my workers tend to stay with me." How long? "The average is about four or five years, some much longer." So the average worker was trained to harvest about four to five years ago and hasn't been trained since? Each day a person has new life experiences. Each day they bring new perspectives to the job. Each day they see and do things slightly differently. After four to five years, how differently are they approaching the decisions of selection and cutting? The potential for **extended indecision** becomes greater the longer the time lapse from being trained in decision criteria. Extended indecision is very expensive.

An important management principle is to spend your time where it will make or save you the most money. The greatest potential for labor savings is in the harvest activities, as these activities comprise half or more of total labor. The harvest systems with the greatest potential for labor ineffectiveness are the selection and cutting systems. All other harvest systems have "no decision" systems which can be developed. A manager should spend time developing and continuously monitoring selection and cutting systems.

Harvest — Stage of Maturity

Table 12-1 lists the optimal stage of maturity for harvesting a variety of species of specialty cut flowers. Flowers for direct sale to final consumers, such as in farmers markets, should be harvested slightly more mature than flowers sold to retailers for resale. Selling to wholesalers requires a slightly less mature flower than a retailer would require. The ideal stage of maturity will also vary with the intended use. Flowers for drying should be harvested when almost fully open, while for fresh use they should be less mature. The information provided in the table should be considered as a general guideline of harvest maturity for retail sales direct to final consumers. This is the stage at which you would sell your flowers at a roadside stand or farmers market.

Table 12-1:
Guidelines for Optimal Harvest Stage of Maturity of Specialty Cut Flowers for Direct Sale to the Final Consumer

Common Name	Stage of Maturity
Aster	flowers fully open
Astilbe	one-half of florets open
Bachelor's Button, Cornflower	flowers just beginning to open
Calendula	flowers fully open
Cockscomb	one-half of florets open
Coreopsis	flowers fully open
Dahlia	flowers fully open
Delphinium	one-half of florets open

Common Name	Stage of Maturity
Dutch Iris	flower buds are colored
Freesia	first bud is fully open
Gayfeather	half of florets open
Gladiola	one to two florets fully open
Globe Thistle	flowers are half open
Goldenrod	one-half of florets open
Heather	one-half of florets open
Hollyhock	one-third of florets open
Larkspur	two to five florets open
Lisianthus	three to five open flowers
Love-in-a-Mist	flowers are open
Marigold	flowers are almost fully open
Peony	puffy, colored buds
Peruvian Lily	one to three florets open
Phlox	one-half of florets open
Pincushion Flower	flowers half open
Purple Cone Flower	flowers almost fully open
Sea Holly	flowers fully open
Snapdragon	one-third of florets open
Statice — annual	one-half of bracts open
Statice — Sea Lavender	majority of flowers are open
Sunflower	flowers almost fully open
Sweet Pea	one-third of florets open
Tuberose	one-half of florets open
Yarrow	flowers are almost fully open
Zinnia	flowers are almost fully open

Always use a sharp knife or shears to harvest flowers. Dull blades tend to crush stem ends and may restrict the flow of water into stems and thereby diminish product salability. Do not lay cut stems on the ground during harvest. Particles of dirt or bacteria may be picked up along with the stems and clog the water conductive tissues.

Flower Care During Harvest

Remember, the quality of the flowers is the best it will ever be at the moment of harvest. After harvest flower quality can only decline as the flower matures and the stem dies. Great care and attention to the smallest detail must be taken to slow the decline of the flowering stem during the harvest activities. The rate at which a flowering stem declines is dependent on the tissue temperature and water status of the flower, stem and foliage. High temperatures accelerate the rate of decline. It is not practical to pull a refrigerated cooler through the fields while harvesting, but other practices can be of value. Plant tissue temperatures will be lower during cooler parts of the day. Harvesting early, during the cool of a morning, will aid in maintaining quality. A note of caution: Do not harvest until after any dew has evaporated off the flowers. Damp flowers packaged or placed into refrigerated storage may develop *Botrytis,* a fungal disease which attacks and destroys salability of the flowers.

Another method of maintaining cooler tissue temperatures is to keep the harvested flowering stems in the shade until transported to the grading/packing area and refrigerated storage. A covered harvest trailer is an excellent method of providing this shade. Figure 12-3 is a drawing of the covered harvest trailer Jerry Longren designed for use at the Kansas State University Research and Extension Center.

Figure 12-3: Covered Harvest Trailer

The other important factor in maintaining quality of the harvested flowering stem is to maintain the water status of the plant tissue. Harvested stems left dry until brought into the grading/packing shed may wilt to a point beyond their ability to recover. Cut stems should be placed into either water or a fresh flower food (floral preservative solution). The typical flower food solution contains water; a simple sugar, which serves as a food source; a chemical to prevent or retard the growth of microorganisms which can plug the conductive tissue; and an ingredient to acidify the water, typically citric acid. Fresh flower preservatives are available from several companies. A list of suppliers is provided in the section of this book listing sources of supplies.

A system of preparing preservative solutions must be developed to provide a consistent concentration of preservative in each harvest container and to control the cost of labor to mix the solutions. A simple system would be to fill a scoop with preservative; scrape excess preservative off level with the top of the scoop; dump it into a bucket; fill the bucket with water to a line; and stir the solution until the preservative is completely dissolved in the water. In this system the amount of preservative being used must be consistently measured, the amount of water being added must always be the same, and the solution must be stirred to completely dissolve the preservative in the water. Any variation in any of these three activities will result in variation of preservative concentration and may affect the uniformity of flower quality. Careful and continuous attention to all details is essential to producing and delivering a quality product.

Another system of preparing preservative solutions is to use an injector with a commercially prepared, concentrated preservative solution. The injector is placed into a bypass line of the water system (with backflow prevention). The draw tube of the injector is placed into a container of the concentrated solution. When the water spigot is turned on, the injector places a measured amount of preservative solution into the water line and the harvest container is filled with a uniform and consistent concentration of preservative solution. No matter how much solution is placed into the harvest container the concentration is always the same. A worker does not measure or stir anything, he simply places the injector draw tube into the purchased container of concentrated solution. Figure 12-4 is a drawing of such an injector system. It shows a second injector for the possibility of utilizing an additional treatment, as might be used for ethylene-sensitive flowers. This system provides consistent uniformity of solution concentration with minimal labor. It is a simplified system for a grower to effectively manage both quality and labor cost.

Figure 12-4:
An Injector System for Dispensing Floral Preservative Solutions

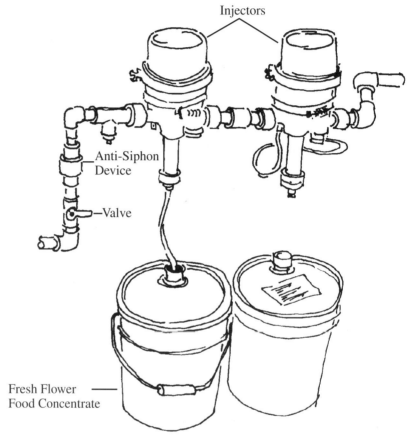

Harvest Containers

Plastic containers are ideal for use in holding harvested flowers. Metal containers should be avoided because of the possibility of rust forming and blocking the stems' conductive tissue. Chemicals in floral preservatives may also react with metal containers. A wide variety of shapes and sizes of plastic containers, which are suitable for flowers, are available. Figure 12-5 shows a range of plastic bucket sizes arranged on a cooler shelf. Differing bucket heights are used to accommodate various crop stem lengths.

Figure 12-5: Plastic Buckets Used For Handling Cut Flowers

Harvest containers need to be stored when not in use. They should be stored in an area and manner which will keep them clean. Stacking plastic buckets by inserting them into each other will store the greatest number of buckets in the smallest possible space. This method saves space and reduces capital investment in warehouse space. However, this container storage system has a couple of serious deficiencies. The dirtiest portions of most containers is the bottom outside surface, which sits on the floor or ground. By inserting containers into each other, this dirty surface is placed inside another container creating the potential for dirt to be inside each and every container. An even stronger reason for not stacking in this manner is the wasted time and high worker frustration level encountered when harvest workers must attempt to pull apart containers which have become stuck together. This wasted time can become very expensive, both in labor cost and in delaying the time of harvest while playing with the buckets.

Despite the potential for dirt contamination many growers continue to stack their buckets because it is the simplest storage system available. If you choose to stack your buckets, design a system to clean the inside of each bucket after it is separated from the stack.

Figure 12-6 illustrates a low-cost, easy-to-build system which greatly facilitates separating stacked buckets that are stuck together. The lip of the top bucket is slid into the slot of the wall-mounted unit, enabling a single worker to pull on the next bucket. This system uses one worker instead of two. When two workers pull on opposing ends of the stuck buckets, they tend to pull in jerky motions from continuously changing positions. This system is performed by a single worker pulling with a more constant force in a fixed and more effective position. Labor to separate buckets may be reduced by as much as 80 percent.

Figure 12-6: Wall-Mounted Bucket Separating Unit

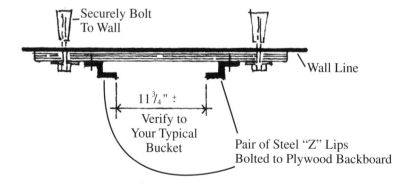

Construction Detail

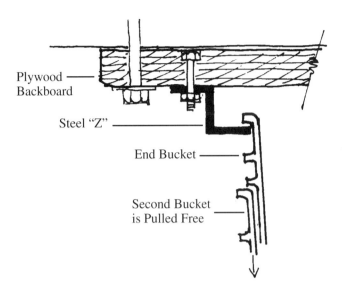

Plywood
Backboard

Steel "Z"

End Bucket

Second Bucket
is Pulled Free

If your local metal supplier or welding shop does not stock Z formed steel, the bucket-separating unit may also be constructed using a flat steel bar or a steel channel. Figure 12-7 illustrates the construction details for these alternative materials.

Figure 12-7: Alternative Construction Methods For Steel Lips

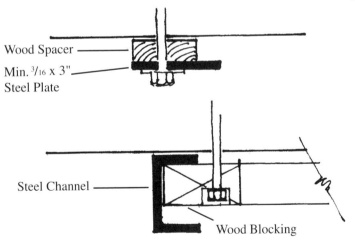

Wood Spacer

Min. $3/16$ x 3"
Steel Plate

Steel Channel

Wood Blocking

Alternate Construction Methods for Steel Lips

Alternative container storage systems exist. Figure 12-8 shows plastic buckets turned upside down and stacked in alternating rows. This system requires more floor space than insert stacking but keeps a greater number of containers cleaner and creates no hassle in separating the buckets.

Figure 12-8: Stacked Bucket System

Harvest containers can also be stored on a rack. Figure 12-9 shows a diagonal and an end view of a simple-to-construct rack made from scrap pipe welded together. This particular rack was a winter project of Jerry Longren, our horticulture research farm manager. This rack system has the advantage of keeping all containers up off the floor away from potential dirt contamination. Each individual container is also accessible at any time without having to move others out of the way. Differing pipe lengths would accommodate containers of differing depths. It makes a great drying rack for containers which have been washed clean.

Figure 12-9: A Welded Pipe Rack for Storing Containers

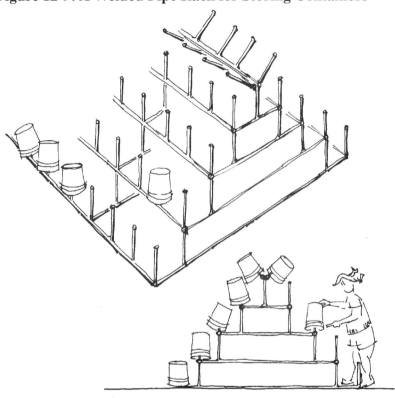

Container Sanitation

Harvest containers and cutting shears and knives should be routinely disinfected. A mild chlorine bleach solution of one part bleach to nine parts water will provide good control of potential disease infection. Horticultural detergents which contain biocides are also available for cleaning buckets. Harvest and storage containers should be washed between each use. Not an exciting job, but necessary to reduce the risk of dirt, bacteria or algae clogging the water-conducting tissue of the stem and flower. Figure 12-10 shows a bucket-cleaning system used by John Zehrer at Star Valley Flowers in Soldiers Grove, Wisconsin. A large tub containing soapy water and power-driven brushes with an adjacent smaller tub for rinsing the containers comprise the system. Parts of the system were originally used to clean milk cans at a Wisconsin dairy and were found in a salvage yard.

Figure 12-10: Container Cleaning System

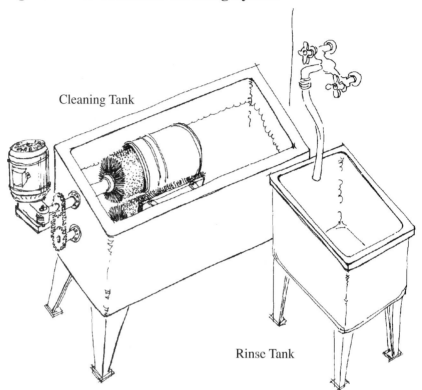

Cleaning Tank

Rinse Tank

Figure 12-11 shows detail of the brush arrangement. The container is placed over one rotating brush to clean the inside while a second powered brush and a stationary brush clean the outside.

Figure 12-11: Brush Detail

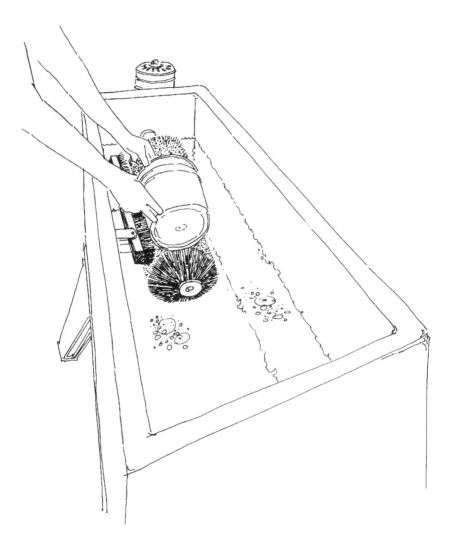

Transport Systems

Flowering stems to be sold as a fresh product must be transported from the plant; to the harvester's arms; to the aisle between production beds; to a roadway; to a holding/storage facility; to a grading/packing area; to refrigerated storage; and finally to the delivery truck. Stems which will be marketed as preserved materials must also be transported in and out of processing areas. Each of these product movement activities require a system to be developed:

a. How will the stems be handled?

b. Will the stems be bunched at the cutting site or left as individual stems for grading later?

c. Will the stems be placed in a container or stacked loose?

d. How many stems will harvesters hold in their arms before placing them somewhere else?

e. How far will harvesters have to walk carrying cut stems before placing them into the next transport subsystem?

f. Will the stems be placed into a preservative solution? When in the transport process will this happen?

g. How will the preservative solution be transported from the site where it is mixed to a container, and the container to the cutting area?

h. In what form and how will the stems be moved into and out of refrigerated storage or processing facilities?

i. How will the stems be moved through the grading and sleeving process?

A transport system and all the subsystems must be developed specifically for each company. The site plan, topography, production system, existing equipment and facilities, workforce and the intended market all affect the transport labor system design. Remember the relay team; don't drop the baton. Transport systems must be integrated with all other aspects of the company. The linkages between each activity are critical. Design each subsystem so as to enhance the performance or lower the cost of the next activity in the system. As an example, the length and width of the production bed affect the labor cost of transport. A wider bed requires the harvester to bend over and reach in farther to harvest flowers from the center portion of the bed than would a narrow bed. A more awkward position will slow harvest and creates a greater distance to move individual flowers. The longer production beds are, the greater the distance flowers may have to be hand-carried to a trailer for transport. This does not mean to say that all production beds should be a single plant row wide by a single plant in length before an aisle, for that may be inefficient space utilization. It does illustrate the interrelationship between site design and transport labor activities.

Figure 12-12 illustrates a transport system designed for a crop to be dried which is "clear cut," that is, it is all harvested at the same time. A three-sided platform is mounted on the three-point hitch of a tractor. The crop is cut and placed directly into the bin with the tractor being backed down the bed as the harvest progresses. The harvest worker does not carry the cut stems anywhere, but merely turns around to place the crop into the bin. Only large quantities of the harvested crop at a time are moved any distance.

Figure 12-12:
A Dried Flower Transport System for a "Clear-Cut" Crop

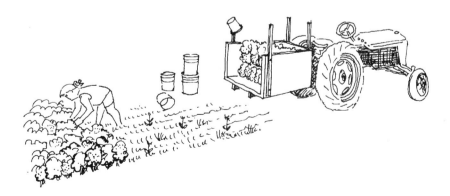

Figure 12-13 is the same figure used earlier as an example of a covered harvest trailer. It illustrates an integrated system combining several subsystems into a single piece of equipment:

- Transports the harvest containers and preservative solution to the production area.

- Provides shade (a cooler environment) for the harvested flowers.

- Serves as a staging area for gathering a large number of flowers before transport to a handling/storage facility.

- Eliminates the need for harvest workers to walk carrying small bunches of flowers and allows for bed length to be increased, reducing the need for cross aisles.

- Allows the workers to hold fewer stems in their arms at a time and thereby increasing cutting efficiency.

Figure 12-13: A Covered Harvest Trailer

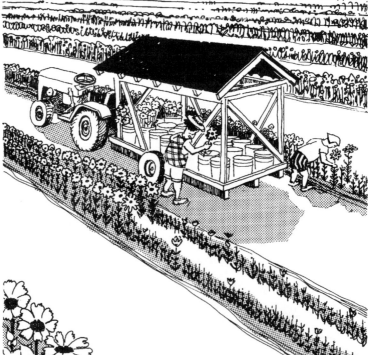

Transport systems should be designed with three tenats in mind:

1. Nothing should move far.

2. Move items in the largest quantities possible.

3. Design for ease of loading and unloading.

The farther anything must be moved, the longer it takes and the greater the labor requirement and cost. This is particularly important where flowers are hand carried by a worker walking down a row in the production field. Walking through constricted spaces between rows on uneven and sometimes muddy surfaces is not conducive to rapid movement of cut stems. The maximum distance anything should be hand carried in the field is 75 feet. Therefore no production bed should be longer than 150 feet between crossways where product is hand carried.

The larger the quantity moved, the lower the unit cost for transporting each item. A single worker can carry a bucket full of flowers, push a loaded cart or drive a tractor pulling a trailer. In any of the three systems — bucket, cart or trailer — the same worker travels at different speeds and transports differing amounts of product. Each of the systems may be the most effective system for a particular setting.

Many transport systems are well designed to move large quantities of materials quickly with minimal labor. The effectiveness of many of these same transport systems is also greatly reduced because the labor activities of loading and unloading were ignored when the systems were designed. Often more labor is required to load and unload than to actually move the materials. Consider the covered trailer illustrated in Figure 12-13. When the buckets of water with floral food are loaded onto the trailer they must be lifted over, under or around the corner posts and angle bracing on every side of the trailer. When the trailer arrives in the field the cut stems must be lifted over, under or around the corner posts and angle braces before they can be placed into the buckets. When the trailer arrives back at the storage and grading area the filled buckets, which are now much taller and heavier because of being filled with the cut stems, must be lifted over, under or around the corner posts and angle braces to unload the trailer. The effectiveness of three separate labor activities has been compromised because the designer of the trailer considered its structural integrity and forgot to consider the loading and unloading activities. Design systems to lower the cost or enhance the quality of all related activities — don't drop the baton.

A Harvest System

The following series of figures illustrate an excellent example of an integrated system for the harvest of grass and grain crops to be sold as dried decorative materials. The system is being used by John Hurd of Avatar's World in Edgerton, Wisconsin. Watching this system in operation impresses one with how simple the process and equipment are. It is even more impressive when one observes how much work is done, with minimal labor, in a very short period of time.

Figure 12-14:
A Rice Harvester — Used to Harvest Grasses and Grains

Figure 12-15: Harvesting and Tying Into Bundles

A piece of equipment designed to harvest rice is used to harvest the crop (Figure 12-14). It operates similar to a sickle-bar mower, clear cutting the crop just an inch or two above the ground surface. A series of fingers moves the cut stems up a slot to a point where they are gathered into a bundle, tied and then ejected from the harvester (Figure 12-15). The machine can be set to tie different size bundles depending on the desired dry weight of the product. A three-legged saw horse (Figure 12-16) with a metal bracket (rectangular sleeve) on the end holds a wood lath suspended parallel to and above the ground. Harvested and tied bundles are spread out, split from the center, and placed hanging by the bundle tie over the lath. Four bundles are hung on each lath. The lathed bundles are then stacked in the field (Figure 12-17).

Figure 12-16: Lath Holder

Figure 12-17: Lathed Bundles

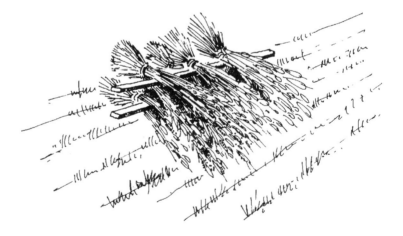

The laths are then picked up and placed onto a specially designed harvest trailer (Figure 12-18). The trailer is built with two rails spaced apart so that the ends of each lath will rest on them. The bundles then hang suspended from the lath between the rails. Loading the trailer is accomplished by walking between the rails and working from the back forward. The use of the laths allows four bundles to be moved at a time. The trailer is moved from pile to pile collecting the lathed bundles. No product is moved by walking any but the shortest distance.

Figure 12-18: Harvest Trailer

The loaded harvest trailer is then pulled into the drying barn where the product is hung to dry (Figure 12-19). Notice the openings in the side of the barn. They are hinged panels, which when left open allow for natural ventilation of the barn to aid in the drying process. The barn was originally a tobacco drying barn adapted for drying decorative plant materials.

Figure 12-19: The Drying Facility

Figure 12-20 illustrates a lath drying rack system in the attic of a barn. It is simply a series of parallel rails which support the ends of laths which in turn support bunches of plant materials. The vertical distance between rails is set to accommodate the stem length of the plants being hung to dry. The lath system facilitates product movement into and out of the drying area. Bunch spacing for proper drying is done one time, out in the field. This spacing is then maintained throughout the transport system.

Figure 12-20: Lath Drying Rack System

Summary

Harvest systems have a great impact on product quality and cost of labor. They must be designed to maintain quality of the plant stem and flower while controlling the cost of the labor to perform the harvest activities. Equipment, materials and labor must be integrated into effective systems. Remember the quality of the product is the highest at the moment it is cut from the plant. The task of harvest systems is to preserve that quality or at least slow the rate of decline. Harvest systems which make the most effective use of labor will speed the product through the processes and help preserve quality. Remember to consider all linkages between systems and don't drop the baton.

CHAPTER 13

POSTHARVEST

Careful handling to prevent damage and rapid decline is important after flowers have been transported from the field to the storage/packing facility. Bruising and breaking flowers destroys their aesthetic and economic value. Wounded plant tissue increases the production of ethylene gas, a natural plant growth hormone, accelerates maturation of flowers and greatly shortens vaselife.

Ethylene

Ethylene is produced by old flowers, decaying plant material and ripening fruit. Controlling your inventory of flowers, using a first in, first out system and discarding flowers past their prime will aid in reducing ethylene damage to your fresh flower products. Good sanitation measures, removing all plant residues from storage areas and not placing any fruit or fruit-type vegetables near stored flowers will reduce the potential for ethylene damage.

Ethylene is also produced by the combustion of gasoline and propane and as a by product of welding. Do not operate tractors, trucks or any engine within the storage/handling area or near air Lvents which provide ventilation for the facility. Do not share building space with maintenance activities.

Ethylene is involved in the maturation of flowers. Reducing the level of ethylene present in a flower will extend its vaselife. Some species are particularly sensitive to ethylene and need to be protected from its effects. Silver thiosulfate (STS) is commonly used to reduce the effects of ethylene on some species of fresh cut flowers. In some ethylene sensitive species, STS may increase vaselife, improve the percentage of buds which fully open, or help inhibit the premature shattering of florets. Table 13-1 lists species of flowers which are particularly sensitive to ethylene.

Two qualities of STS must be considered when designing a system to treat fresh flowers. STS is not a very stable compound. It has a shelf life, after which it shouldn't be used. STS should be purchased in quantities which will be used within its projected shelf life. STS also has the potential to pollute groundwater and soil. Approved disposal systems must be followed. They can be purchased along with the STS solution from suppliers.

Table 13-1:
Flower Species Particularly Sensitive to Ethylene

Achillea	Daucus	Lysimachia
Agapanthus	Delphinium	Phlox
Allium	Dicentra	Penstemon
Alstroemeria	Eremurus	Physostegia
Antirrhinum	Freesia	Ranunculus
Aquilegia	Gladiolus	Scabiosa
Astilbe	Godetia	Solidago
Bouvardia	Gypsophila	Stock
Campanula	Lavatera	Sweet Pea
Carnation	Lily	Veronica
Centaurea	Limonium	

Fresh Flower Food

Cut stems should be placed into either water or a fresh flower food (floral preservative solution). The typical fresh flower food contains water; a simple sugar that serves as a food source; a chemical to prevent or retard the growth of microorganisms that can plug the conductive tissue; and an ingredient to acidify the water, typically citric acid.

The quality of your water can influence the effectiveness of the fresh flower food solution on prolonging flower appearance. Each of the commercially prepared fresh flower food solutions may react differently with any calcium, magnesium or other salt naturally occurring in your water. Many community water systems routinely add fluorine or chlorine to the water. These added chemicals may react differently with each manufacturer's fresh flower food preparation. The alkalinity of the water will affect the ability of the acidifying agent to lower the pH of the water to desired levels. The water you use to make the solutions should be analyzed for total dissolved salts, content of individual salts, pH and alkalinity. Ideally the final food solution should have a pH in the range of 3.0 to 4.5.

When a flowering stem is cut from the plant, it is severed from its food supply. The food source must be replaced. Simple sugars are used as the source of nutrition for fresh cut flowers. They provide the energy to complete flower development, open buds and maintain color. Fresh flower food solutions used to maintain flowers typically contain 0.5 percent to 1 percent sugar. Food solutions used as pulse treatments to encourage a greater number of buds to open on flowers like gladiolus may contain up to 20 percent sugar. It should be noted that flowering stems are placed in these high concentration solutions for only relatively short periods of time. The solution is "pulsed" in and the stem removed to water or a maintenance solution with a low concentration of flower food. Some flowering species, such as gerbera and asters, do not benefit from sugar in the solution and may respond with shortened vase life.

Each grower should trial several commercial fresh flower food solutions with their water and product mix of flowering species. Purchase a variety of food products, mix according to directions, and place three to five vases of flowers containing each solution in a well-lighted room at a constant temperature. Also fill some vases with tap water to use as a reference to test whether or not the food solutions are an improvement. Record vase life and the percentage of buds opening, and note changes in color of flowers and foliage. Repeat the test for each of the flowering species that you grow. Choose the solution that performs best for the greatest number of species within your product mix. An accurate measurement of the recommended concentration of fresh flower food is important. Too much or too little of any ingredient in the solution can seriously affect flower quality. A complete, uniform mixing of the food solution is essential to consistent, satisfactory results. A discussion of mixing systems is presented in Chapter 11. Fresh flower foods (preservatives) are available from several companies. A list of suppliers is provided in the section of this book listing sources of supplies.

Recutting Stems

Whenever practical, recut all stems under water. Cutting stem ends underwater prevents air bubbles from entering the stem and blocking the conductive tissue. One to three inches of the stem should be removed to be assured of removing any air bubbles present. Recutting flower stems under water removes potential air blockage. However, some flowers will hydrate properly when cut in air. Equipment can be made to recut large volumes of flowers underwater without unreasonably increasing labor. Many small growers may find the practice of recutting under water to require a greater use of labor than they can justify. Caution should be used in making this determination. Is the practice truly not cost effective or is the decision being made inappropriately, on a nuisance factor? Test your recutting methods periodically by comparing vase life of your flowers to the alternative recutting method.

Figure 13-1 illustrates a commonly used "guillotine cutter". After bunching, the bottom one to three inches of the stem ends are cut off to remove any stem blockage and to even-up the ends to assure all stems an opportunity drink. Uneven ends may result in the shorter stems being suspended above the solution and becoming wilted, with loss of quality.

Figure 13-1: A Guillotine Type Flower Stem Cutter

Bunching and Sleeving

Stems should be graded and tied into uniform bunches. Bunch size should be determined by the standards of the marketplace. Either a specific number of stems or a standardized weight per bunch is used to determine bunch size. A standard bunch of many flowers (roses, carnations) consists of twenty-five stems. Other flowering species (liatris, dutch iris, peony) are sold as ten stems to the bunch. Gladiolus are typically sold in ten stem bunches in the wholesale trade but are often sold in five stem bunches at farmers markets. Growers selling in small or local markets may bunch according to whatever standards suit their particular market situation. Growers wishing to sell in regional or national wholesale markets will be required to grade and bunch according to industry standards. Many leaders within the industry would like to see a standardized bunch of flowers become universally defined to consist of ten stems.

When tying flowering stems into a bunch, place the tie three to four inches up from the stem ends to allow room for recutting without retying the bunch. After tying, the bunch may be placed into a funnel-shaped sleeve to protect the flowers and stems from breakage during handling, storage or packing activities. Figure 13-2 shows a bunch of flowers being placed into a plastic sleeve. The easel type stand with backplate allows for effective bunch placement into the sleeve with reduced breakage. A simple, low-cost, bunch sleeving system.

Figure 13-2: A Simple, Low-Cost, Bunch Sleeving System

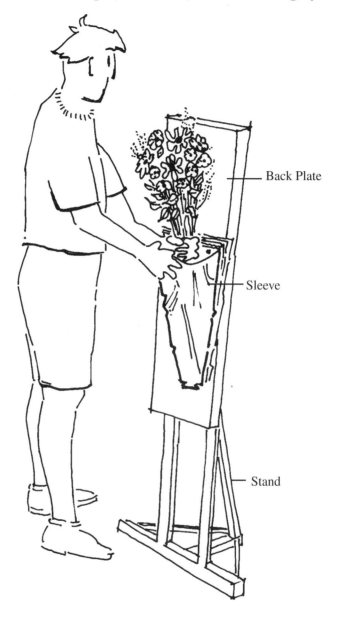

Back Plate

Sleeve

Stand

Storage Containers

The same inventory of containers used for harvesting flowers can be used for storing the graded and sleeved bunches. The containers should be cleaned before use. Do not use the same container that was used to transport the flowers from the field before it has been recleaned. A discussion of containers and a container cleaning system is presented in Chapter 12.

Solution Depth

The fresh flower food solution in the storage container should be deep enough to cover the ends of all stems with sufficient margin for error, and to allow for uptake without having to constantly refill. This is not to say the container should be filled to any great depth. Excess solution is wasteful and costly in materials and labor, as it should not be reused. The deeper the solution, the greater the potential amount of dirt and debris which may wash off submerged stems and leaves. Rinsing stems and leaves under tap water before recutting and placing into containers with solution will aid in keeping storage solutions clean. Leaves should be removed from the stems up to a point just above where they won't become submerged in the solution. A no-decision system should be developed for placing the correct amount of fresh food solution into the storage buckets. A fill-to line marked on the inside of all buckets is part of such a system.

Summary

Postharvest systems should be designed to provide proper treatment of each plant species to prolong quality of the flowering stem and to make the most effective use of labor possible. Often growers concentrate on providing proper postharvest handling and storage conditions to their floral products and ignore the labor activities required to provide those conditions. Chemicals for the STS and fresh flower food solutions must be unloaded from delivery trucks, transported to a storage area, and transported from storage to the area where they are mixed with water for use. Proper amounts must be measured and completely dissolved, solutions placed into buckets to proper depth, flowers graded, bunched and sleeved, bunches placed into buckets of solution, and buckets of flowers transported to refrigerated storage. Effective labor systems and subsystems must be developed, implemented and monitored for each activity. Too frequently, excessive labor expense is incurred in these postharvest activities. Growers, as plant people, tend to concentrate on growing activities and lose interest in effectively managing other areas of the business. Remember one-half or more of total labor is used in the Harvest (including postharvest) portion of the Stevens Labor Model. Don't lose profit by not managing labor at the end of the production process.

CHAPTER 14

REFRIGERATED STORAGE

Cold temperatures are an important factor in prolonging the quality of harvested flowering stems. Lowering the storage temperature will increase flower longevity by:

- decreasing the rate of respiration and the utilization of carbohydrates in the plant tissue

- decreasing the amount and the effectiveness of ethylene produced by the flowers

- decreasing the amount of transpirational water loss

- slowing the growth of microorganisms in the fresh flower food solution

- decreasing the rate of flower development and senescence

For all of the above reasons, harvested flowers need to be moved from the field to cold storage as soon as possible. Any delay in lowering plant tissue temperatures will accelerate the senescence process and reduce longevity. Handling/storage facilities should be located near production areas to facilitate moving the product into refrigerated storage as soon after harvest as possible.

Refrigerated Storage Facilities

Refrigerated storage facilities may be custom-constructed to fit a space or purchased as a prefabricated unit. Or, a refrigerated truck body can be purchased and adapted for use. The choice of which type to use depends on your individual needs, work facility and available capital. Figure 14-1 illustrates a common type of prefabricated walk-in cooler. A single walk-through door provides access to the refrigerated space. A compressor and condensing unit is mounted outside on a wall or at ground level with the refrigeration evaporator coils suspended from the ceiling near one end of the interior space. Many prefabricated units are constructed on skids so they may be moved if required.

Figure 14-1: Prefabricated Refrigerated Storage Unit

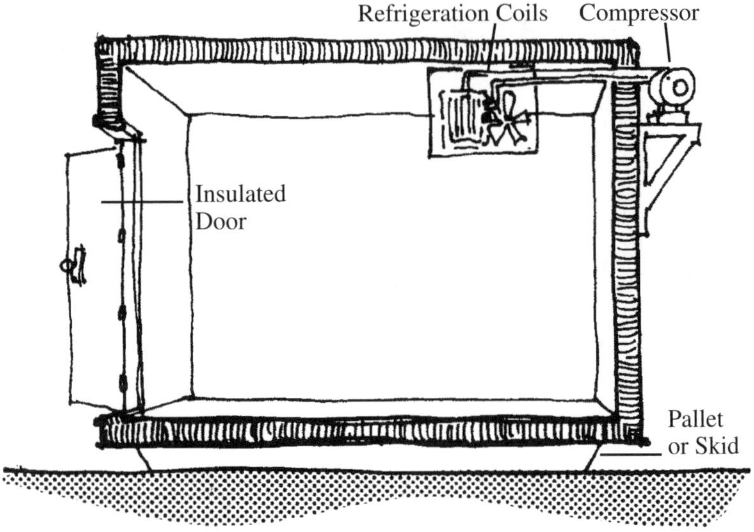

Refrigeration Coils   Compressor

Insulated
Door

Pallet
or Skid

Cut-Away Side View

Ease of access to the storage unit is important for effective labor utilization. Figure 14-2 illustrates a used refrigerated semi-tractor trailer being used for cold storage. Since the trailer is on wheels, it is necessary to provide a means of elevated entry to the storage space. A dirt berm with approach ramps on both sides of a level, elevated landing enables a tractor to pull the harvest trailer up to the doors for easy access to the storage space. This is a simple, low-cost means of providing refrigerated storage.

Figure 14-2:
A Refrigerated Semi-Tractor Trailer Used as Storage Space

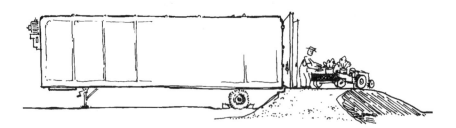

To maximize the effect of refrigerated storage on flower longevity, it is necessary to reduce the tissue temperature of the flower to the optimal level as rapidly as possible. Respiring plants give off heat. Large quantities of flowers brought into refrigerated storage at one time can cause temperatures within the storage space to rise. Fluctuating storage temperatures can result in condensation moisture forming on flower petals, leading to fungal disease problems in storage and to the icing over of evaporator coils and loss of cooling efficiency. A system to rapidly precool flowering stems is often required.

Constantly opening and closing cooler doors to store flowers allows warm air to enter the cooler and cause similar problems. Figure 14-3 illustrates a two-space refrigerated storage system. The first space is used to precool newly harvested stems and for short-term storage. The second space, entered through the first, is for long-term storage of precooled flowers. The door to this second space is opened much less frequently, and the air which enters when the door is open is cooled air. Energy is saved and fewer disease problems arise during long-term storage.

Figure 14-3: A Two-Space Refrigerated Storage System

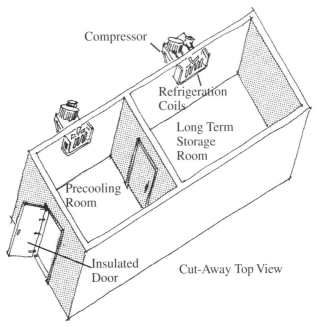

Compressor

Refrigeration Coils

Long Term Storage Room

Precooling Room

Insulated Door

Cut-Away Top View

Shelf Systems for Refrigerated Storage

Refrigerated storage space is expensive to purchase and operate. The space must be utilized to the maximum extent possible. Three-dimensional space, not just floor space, must be put to use. Shelving of some kind solves this problem. Figure 14-4 shows a prefabricated cooler with two types of shelf systems: one for dry storage and the other for wet storage (in buckets of solution).

Figure 14-4: Refrigerated Storage Shelf System

Figure 14-5 shows a shelf system installed in a wide cooler which utilizes a central shelf island between two aisles. These two examples both show shelves for wet and dry storage in the same cooler. This is for illustration purposes only and does not imply that this would or should always be the case. Like everything else, a shelving system should be designed for specific needs and integrated with other systems.

Figure 14-5: Shelf System for a Wide Cooler

Figure 14-6 illustrates a stair-step type shelf system that is particularly suited for displaying the flowering stems while in storage. It might be used in a retail or wholesale situation where the customer comes to the facility to select their own flowers. The end view provides construction detail while the frontal view illustrates how the product would appear to the customer.

Figure 14-6 A Stair-Step Shelf System

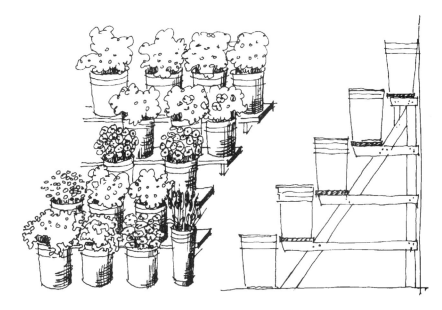

The Refrigerated Storage Environment

The environment within the refrigerated storage facility must be controlled to maintain floral quality. Temperature, humidity, air circulation and the presence of ethylene all affect the longevity of stored flowers.

Temperature

As stated earlier, temperature is an important factor in prolonging the quality of fresh cut flower stems. Cold temperatures reduce respiration rates, ethylene production and effectiveness, and transpirational water loss. The optimal storage temperature will vary between flowering species. It is not practical for most growers to have separate coolers for a variety of storage temperatures. A single cooler set to a temperature safe for most species will suffice for the majority of growers. A temperature setting in the range of 35°F-39°F (2°C-4°C) should be acceptable for most flowers. If temperatures are set lower, closer to freezing, equipment and management of the system must be of sufficient quality to ensure against any malfunction that could damage the flowers by freezing water in the plant tissues.

Relative Humidity

Flowering stems lose water through transpiration or the evaporation of water from small openings (stomata) located primarily on the underside of the leaf. The rate of transpirational water loss is affected by temperature, relative humidity and air circulation. Lower temperatures reduce the rate of transpiration. The lower the relative humidity, the higher the rate of transpiration, the greater the water loss and vice versa. Transpiration can be significantly decreased by saturating the air in the storage environment with water vapor. Relative humidity levels of 85 percent to 95 percent will reduce water loss and maintain quality. Equipment that adds humidity to the storage environment is available and can be beneficial. It must be designed by competent personnel so that it is matched to the evaporator coils. If the equipment is sized or installed incorrectly, the water added will be quickly removed by the coils and excessive ice will form on the coils. High relative humidity levels are desirable, but remember that wet flowers and foliage can lead to disease problems, especially Botrytis.

Ethylene

Many flowering stems are negatively affected by even very low concentrations of ethylene gas. Ethylene must be controlled in the storage environment or the quality and longevity of the flowers will suffer. The lower the temperature, the less ethylene produced by plants. Prolonged storage may increase flower sensitivity to ethylene. Maintaining low storage temperatures alone will not sufficiently control the negative effects of ethylene. Other steps are necessary.

Damaged plant tissue produces ethylene. Broken and torn leaves, stems and flowers produce ethylene which not only shortens their life but also the life of other flowers in the general area. Gentle handling of product in storage will decrease the amount of ethylene produced. Proper sanitation, removing all plant debris from the cooler, will aid in reducing ethylene levels.

Flowers can be treated with a product, such as STS, that prevents or blocks ethylene from attaching to an ethylene action site and thereby preventing its negative effect. Flowers should be treated with such materials prior to being placed into storage.

Ethylene scrubbers or absorbers can be installed inside coolers to remove the ethylene gas. To be effective the system must include pumps which force air from inside the cooler through the absorptive material at a nominal air exchange rate. Such systems may not be economically justifiable.

Exchanging the air inside the cooler with outside air containing less ethylene, in conjunction with proper sanitation and product handling may be the best method of controlling ethylene in refrigerated storage facilities.

Air Circulation

Circulation of air throughout the cold storage room is necessary to ensure a uniform environment. The temperature and atmosphere must be maintained at uniform levels around each flower in storage. If the difference in temperatures taken at various points around the cold storage room is greater than one degree fahrenheit, the air circulation system is not functioning like it should. A fan-forced air circulation system and proper spacing of stored flowers and containers are normally required to attain this degree of uniformity. Buckets should be spaced two to four inches apart and set up at least two inches off the floor to permit air to flow along the floor. Flowers should not be allowed to touch walls and buckets should be placed six to eight inches in from the wall. Do not place any stored materials within six feet of the front of the cold air outlet or the product may suffer desiccation or freeze damage. Keep all stored materials one-and-a-half to two feet from the ceiling.

All stored materials should be spaced uniformly. Too narrow spacing restricts air flow and encourages elevated product temperatures. Too wide spacing invites uneven air flow. Air follows the path of least resistance, therefore, more refrigerated air flows past widely spaced containers than closely spaced containers and uneven product cooling occurs. Uneven air flow also means a non-uniform atmosphere — non-uniform levels of ethylene and relative humidity surrounding the stored flowers. Non-uniformity leads to variable quality which the customer will perceive as poor quality.

The uniform spacing principle applies to all stored product, not just storage containers. All containers should have about the same amount of product. There will be less air circulation around individual flowers when ten bunches are placed in a bucket than when a bucket contains five bunches. Uniformity in all ways must be maintained.

Light

Light does not significantly enhance either the quality or the storage longevity of most fresh cut flowers. Installing lights, other than enough to see what you are doing when working in the cooler, is of marginal benefit at best.

Summary

Refrigerated storage should be considered as a system with several subsystems of temperature control, ethylene control, relative humidity control and air circulation. Each of these subsystems must be developed as an integrated part of each of the other subsystems. None can stand alone and be effective. Remember the difference between success and failure, profit and loss, is attention to every detail. Setting the cooler thermostat to 35°F (2°C), adding water vapor to provide 90 percent relative humidity, treating ethylene-sensitive flowers with STS, and placing a fan in the cooler to blow air around, will not yield consistent, quality product coming out of the cooler if you fail to provide for uniform distribution of flowers and circulation of the air within the refrigerated space.

Remember that at the time of harvest the quality of a fresh cut flower is the best it will ever be. The task of the grower is to design, operate and monitor harvest systems which will slow the flower's decline to the greatest extent possible. The following graphic representation of a fresh cut flower harvest system illustrates a number of steps that must be accomplished effectively to minimize labor and preserve the quality of the flower.

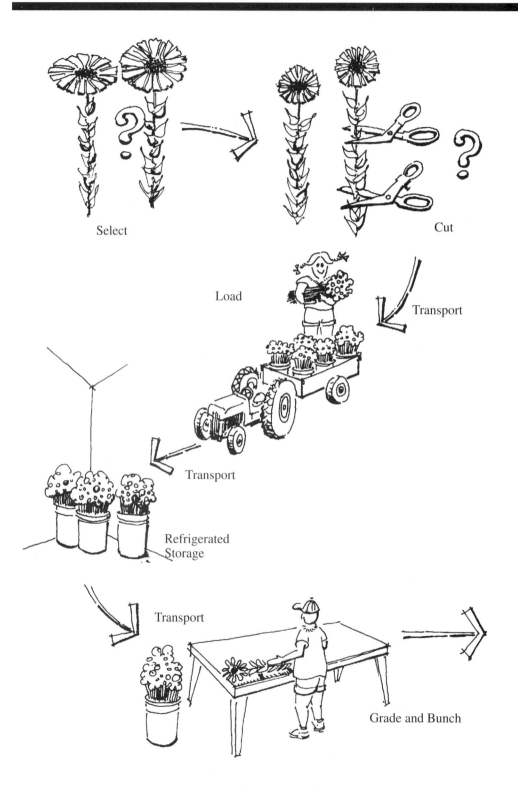

Select

Cut

Load

Transport

Transport

Refrigerated
Storage

Transport

Grade and Bunch

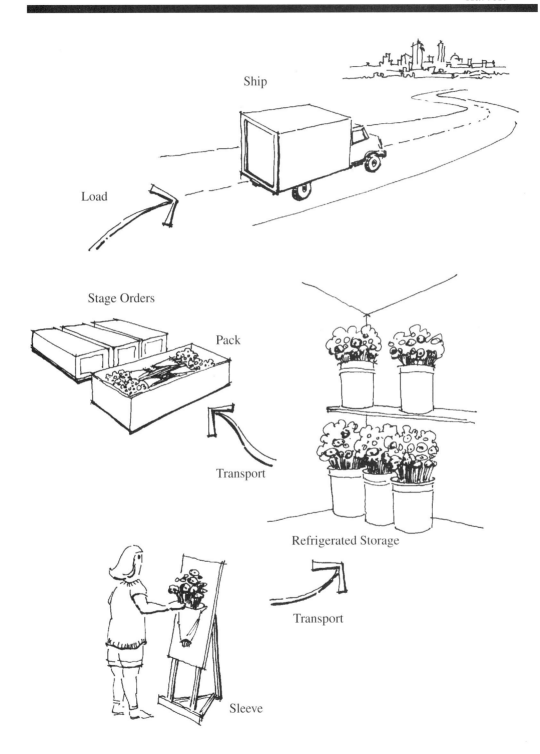

Ship

Load

Stage Orders

Pack

Transport

Refrigerated Storage

Transport

Sleeve

CHAPTER 15

PRESERVING

Preserve *— 1. To maintain unchanged. 2. To prevent organic bodies (plants) from decaying or spoiling. 3. To treat fruit or other plant parts so as to prevent decay.*

The desire to have the flowers of summer in the house during the winter leads many consumers to purchase preserved plant materials. Florists, interior decorators, furniture stores and mail order catalogs all display and offer for sale arrangements of preserved plant materials. The expanding market for craft supplies has greatly increased demand for preserved floral materials. These market forces have created a strong demand for preserved floral products.

Forces in the agricultural economy have caused producers to seek alternative crops and value-added activities. Growers in very rural areas may lack the population density to support fresh cut flower crops. By removing the perishability factor, rural growers can access national or international markets.

Many floral products have markets as preserved materials. Preserved floral products can be divided into several classes:

- Flowers (statice, hydrangea, *celosia,* peony, *gomphrena,* strawflower, zinnia)

- Ornamental Grains and Grasses (flax, wheat, rye, barley, millet)

- Foliage (eucalyptus, ferns, cedar, assorted leaves)

- Herbs (ambrosia, *artemisia,* marjoram, oregano, yarrow)

- Vegetables (ornamental corn, gourds)

- Fruits (apple and citrus slices, cones, berries, pods, seeds)

- Bast Fibers (raffia, jute, hemp)

- Wood and Vine Products (baskets, grapevine wreaths, excelsior, driftwood, woodchips and shavings for potpourri, decorative bark)

- Mosses and Lichen (Spanish moss, reindeer moss, black lichen)

Flowers intended for preserving must be the same quality as those sold as fresh flowers. Quality preserved material begins as quality fresh material. Preserving flowers that were too poor quality to be sold fresh is not an acceptable option. Quality is the best it will ever be at the time flowers are harvested. Preserving them will not all of a sudden make them better. Preserved floral goods should have a useful life of at least one year.

Variety Selection

Just as in fresh flower production, production of preserved floral products begins with the selection of the proper plant variety. Some flowers that do very well as fresh flowers do not produce good preserved materials. For example, the rose variety Royalty is a red variety grown for the fresh-cut, long-stem florist market but it does not produce a good dried red rose. Upon drying, it turns purple-black. The Mercedes variety of rose, however, dries a true red. Table 3-1 in Chapter 3 lists rose varieties for drying. Unfortunately, major seed producers offer very little information about recommended varieties for preserved floral production. The best information is found in literature developed for floral designers and crafters who use preserved materials.

Growing

Any factor that damages the plant while it is growing also damages the final preserved product. Row and plant spacing help determine stem length. Insect and disease problems damage preserved products just as they do fresh materials. Botrytis can discolor fresh flowers, rendering preserved material unacceptable. Larvae on plant material may not be detected until the product has been harvested, processed and shipped. Any blemish present on a stem, leaf or petal will be present on the preserved product. In some cases the blemish will be even more apparent. When plant materials are colored with a dye, blemished (damaged) tissue does not absorb the dye in the same manner as undamaged tissue. The blemish becomes more pronounced and the low quality product must be trashed. An expensive waste of time and materials.

Harvest

Quality and stage of development at time of harvest is important. Flowers preserved almost immediately after harvest are of higher quality, especially if a glycol process is involved. Growers who buy fresh material rather than growing it themselves must make sure the material arrives in good condition. Quality preservation sometimes means that fresh plant material must be shipped by air to arrive in time for processing. Systems need to be developed to facilitate moving the plant materials from harvest through the preservation process.

Preservation Methods

Preserving floral products is a labor intensive process which includes air drying, the use of glycols, desiccant drying and freeze drying. Commercial processors most commonly use the methods of air drying or glycerin preserving. Air drying is the lowest cost way to preserve plant materials. Preserving with a glycol is the only process that results in a supple finished product.

Air Drying

Air drying refers to the release of water in plant tissues to the surrounding environment by evaporation. Simple drying sheds, well-ventilated greenhouses and warehouses are often used for air drying. Rapid-dry chambers with controlled heating, ventilation and dehumidification may be used but require greater capital investment. The economics of using low investment cost, naturally ventilated structures that dry product slowly versus higher investment cost, controlled environment structures that dry materials rapidly need to be examined for each specific situation. Figure 15-1 illustrates a simply modified structure for drying decorative plant materials. A fan/blower assembly has been placed in each of two opposite corners. An air intake tube has been extended up to draw in the hotter air from near the roof. The fan then blows this hotter air down a perforated poly-tube to distribute the hot air along the floor of the drying structure. With natural convection the hotter air then rises up through the plant materials and increases the rate of drying.

Figure 15-1: A Simply Modified Drying Structure

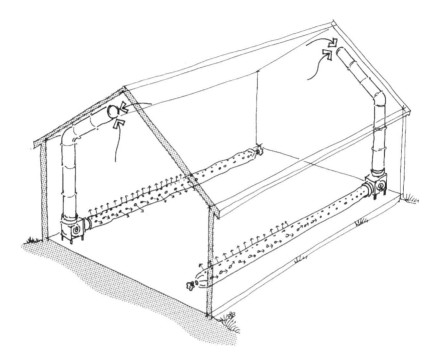

Figure 15-2 illustrates how a drying rack system might be placed into the structure of Figure 15-1. This system utilizes the lath transport/hanging system shown in Chapter 12 on harvest activities. The laths containing flowers would normally be hung starting from the top rails and working your way down to lower rails as the structure fills with drying product.

Figure 15-2:
Lath Hanging/Transport System Placed in the Drying Structure

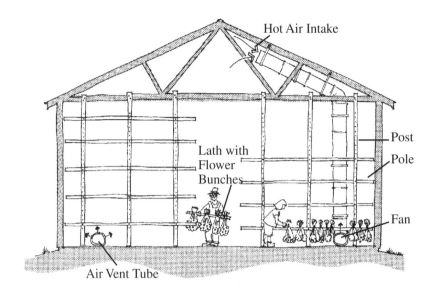

Drying sheds range from extremely simple to very elaborate. Small producers use converted garages, basements and attics. Large producers often adapt simple greenhouses or allocate industrial warehouse space for drying purposes. Regardless of the complexity of their design, all drying sheds have a few characteristics in common. The basic elements to consider when constructing a drying facility are protection and ventilation, and the control of light, temperature and humidity.

Protection

Drying sheds must protect plant materials from anything that could harm them, such as excessive sunlight, wind, rain, dust or insects. Concrete floors, though expensive, act as a heat sink, controlling the buildup of heat during the day and preventing excessive temperature loss at night. Concrete floors can be washed, preventing dust problems. Dirt floors produce so much dust that they are impractical. Many flowers and foliages are sprayed with or dipped into polymer sealants and flame retardants before being placed in the drying shed. Dust particles attracted to these materials become permanently attached. Dust or dirt on dried decorative materials reduces their visual impact and therefore their marketability. Openings in the structure may need to be screened to prevent entry of insects which may feed or deposit eggs on the plant materials.

Ventilation

While drying, plant materials release their moisture to the surrounding air. Relative humidity will increase if there is insufficient air exchange with dry external air, and plants will dry slower. Most drying sheds are constructed to take advantage of natural ventilation and have fans to ensure adequate air circulation. Air exchange may need to be limited in periods of high humidity.

Exposure to Light

The light requirements of drying plants vary. Many drying facilities can adjust the amount of sunlight reaching plants. Plant pigments are very unstable and are easily altered by sunlight. Most items fade to an off-yellow. Drying in dark conditions is necessary to retard the fading of the natural color of many flowers. Processors can also take advantage of sun-bleaching to lighten material before dyeing (immersion dye processing).

Temperature and Humidity

The rate of drying increases with increasing temperatures and decreases with increasing humidity. Plant materials with heavy cuticles, large stem diameters and high moisture content require longer drying times than delicate plants and plants with low water content. Ideal temperatures range from 90°F (32°C) to 150°F (66°C). Plants retain color better when dried quickly and tend to have less petal shatter. Because most small producers rarely correct extreme humidity, the humidity level of the drying facility is that of the outside air plus the influence of moisture released from the drying product. Large manufacturers install humidity and temperature-control equipment. In general, humidity levels should be kept low to promote evaporation. Humid locations usually require climate-control equipment.

Bunching

Materials to be dried are generally bunched and hung in the drying structure immediately after harvest. Date each section to keep track of drying time. Bunches should be small enough and spaced widely enough to ensure adequate air circulation. Dried products are brittle; they should be bunched in a size that will not require much handling after drying. You can determine the water vs. dry fiber content of the plant material, and then use that to determine the bunch weight of fresh-cut material required to dry down to the desired final shipping weight.

To determine the water vs. dry fiber content of a plant material, harvest a group of stems and tie them into ten bunches of average size. Immediately weigh each bunch and record this fresh weight. Do not delay in weighing the bunches. Any time delay will allow the plant material to lose some water and introduce error into your calculations. After determining the fresh weight of each of the bunches, hang them to dry. After allowing them to dry completely, weigh each of them again. Divide this final dry weight by the bunch's fresh weight to determine the percentage of dry fiber (dry fraction) in the original fresh cut plant material. Repeat the calculation for each of the ten bunches and then average the results. It is this average value that should be used to determine the size (weight) of the fresh-cut bunch to be used for drying.

Using *Limonium sinuata,* annual statice, as an example, we measure ten bunches and get the following information.

Bunch Number	Fresh Weight	Dry Weight	Percentage of Dry Fiber
1	0.75 lbs	0.23 lbs	0.307 or 30.7%
2	0.90 lbs	0.27 lbs	0.30 or 30.0%
3	0.81 lbs	0.25 lbs	0.309 or 30.9%
4	0.92 lbs	0.28 lbs	0.304 or 30.4%
5	0.70 lbs	0.21 lbs	0.30 or 30.0%
6	0.77 lbs	0.23 lbs	0.299 or 29.9%
7	0.98 lbs	0.30 lbs	0.306 or 30.6%
8	0.85 lbs	0.26 lbs	0.306 or 30.6%
9	0.83 lbs	0.25 lbs	0.301 or 30.1%
10	0.67 lbs	0.20 lbs	0.299 or 29.9%

To calculate the average (mean) percentage of dry fiber content, add the individual bunch values and divide the total by ten.

0.307 + 0.3 + 0.309 + 0.304 + 0.3 + 0.299 + 0.306 + 0.306 + 0.301 + 0.299 = 3.031. 3.031 divided by ten equals 0.3031 or 30.31 percent.

This means that in this example the final dry weight of a bunch of the annual statice will be 30.3 percent of its fresh weight at harvest.

To determine how much fresh cut material should be placed into a bunch, simply divide the final desired bunch weight by the average (mean) percentage of dry fiber in the material. If you wanted to offer for sale eight-ounce (0.5 lb.) bunches of dried statice, you would divide the desired final sale weight of 0.5 lb by the average dry fiber percentage of 0.3031 and get 1.65 lbs. (26.4 oz.) as an answer. You would need to place 1.65 pounds or 26.4 ounces of fresh cut annual statice into each bunch so that when dried, a bunch would weigh eight ounces (½ lb.). To sell four-ounce bunches of dried statice, divide 0.25 by 0.3031 and get an answer of 0.824 pounds or 13.2 ounces. A four-ounce bunch of dried statice would require 13.2 ounces of fresh cut statice to be dried.

You may want to repeat the experiment at different times of the harvest season to double check for variation. If the variation is very small, you may choose to ignore it. If there is more than a plus or minus two percent variation, then either the experiment needs to be repeated and more closely controlled or you will have to adjust the bunch size upwards to allow for the variation so as not to cheat the customer on the final weight of a bunch.

It should be noted that when calculating the average (mean) percentage of dry fiber (dry fraction) in a fresh plant material you should not round off decimals to simplify the calculations. If you were to round up to 22 percent from 21.5 percent and then use that value to determine the fresh weight bunch size, the amount of fresh material placed in a bunch would be slightly smaller, and the resulting weight of the dried bunch would be less and may then be under the advertised bunch weight of the product. You would then either be cheating your customers or would have to break open each bunch to add additional stems to meet your advertised weight. If you were to round the dry fraction to 21 percent from 21.49 percent and use that value, then the amount of fresh material placed into a bunch would be greater, and the resulting weight of the dried bunch would be greater than your advertised weight. You would be giving away product unnecessarily.

Drying Time
 Required drying times vary with the type of plant, location, drying shed design and season of the year. Most plants dry in one to three weeks. If your drying facility is full of product and you are harvesting more each day with nowhere to put it, you have three choices. One, you can choose not to harvest the remainder of the crop and allow it to rot in the field. Two, if you have sufficient capital, i.e. money, you can construct additional drying buildings. Or, three, you can shorten the time required for drying each crop and thereby move more product through the same size drying facility. This also serves to lower overhead costs. Drying time is affected by any environmental factor which influences the rate at which water evaporates. Temperature, air circulation and relative

humidity of the air surrounding the plant materials all affect drying time. To shorten drying times, you can raise the air temperature, increase the air circulation, or lower the relative humidity in the air around the product. Many growers dry crops in attics of barns, old chicken coops, metal grain bins or similar structures. Most of these situations have high daytime temperatures. Increased heat also lowers the relative humidity by increasing the air's capacity to hold moisture. The relative humidity is generally at its greatest in the microclimate immediately surrounding the surface of the plant tissue. The most economical means to lower the humidity in this microclimate is to blow it out. Increase the air circulation around the surfaces of the product being dried. The air inside the drying structure should also be replaced with air from outside. Improving air movement to shorten drying times is then a two-step process: ventilation, moving the air from outside into, through and back out of the drying facility; and circulation, moving the air through the microclimate surrounding the plant surfaces of the crop being dried. It usually requires more than a single fan to accomplish both ventilation and circulation.

Failure to adequately dry a plant can lead to mold problems if the material is sleeved and boxed. If you know the fiber percentage of a plant, you can monitor drying by periodically weighing sample bunches.

Mold and Insects

Poor air circulation, high humidity, large bunch size and overcrowding encourage mold growth. Make every effort to ensure that no insects or larvae are on plant materials during drying. Some processors apply pesticides immediately after harvest or fumigate after drying. Most fumigants require licensing and so are used only by larger processors. While methyl bromide is the most commonly used fumigant, it may be removed from the market due to its toxicity. Drying structures that raise the temperature above 110°F (43°C) can eradicate pests with sufficient exposure time. Information presented at the Association of Specialty Cut Flower

Growers 1993 National Conference in Kansas City, Kansas, suggests the following temperatures and times for pest eradication:

Drying Temperature	Required Exposure Time
110°F (43°C)	24 hours
120°F (49°C)	3 hours
150°F (66°C)	20 minutes

The drying structure must also be sealed to prevent insect entry. All cracks and openings around doors, eaves and windows must be sealed or covered with fine mesh screening material. Insects will feed on materials and/or lay eggs on the plant tissue. The insect eggs may then hatch out while the material is in storage or after it has been delivered to the customer. Insect pests on preserved plant materials are a major problem and systems to deal with them must be an integral part of your overall preservation process.

Glycol Preserving

Glycol preserving refers to the replacement of the water in plant tissues with glycol. The glycols which have been used commercially are glycerin, ethylene glycol, diethylene glycol and propylene glycol. Research in the author's lab at Kansas State University indicates that the use of glycerin provides the most consistent and uniform, high-quality preserved product. Glycerin has a very high boiling point and does not readily evaporate at ambient temperatures, providing a long-term preservation effect. Glycerin-preserved plants remain soft and pliable, much like they are in the fresh state.

If you plan to preserve with glycerin, harvest in the morning or early evening, and do not use postharvest preservatives. The stage of development is important; in general, harvest later in the season, when the plants are more mature. Very soft, succulent growth will take up the glycerin and become preserved, but it may not have enough structural strength in the stem to support its own weight and will subsequently droop over. Mature stems whose growth has slowed tend to glycerin-preserve with stronger, more substantive stems. Each type of plant is different. You will need to experiment with each of your products to determine the ideal harvest stage of maturity for preserving with glycerin. For example, grasses should be cut between pollen shed and their dough stage of seed development for systemic preserving. When maturity has progressed beyond the dough stage, the stem, foliage and seed head are less able to systemically absorb the glycerin and dye solution.

Two methods are commonly used to preserve floral products with glycerin: systemic absorption and immersion. With systemic absorption, plants systemically absorb a glycerin-bearing solution. Many plants don't absorb the solution efficiently and so are processed by immersion in a glycerin solution, where the glycerin enters the plant by diffusion. This immersion process is also carried out with many dried materials.

Systemic Absorption
The following table (15-1) lists some species that can be preserved with glycerin using systemic absorption.

Table 15-1:
Plant Species For Systemic Preservation With Glycerin

Annual Statice	German Statice	Pepper Grass
Boxwood	grasses	Poplar
Broom Bloom	Juniper	Salal
Candytuft	leaves	Sweet Annie
Caspia	Lepidium	Yarrow
Cedar	Myrtle	
Eucalyptus	Oak	

Instructions for Preserving With Glycerin by Systemic Absorption —Condition of Plant Material Prior to Treatment. Use only high-quality plant materials. Preserving with glycerin will not improve the quality of the crop. It will only preserve the plant material in its present condition. If the edges of the leaves, the leaf margins, are damaged or dried out before beginning treatment, they will remain so after treatment. The main portion of the leaf blade will absorb the glycerin and remain soft while any dry edges will remain dry, become brittle and easily break off, destroying the salability of the product. Leaf spots or the physical evidence of insect or disease damage will not absorb the glycerin solution and often become more apparent after the preservation process. Do not waste time and materials attempting to preserve poor quality crops.

—Choice of Containers. The container should be made of plastic or glass and not metal. It should be tall and narrow to allow for a greater depth of solution without requiring a large quantity of the preservative. Large-diameter containers tend to result in greater amounts of unused glycerine solution, which can become contaminated with bacteria and have to be discarded. Clean and rinse all containers before use. Bacteria and debris left in the container may plug the conducting tissues of the stem, preventing or reducing the uptake of the glycerin preservative solution. Figure 15-3 illustrates a tall and narrow container being used to preserve a one-pound bunch of eucalyptus.

Figure 15-3: A Container for Preserving with Glycerin

—The Glycerin Solution. When mixing a glycerin solution for systemically preserving plant materials, it is important to determine the amount of each ingredient to add by weight, not by volume. Use glycerin which is at least 96 percent pure. Most processors seem to prefer glycerin from a vegetable source rather than from an animal source.

Begin by heating a quantity of water to 140°F (60°C) or slightly warmer for ease in mixing with the glycerin.

Weigh a quantity of glycerin and mix with the heated water in a ratio of one part glycerin (by weight) to anywhere from one and a half to four parts (by weight) of water. The higher glycerin concentration solutions are normally used on softer herbaceous plants with the lower glycerin concentration solutions being used on woody plant materials.

Mix in a bacteriostat, ¾ gram per gallon solution of 8 hydroxyquinoline citrate (8-HQC) and if no dye is being placed into the solution, a bactericide (½ fl. oz. per 20 gal. of Physan 20 or Greenshield) may also be added.

Modify the pH of the preserving solution by adding citric acid (powder) until the pH of the solution falls into the range of 3.0 to 6.0 pH. When preserving a plant species for the first time, a pH of around 3.5 to 4.0 is a good starting point.

Many sources recommend adding a wetting agent (surfactant) to the solution. In my research at Kansas State University, I have found some species of plants benefit from the addition of a surfactant while others, particularly woody species with aromatic oils, have absorbed significantly less glycerin/dye solution and yielded a higher percentage of unacceptable stems when a surfactant was included in the preserving solution. Our research has shown considerable variability in results between plant species depending on which surfactant has been used. Growers should try more than one surfactant each time they begin to preserve a new plant material.

Typical Systemic Glycol Preservative Formulation

1. Glycol/water mixture:
   a. glycerin   20%-40% by weight.

   b. water   Balance of solution.
   Trial at a 25% glycerin,
   75% water solution (by weight).

2. pH modification:
   a. citric acid   Add sufficient amount to adjust the pH
   of the solution to 3.0-6.0. Trial at a pH of
   3.5-4.0 for most species.

3. Bacterial control:
   a. bacteriostat   ¾ gram of 8 hydroxyquinoline citrate
   (8-HQC) per gallon of solution.

   b. bactericide   ½ fl. oz. of Physan 20 or Greenshield per
   20 gallons of solution. Use only if no dye is
   being placed into the solution.

4. Wetting agent (surfactant):
   a. Tween 20   0.1 grams per gallon of solution.
   Check quality of preserved product with
   and without the wetting agent in the
   preserving solution.

5. Dye (optional):
   a. Systemic type   5-20 grams per gallon (1.3-5 grams per
   liter). Trial at 7 grams per gallon and adjust
   for the depth of shade desired. Predissolve
   the dye in hot water.

—Bunch Size and Amount of Solution. Bunch size of glycerin-preserved plant materials is determined the same way as it was for air-dried materials. Weigh ten bunches of fresh-cut material. Preserve the bunches with glycerin, allow to dry and weigh again. Determine the weight change between fresh-cut and glycerin-preserved for each bunch and convert this to a percentage of the initial fresh weight. Average the weight change percentages. Use this number as a factor to determine what the initial fresh weight of a bunch should be to end up with a preserved bunch weight equal to what is desired in the marketplace.

How much glycerin solution is required to preserve a bunch of plant material? Glycerin is expensive. Putting more glycerin into the plant than is necessary is wasted expense. Leaves preserved with too much glycerin may absorb water vapor and bleed glycerin and dye out onto the customer's furniture or walls. Not putting enough glycerin into the plant to properly preserve it will result in a product that turns brittle. Use one gram of a 25 percent glycerin solution (weight basis) per gram fresh weight of plant material as a starting point. Make slight adjustments to this amount as you gain experience working with each of your preserved products. When you put glycerin into fresh plant materials, yu are replacing some of the water in the plant with glycerin. The percentage of water in the plant which is replaced by glycerin is known as the Z value. The optimal Z value is a number which will fall within a range of values. Preserved material with a Z value below the minimum number in the range will become brittle. Materials with a Z value above the maximum number in the optimal range will contain an excessive amount of glycerin and have a very high potential for bleeding.

Knowledge of the optimal Z value for a product will enable processors to:

- lower the total cost of glycerin

- reduce customer complaints because of dry or brittle product

- reduce customer complaints because of bleeding

- eliminate surplus (waste) glycerin and the attendant disposal problems

- fine tune their production processes to a more predictable assembly-line approach to glycerin-preserving

The Z value of a product you have preserved with glycerin can be calculated by the following procedure.

1. Cut ten bunches of plant material and label them 1 to 10. The bunch size should be the same as you would normally preserve as a commercial bunch.

2. Weigh and record each bunch's fresh weight.

3. Dry the bunches in a warm oven for a sufficiently long enough period to remove **all** water from the plant tissue.

4. Subtract the dry weight of each bunch from its fresh weight to determine the weight of the water contained in the fresh plant material.

5. Divide the weight of the water contained in a bunch by the fresh weight of the bunch to determine the percentage of the fresh weight which is comprised of water. This number is known as the water fraction.

Bunch Number	Fresh Weight	Dry Weight	Water Weight	Water Fraction
1	459g	170g	289g	0.630
2	455g	168g	287g	0.631
3	453g	172g	281g	0.620
4	458g	165g	293g	0.640
5	456g	160g	296g	0.649
6	462g	171g	291g	0.630
7	457g	174g	283g	0.619
8	460g	170g	290g	0.630
9	465g	181g	284g	0.611
10	470g	174g	296g	0.630
				6.29

6. Add the water fractions for each of the 10 bunches and divide the total by 10 to get the average water fraction for the fresh cut material.

6.29 divided by 10 = 0.629 which is the water fraction or the mean percentage of water contained in the 10 bunches of eucalyptus.

7. Cut and weigh a new bunch of fresh plant material.

    465 grams (453.6 grams = 1 pound)

8. Weigh out the amount of glycerin solution that you would normally place in a container to preserve a bunch of material.

    500 grams

9. Place the fresh cut bunch into the solution and preserve as you normally would.

10. Remove the newly preserved bunch from the container and weigh any remaining solution.

    30 grams of solution remain

11. Subtract the weight of the remaining solution from the weight of the initial total solution to determine the weight of solution absorbed by the plant material.

    500 - 30 = 470 grams of solution absorbed by the bunch of eucalyptus

12. Divide the weight of the solution absorbed by the fresh weight of the bunch to get the unit weight of solution absorbed per unit weight of plant material. Note that this measurement is similar to the suggestion earlier in this section that you should use one gram of solution per gram of fresh weight as a starting point in determining how much solution to use.

    470g solution divided by 465g plant material = 1.01g solution per gram fresh plant weight

13. Multiply this unit solution weight per unit fresh weight number by the percentage of glycerin contained in your preserving solution (expressed as a decimal). This is required because in absorbing the preserving solution the plant material absorbed

both the glycerin and the water in the solution. You must factor out the water because it will evaporate as the plant material dries. The answer is the actual amount of glycerin you have placed into the plant tissue.

1.01g x 0.25 = 0.253g

14. Divide the weight of the glycerin placed into the tissue by the average water fraction from step 6 to arrive at the Z value of your bunch of glycerin-preserved material.

0.253 divided by 0.629 = 0.40 which is the Z value of this bunch of preserved eucalyptus.

Z values are different for each plant species. The optimal Z value range for most plants is unknown at this time. Research into optimal Z values is currently being conducted by the author at Kansas State University. A complete mathematical derivation discussion of the Z value concept can be found in the book *Preserving Flowers and Foliage with Glycols & Dyes* by Mark Koch.

—The Preserving Environment. Transpiration, the evaporation of water from the leaves, is the force that drives the systemic preservation process. Water, in the form of vapor, must move out of the plant in order to make room for the glycerin solution to move in. The preserving environment should be one which encourages transpiration at a controlled rate. If the transpirational rate is too slow, the plant tissue may die and shut down the system before enough glycerin has been absorbed. If the transpirational rate is too high, water will be lost faster than the preserving solution is absorbed and portions of the leaves will dry out and not be able to absorb the glycerin. The preserving environment must be uniform around each and every leaf or each leaf will transpire at a different rate. Different transpiration rates will result in different absorptive rates and different amounts of glycerin entering each leaf. This non-uniformity of glycerin content will result in a poor quality product.

The ideal preserving environment will have an air temperature of 60°F to 85°F (16°C to 29°C), have neither excessively low nor high relative humidity, be out of direct sunlight and have excellent air circulation.

—Temperature and Humidity. The optimal temperature and humidity combination in the preserving environment varies with the species of plant being preserved. Eucalyptus preserves well under a warmer temperature and lower relative humidity range than Port Orford Cedar, which preserves better in a cool, humid environment. Eucalyptus grows well under desert-like conditions while Port Orford Cedar grows in the cool damp conditions of coastal Oregon. In general most plant species will preserve with a high-quality product in an environment of 65°F-85°F and 20 percent to 40 percent humidity.

—Air Circulation. Air circulation requirements within the glycerin-preserving structure (room) are similar to those for air drying but with key differences. The primary difference is that for glycerin preservation, the environment must be consistently uniform around each leaf and adjusted to control the rate of transpiration. For air-drying purposes the environment is designed to accelerate the transpirational rate to remove all water from the plant material at the fastest possible rate. Uniformity around each leaf is not critical as long as each leaf eventually becomes dry. For both glycerin preserving and air drying, water vapor must be blown off the leaf surface and the air within the room must be circulated.

Water vapor, leaving the plant by transpiration, exits through small pores called stomates located primarily on the underside of the leaves. Bunches of flowers hung to dry are typically hung upside down. The lower leaf surfaces containing the stomates are then pointed upward. Air circulation to remove transpirational water vapor should be directed across these leaf surfaces, which are now on top. For air drying, the optimal direction for air flow is down and across the upward-facing lower leaf surfaces.

In the glycerin-preserving process, the stems are placed upright in containers. The lower leaf surfaces with the stomates are pointed down. Air circulation to remove transpirational water vapor from plant materials being glycerin-preserved must be directed up and across these downward-facing lower leaf surfaces. Air circulation systems designed for air drying may be unsatisfactory for glycerin preserving.

Bunch and container size also impact air circulation in the glycerin-preserving process. Bunch size must be small enough and container diameter large enough to allow air to circulate uniformly around each leaf in the bunch. Stems must be placed loosely in the container or the leaves on the inside of a tight bunch will not transpire at the same rate as leaves on the outside, and therefore will not receive the same amount of glycerin. Too narrow of a preserving container will have the same effect by holding the stems too tightly together to allow for uniform transpiration at each leaf.

—**Light.** Light is important in the systemic absorption of a glycerin solution. Plants absorb glycerin/dye solution at a greater rate under conditions of light than they do in the dark. Figure 15-4 illustrates the effect that the presence or absence of light has on systemic absorption by eucalyptus of a 25 percent glycerin solution containing a red dye. The experiment was conducted in a growth chamber at a constant 72°F and 50 percent relative humidity with continuous and uniform air circulation moving from the bottom to the top of the chamber. The eucalyptus stems were preserved under a 12-hour light and 12-hour dark alternating cycle.

Figure 15-4:

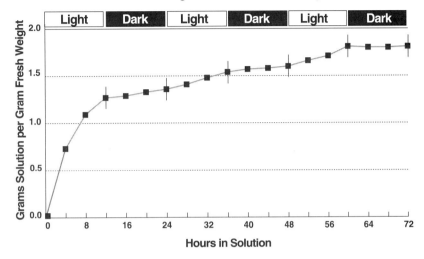

Effect of Light on Solution Uptake
12 Hours Light & 12 Hours Dark Per Day

The very rapid uptake of the solution in the first twelve hours is due in part to a high water-potential deficit due to the time lag from cutting the branches off the tree until placing them in the preserving solution. In other words, the branches dried out to some degree before being placed into the glycerin/dye solution. The difference was also due to being in the light. Eucalyptus branches which were preserved in the dark absorbed 46 percent less solution during this initial 12-hour period.

Notice how the rate of absorption decreases in the periods of dark and increases during the periods of light. The presence or absence of light has a definite effect on the systemic absorption of glycerin/dye solution by eucalyptus stems. When stems are cut off the parent plant, they begin to die. A high-quality preserved branch must have uniform glycerin and dye distribution throughout the tissues of the leaves. The quicker the preserving solution is absorbed into the plant tissue after the branch has been cut from the plant, the more likely the glycerin and dye will be uniformly distributed and yield a high-quality product. Research into determining the most economical length of this initial light period continues. Other factors of light intensity and quality are also under investigation.

The Process — Clean the containers and fill them with an amount of preserving solution equal in weight to the fresh weight of the plant material to be preserved. This is a general guideline for solutions with glycerin concentrations of 25 percent to 33 percent. The optimum amount of glycerin preserving solution will vary with the concentration of glycerin in the solution and the desired Z value of the preserved product.

Rinse the lower portion of each bunch to remove any dirt or debris which might contaminate the preserving solution. Recut all stems immediately before placing them into the preserving solution. About one-and-a-half inches of stem should be removed to be assured of removing any potential blockage of the conductive tissue.

Preserving time for most plant materials is three to seven days. Leave the material in the glycerin solution until the plant quits taking up the solution. Rinse stems and hang to dry. Dry the materials completely to prevent mold from forming. Store away from areas of high relative humidity. Screen warehouses to exclude insects such as Indian meal moth.

Preserving by Immersion in Glycerin Solution

Plants that don't absorb glycerin systemically may be preserved by immersion. Add glycols to very hot water about 180°F to break down any waxy cuticle which may be present on the leaf surface. While not essential, maintaining a high solution temperature will produce better results. Add acidifier, bacterial control agent, surfactant and dye, stirring thoroughly. Rinse the plant materials to be preserved in a water/surfactant mixture to clean the surface for more uniform penetration of glycerin/dye and improved appearance of the final product. Once the plant materials have been preserved, they can no longer be washed or bleeding will likely occur. Immerse the materials in the glycol solution so they are completely covered by the solution. Immersion times for most plants is one to 24 hours. Allow preserved materials to dry thoroughly before storing.

Typical Immersion Glycol Preservative Solution

1. Glycol/water mixture:

   a. glycerin   10-50% by weight.

   b. water   Balance of solution. Trial at the more concentrated end of the range.

2. pH modification:

   a. citric/acetic acid   Add sufficient amount to adjust the pH of the solution to approximately 4.5.

3. Bacterial control:

   a. potassium sorbate   0.1-0.15% powder or 0.2-0.3% liquid form.

   b. propylene glycol   17% of the total solution (by weight) Use potassium sorbate or propylene glycol but not both.

4. Wetting agent (surfactant):

   a. nonionic/cationic   0.1% of solution (by weight), equivalent to approximately 1 teaspoon or 3.8 grams per gallon. Do not use an anionic wetting agent.

5. Dye (optional):

   a. basic (cationic)   0.15-3.0% of weight of plant material to be dyed, depending on depth of shade desired.

Desiccant Drying

Desiccant drying involves the transfer of water from plant tissues to a material with a high affinity for water, such as silica gel or sand. Plants remain completely embedded in the medium until all the water has left the plant. Flowers with delicate petals or high water content which are difficult to air-dry can be preserved with these desiccants. A primary advantage of drying with desiccants is that because every petal is supported by the drying media, the flower retains its original form. Flowers to be dried with a desiccant can be harvested at a more mature stage. Examples of flowers which preserve well with this method are peonies, pansies and zinnias. This method has limited applications in commercial production due to high labor costs. However, for uses where the market will bear a price premium equal to or greater than the additional cost to desiccant-dry over air-dry, this method can be profitable. Systems to minimize labor must be developed to make this method economically feasible.

Freeze Drying

Freeze drying is the removal of water from plant tissues by way of sublimation. Specially engineered chambers create conditions in which water passes directly from the solid state to the vapor state. A vacuum reduces pressure in the chamber to a level at which the boiling point of water is below the freezing point of water. Applied heat energy in the form of electromagnetic radiation allows the water in the plant tissues to evaporate.

Freeze drying avoids the shrinkage normally associated with air drying and can be useful for delicate flowers. Flowers which have been properly freeze-dried are of high quality and may receive premium prices in the marketplace. Capital investment is large and high volumes of materials may need to be processed to make freeze drying economically viable.

Polymer Coating

Primarily developed for freeze-dried products, polymer coatings are gaining wide acceptance with many dried floral products, especially delicate flowers, air-dried items that shatter, and fruit slices. Polymer coatings prevent shattering and water reabsorption. The coatings are applied by spray or immersion. The cost of coating materials varies significantly. Water-born polymers require little capital investment or training but are limited to application to a few products. Solvent-born polymers require significant capital investment and training but may be applied to a wide range of products. To be of benefit, polymer coatings must be applied to a preserved product. This process will require systems to be developed to apply the coating while maintaining the integrity of the flower.

Summary

The preservation process requires labor, equipment, facilities and materials, in addition to those of producing fresh materials. Markets must be developed which will pay a price premium at least equal to the cost of preserving your products, or you'll lose money by preserving them.

The largest cost for preserving decorative plant materials is labor. Labor may comprise as much as 50 percent of the cost of producing these materials. Systems must be developed to minimize and control labor, or a firm can quickly become unprofitable. Linkages between systems are critical to keeping the labor requirements to a minimum. Each of the harvesting and transporting systems should be designed to facilitate the preserving processes.

For further information on glycols and dyes:

Preserving Flowers & Foliage with Glycols & Dyes
A Manual for the Commercial Producer
by Mark Koch

available from: Robert Koch Industries, Inc.
4770 Harback Road
Bennett, CO 80102

CHAPTER 16

COLOR PROCESSING

Color processing involves bleaching, dyeing and painting. Coloring flowers can greatly broaden a product mix without increasing the number of varieties grown. A greater proportion of a white-flowered variety can be grown and then custom-colored to meet demand in the marketplace. Stems of flowers to be dried can be dyed green. Dried materials can be painted gold or silver. New products can be added through the creative addition of color.

Bleaching

Bleaching refers to the chemical decolorizing of plant materials to increase brightness (whiteness). Bleaching allows plant materials to be subsequently colored in very light or pastel shades. Bleached plant materials are in increased demand and are often required for subsequent dyeing. Bleaching is usually carried out in large vats. Hydrogen peroxide, sodium hypochlorite and calcium hypochlorite are the bleaching chemicals most often used. Bleaching plant materials is complex; training and significant capital investment are required.

Dyeing

Dyeing is relatively simple and requires little capital investment. Either fresh or dried plant material may be colored with dye. Dyes can be placed inside fresh cut plant tissues through systemic absorption, by placing stem ends into a water-and-dye solution and allowing the stem to "drink" the dye. This is the process by which white carnations become Irish green for St. Patrick's Day or are custom-colored to match a bridesmaid's dress. Plant materials also can be immersed in a water-and-dye solution allowing the dye to become absorbed into all parts of the plant. With either method the resulting color is a combination of the dye color and the plant's natural pigmentation (substrate color). Dyes do not completely mask the substrate; dark plant material cannot be dyed a lighter shade without bleaching the material first. Flowers can be dyed and then sold as a fresh cut flower or dried and sold as a preserved product. Little training is required, but a lack of training will result in poor quality. Although dyeing often produces a more attractive product than painting, certain foliage and flowers respond better to painting.

Painting

Painting involves spraying or immersing plant products in a diluted solution of water-soluble latex paints. Painting does not require bleaching to produce light shades on dark material, but excess paint often gums up delicate flowers. A major disadvantage of painting is that all parts of the painted plant material appear the same. The leaves and stems will not look different, as they do in their natural state.

Systemic Dyeing with Acid Dyes

Acid dyes are widely used to systemically dye fresh cut flowers such as carnations, feverfew and waxflower. They may also be used with other fresh cut flowers to provide specific colors for holidays or to create new and unusual colors for everyday applications. The following guidelines have been developed for effective coloring of fresh cut flowers. By following these simple measures, dye solutions may be used very efficiently, thereby reducing waste and adding to the cost-effectiveness of your dyeing program.

These instructions are for dye-and-water solutions only. For detailed instructions regarding use of acid dyes with glycerin preservatives, consult the section on glycol preservation in Chapter 15.

Condition of Flowers Prior to Dyeing

To obtain the best results, only high-quality flowers should be used. Adding color to a poor quality flower will not improve it, only change its color. Flowering stems should be left out of water for a brief period of time to enhance uptake of the dye solution.

Choice of Containers

The choice of container is important. The container should allow for adequate depth of solution, while not requiring a large volume of solution. Containers with very large diameters tend to be inefficient. Tall, narrow buckets provide support for long-stem flowers and require less solution to achieve the same depth. Use plastic or glass containers, not metal.

Clean all dye containers thoroughly and rinse them with clean water before preparing the dye solution. Dirty containers may contain bacteria or debris that can plug conductive tissue. If you use bleach to clean containers, you must thoroughly rinse these containers to avoid bleaching the dye solution.

Water Quality

Systemic dyeing works best when the dye solution is prepared with warm water. Avoid hard water when systemically dyeing fresh cut flowers. Hard water — water that contains salts of calcium or magnesium — makes dye solutions less effective.

Surfactant (wetting agent)

A surfactant is generally added to the dye solution at a concentration of 0.1 percent by weight. This would be equivalent to 0.12 fluid ounces per gallon of solution.

Dye Requirements

Dye is generally used at the rate of one to two ounces per gallon when systemically dyeing fresh cut flowers. Base the amount of dye you use on the weight of material to be dyed. The amount of dye should be 0.5 percent of the weight of the material. Depth of shade depends on amount of dye and the length of time the flowers are in the dye solution. Higher dye concentrations will result in shorter dyeing times. Lower dye concentrations give you more control over the rate of dyeing, making it easier to produce soft, delicate shades without over-dyeing. In general, one pound of dye will treat about 15,000 carnations.

Handling Dyes

When handling dyes, follow common safety rules. Wear rubber gloves, safety glasses, protective clothing such as an apron, and a NIOSH approved dust mask. Dyes can stain skin and clothing. Most dyes are not considered hazardous but may cause irritation for some people. Consult the Material Safety Data Sheet (MSDS) for the dyes you use before using these products.

When adding dye to water, add and dissolve small amounts of dye at a time; don't add it all at once. Stir the solution thoroughly. Unless the dye is completely dissolved, it will not function properly. It is often helpful to predissolve the dye in a small amount of very hot water before adding it to the dye buckets.

The Dyeing Process

Recut the stems of the flowers just before placing them in the dye solution. Trapped air bubbles in the lower portion of the stems can block conductive tissue, thereby preventing solution uptake. Leave flowering stems in the dye solution until color is lightly distributed throughout the flower, being careful not to over dye. The dyeing process normally takes 30 minutes to one hour. Expect considerable variation among plant species. After removing flowers from the dye solution, rinse stems in clean water and place in a solution of water and a commercial cut flower preservative. This will bring the remaining dye up from within the stems into the flowers.

To achieve pastel shades, don't leave the flowers in the dye solution too long. When the flower is removed from the dye solution, dye that is still in the stem will travel to the flower, increasing the color intensity.

Immersion Dyeing With Basic Dyes

Basic dyes are often used to color dried flowers and foliages. Immersion dyes provide brilliant color and total coverage. Some materials, like wood chips, are porous enough to dye at moderate temperatures, but most dried flowers and foliages are covered by a heavy, waxy cuticle that must be broken down by a moderate to high dyebath temperature. For most items, a minimum dyebath temperature of 160°F (71°C) will sufficiently open the cellulose fibers and allow the dye to diffuse into the material. A temperature of 180°F (82°C) is best. Note that high temperatures will damage fresh flowers, which are usually dyed in an alcohol solution.

Two types of operations are routinely used to dye floral products: continuous dyeing and batch dyeing. A continuous dye operation uses the same dyebath to dye several batches of goods, while a batch operation dyes a single batch of material in the dyebath. With a batch system, the material remains in the solution until nearly all of the dye has left the solution in favor of the substrate — a process called exhaustion. A batch operation is both simpler and slower than a continuous dye operation.

In a continuous dye operation, you must periodically add dye to the dyebath because the dye continuously leaves the dyebath in favor of the substrate. The concentration of dye in the dyebath does not remain constant. The rate at which dye leaves the dyebath, called the diffusion rate, depends on temperature, initial dye concentration, pH of the dyebath, affinity for the substrate and the fibrous nature of the product. With a continuous operation, the material remains in the solution until it reaches the desired depth of shade. The higher the initial dye concentration and the hotter the dyebath temperature, the faster the dyeing proceeds.

While the continuous system is much faster, it is also more difficult to obtain uniform dyeings because the dye concentration continuously changes. You must conduct tests to determine when to add dye to restore the dye concentration to its original level. You will also need to add water to replace the water consumed in the dyeing process.

Regardless of the type of operation, dyeing is a three-step process. The material is first wetted-out in a water and surfactant mixture, then transferred to the dyebath for a predetermined amount of time, then rinsed and allowed to dry.

Wetting the Material Before Dyeing

Before dyeing, wet materials in a water/nonionic surfactant mixture. Although this step is optional, it helps achieve a more uniform dyeing. Heating the solution will give better results. After wetting, plant fibers have a more uniform consistency and tend to absorb dyes at a more uniform rate. Impurities in the materials are removed, helping to prevent contamination of the dyebath. Prepare the solution by adding a nonionic surfactant to water, at a rate of $\frac{1}{10}$ of one percent of the weight of solution. Most nonionic surfactants can be used. An excellent surfactant is Polysorbate 80, often used as an emulsifier with flavor oils in the food industry. Soak materials for five to 10 minutes.

Determining Dye Requirements

Dye requirements vary considerably depending on the type of dyebath and the nature of the material being dyed. In general, add dyes at a rate of 0.5 percent to 3 percent of the weight of the product. For example, the dye required for 100 pounds of material is 0.5 to 3 pounds. While it is best to determine dye requirements as a percentage of the material being dyed, it is also customary to state dye concentration based on the dyebath — for example, 4 grams per gallon. When calculating dye concentrations based on the dyebath, add dyes at the rate of two to 20 grams per gallon. Using a higher concentration of dye decreases the time required to achieve the desired depth of shade. Using a lower dye concentration requires longer dyeing times, but generally results in more color uniformity. Heated water solutions generally require less dye than do cold water dyebaths.

Always predissolve dyes before adding them to the dyebath. Form a paste with acetic acid and then add hot water, preferably boiling, to liquefy the paste. It is imperative that the dye be thoroughly dissolved before you add it to the dyebath. The amount of acetic acid you should use is the amount required to reduce the pH of the dyebath to about 4.5.

Preparation of the Dyebath

Two types of dyebath solutions are commonly used: a water solution and an alcohol solution. The water solution is typically used to dye dried flowers and the alcohol solution is used for fresh flowers such as Marguerite daisies. The alcohol solution system is best left to experienced personnel and may pose significant safety factors due to the flammability of the alcohol.

Water Solution Dyebath

This simple solution consists of water, dye and a nonionic surfactant. The dyebath performs best when heated, although ambient temperatures work adequately for certain items. A dyebath temperature of 140°F-180°F (60°C-82°C) is recommended. To keep the color uniform, hold the dyebath temperature constant. There are two reasons to heat the dyebath. First, heat breaks down the waxy cuticle covering the plant. This cuticle is very difficult to penetrate at low temperatures. Second, heat opens the cellulose fibers to allow the dye molecules to diffuse into the substrate. Materials dyed in cold-water dyebaths generally require substantially longer immersion times and often display a lack of color consistency. Cold-water dyeing is generally a staining of the outer fibers, while true dyeing occurs when the dye actually penetrates the plants fibers.

Prepare the dyebath by first adding the surfactant to the required amount of water. As with the wetting solution, add the nonionic surfactant at the rate of ⅒ of 1 percent of the weight of water. Measure the dye required and predissolve before adding to the dyebath. It is important that the dyebath be thoroughly blended before use.

Rinse

After dyeing, rinse materials thoroughly in water. This will reduce the possibility of the dye running or coming off the material later. Properly dyed products will not show noticeable loss of color after rinsing. Some producers also include a bactericide in the rinse water to help prevent mold from developing. This is especially important if glycerin has been added to the dyebath as a softening agent. After rinsing, allow the materials to dry completely before packaging. Dip-dyed materials should never come into contact with excess moisture.

Summary

Color processing floral materials can add considerable depth to a product mix without requiring more varieties to be grown. Adding color to products requires additional materials and labor and therefore greater cost. Systems for adding color should be carefully linked with those for harvesting and preserving so as to minimize associated costs.

Preserving and color processing are terminal stages in the series of activities for producing a preserved product. Do not drop the baton at the end of the production process. Design a preserving system that effectively uses labor and results in a high quality product.

The following graphic representation of a dried flower harvest system illustrates the series of steps required to harvest and process a dried flower crop. Each step requires the crop to be handled and transported. Often 50 percent or more of the total labor to produce a dried floral product is expended in the harvest systems. Profitability can be maintained or lost in the design, operation and monitoring of each of the activities and the interrelationships between the activities that comprise the harvest system.

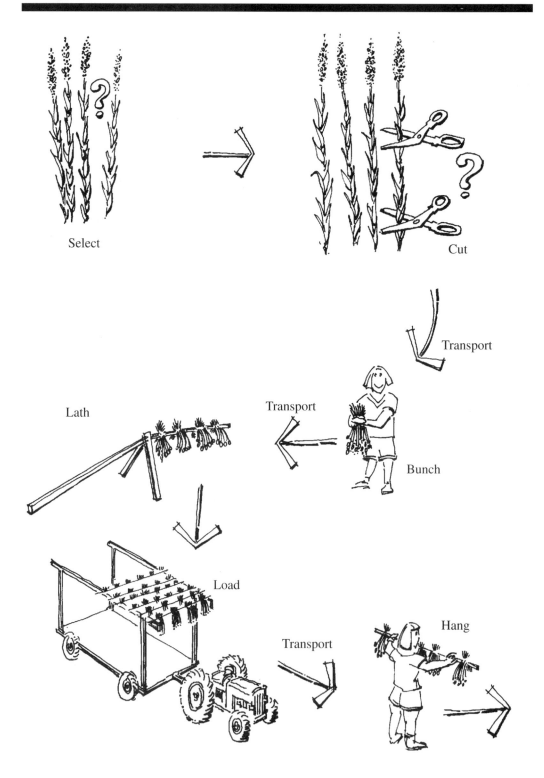

Select

Cut

Transport

Lath

Transport

Bunch

Load

Transport

Hang

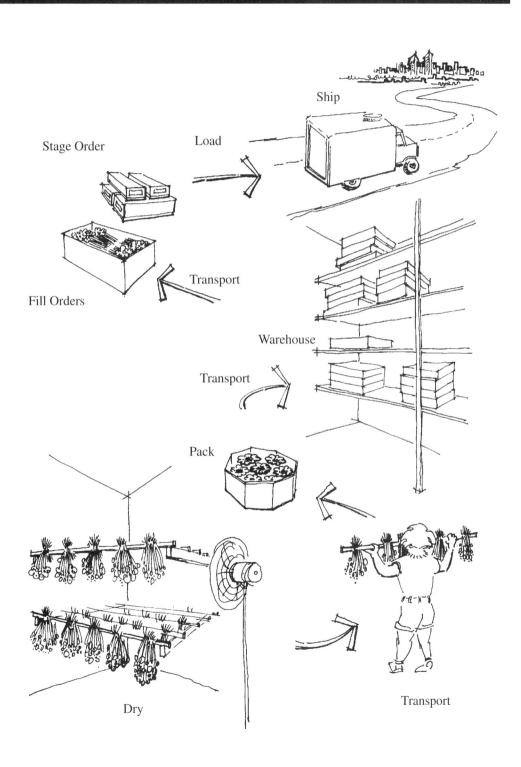

Ship

Load

Stage Order

Transport

Fill Orders

Warehouse

Transport

Pack

Transport

Dry

Appendix A

CROPS

A-1   *Achillea* (Yarrow). 245

A-2   *Gladiolus* 253

A-3   *Liatris* (Gayfeather) 266

A-4   Peony. 276

A-5   Annual Statice 299

A-6   Sunflower 305

A-7   Zinnia 317

A-8   Woody Ornamental Branches. 327

INTRODUCTION

Appendix A provides basic information on a few representative crops. The crops presented represent a cross section of potential crops including: annuals, perennials and shrubs; plants propagated from seed, corms and transplants; and design forms of line, focal and filler flowers. The list is not intended to be a list of crops for a beginning grower to start with or a list of crops which should be in every grower's product mix. It is a sample of crops which represent the broad spectrum of specialty cut flowers currently in commercial production.

Little research-based information exists for most specialty cut flower crops. The section on sunflowers contains more detailed information than sections on other crops. This is because sunflowers are an important agronomic crop. Considerable research has been conducted on sunflower production because of the economic value of its seeds and oil. The results of this research have been interpreted and presented here for use in producing the crop as a cut flower. Earlier in this century, peonies were a significant cut flower crop and the U.S. Department of Agriculture developed grades and standards for its commercial sale. These are presented for use by growers of peonies and as a reference to consider for the grading of other crops.

The author recommends that growers seeking production information on specific crops refer to the book *Specialty Cut Flowers* written by Alan Armitage and published by Timber Press.

A-1 *ACHILLEA* (YARROW)

Modern society may appreciate the way yarrow appears in a vase, but older cultures valued it for medicinal and even magical purposes. Homer's hero Achilles distributed yarrow among his soldiers to stanch the blood from their wounds, which gave the plant its genus name, *Achillea*. Navajos regard it as a general panacea; the English call it allheal. Pioneers drank it to cure just about anything. It has also been used as an astringent, as an anti-inflammatory agent, and as a salve to heal cuts, burns and bruises. The dried root of one species, *Achillea ptarmica* (sneezewort), was even once ground and used for snuff, which resulted in a runny nose.

Yarrow, a hardy perennial, typically has flattish clusters of yellow, white or reddish flowers. It has gray or green, finely divided leaves with a lingering, spicy fragrance. Yarrow varies in size, from the creeping, alpine variety used in rock gardens to the four foot-tall kind used in wild gardens, in borders and in cut flower arrangements. It thrives in ordinary garden soil, open sunlight and well-drained conditions. Once established, yarrow can survive drought and neglect.

Achillea consists of more than one hundred species of perennial herbs found throughout Europe, North and West Asia, and North America. Only four or five species of this specialty cut flower crop are currently being grown in the United States, though numerous cultivars have been produced through breeding and selection.

VARIETIES TO GROW

The primary question to answer while exploring which varieties to grow is: What do consumers want to buy? Some varieties of *achillea* have dual use as fresh cuts and as dried flowers. Examples are listed below.

Achillea ageratum (Sweet Yarrow) — used for medicinal purposes but not considered useful as a cut flower.

Achillea x 'Coronation Gold'
'Coronation Gold' — 24-36"; smaller, deep yellow flowers; gray-
   green, fragrant foliage.

Achillea clypeolata x taygeata
'Moonshine' — 18-24"; sulfur-yellow flowers; silvery-green, fern-
   like foliage.

Achillea filipendulina
   Cultivars:
       'Gold Plate' — 24-60"; yellow flowers; excellent but very
          large flower heads which may limit their use.
       'Parker's Variety' — 36"; wide, golden-yellow flowers.

Achillea millefolium
   Cultivars:
       'Cerise Queen' — 24"; cherry-red flowers.
       'Fire King' — 18"; deep red flowers that fade with age
          and hot weather.
       'Heidi' — 18"; dark violet flowers.
       'Kelwayi' — 18-24"; dark red flowers.
       'Lavender Beauty' — 18-24"; light lavender flowers.
       'Lilac Beauty' — 18-24"; lilac flowers.
       'Paprika' — 24"; red flowers with yellow centers.
       'Red and Gold' — 24"; bright red flowers with gold centers.
       'Rose Beauty' — 24"; pink flowers.
       'Summer Pastels' — 24"; pastel color mix; best used as
          fresh — tend to fade when dried.
       'Weserandstein' — 18-24"; light rose flowers.
       'White Beauty' — 24"; creamy white flowers.

Achillea millefolium x Achillea clypeolata
   Cultivars ('Galaxy Series'):
       'Appleblossom' — 36"; mauve flowers.
       'Beacon' — 24-36"; red flowers.
       'Great Expectations' — 24"; pale yellow flowers.
       'Salmon Beauty' — 36"; salmon-peach flowers.

Achillea ptarmica (Sneezewort)
Cultivars:
'Ballerina' — 12-15"; very short stems; clear white flowers.
'The Pearl' — 24"; profuse, white, double flowers; may be raised from seeds or cuttings.

Achillea taygeata
Cultivar:
'Debutante' — 24"; mix of ivory, cream to lemon-yellow & gold, all shades of pink, rose, salmon, lilac, purple, red, scarlet, coral and orange flowers.

WATERING

Overhead watering is not recommended. It may physically damage the flowers, cause spotting on the petals, splash soil onto the foliage and promote the spread of disease. Drip irrigation is recommended because it places the water on the ground where it is needed and not on the flowers or foliage.

The amount and frequency of water required will vary with the weather and stage of maturity of the crop. Base the irrigation schedule on the soil moisture status in the root zone and irrigate to provide sufficient but not excessive water to the crop. Insufficient water will reduce the production and quality of a crop, whereas a consistently saturated soil will reduce growth and promote the development of root rot. In general, yarrows do better if kept moderately moist.

FERTILIZER

Before initiating any fertilizer program, always test the soil for nutrient content. The increased water requirement of cut flowers creates an increased requirement for fertilization. The application of fertilizer should coincide with crop needs.

One to 1½ pounds of nitrogen per 1,000 sq.ft. of production bed space applied in spring should be sufficient for the crop. Crops growing in sandy soils or in areas of heavy rainfall may require a second application in late June. Use calcium nitrate as a portion of the nitrogen requirement; the added calcium will aid in increasing stem strength. Apply phosphorus and potassium, if needed (determined by soil test), at the same time.

If fertilizer is injected into drip lines, 150-200 ppm of nitrogen in a constant feed program is ideal. Again, depending on soil test results, a complete fertilizer may be used to supply phosphorus and potassium.

Avoid late summer application of any fertilizer. Plant growth in September and October needs to gradually decrease toward dormancy to promote cold hardiness for winter survival.

WEED CONTROL

Growers must control weeds in the field production of yarrow, as competition with weeds reduces the quantity and quality of floral production. A bed full of weeds also increases the time required to harvest, raising labor costs. Several options are available to combat weed growth: herbicides, barriers or mulches, hoeing and hand-weeding.

Due to limited production of many species of specialty cut flowers, only a few herbicides are labeled for use. DCPA (Dacthal), Fluazilop-P (Fusilade), Trifluralin (Treflan) and Fenoxaprop (Acclaim) have all been registered for use on *Achillea* spp. (yarrow). Chemical labels are subject to change — read the label before purchasing or using any chemical to be certain it is registered for your intended use. Not all chemicals are registered for use on all species. Contact your county extension agent for an update on herbicides currently labeled for yarrow production.

Weed barriers and mulches prevent weed growth and have the added benefit of restricting soil splash from rain and irrigation on foliage and flowers. The greatest benefits in weed control from these materials occur in the first growing season while the yarrow plants are becoming established.

While hoeing and hand-weeding are excellent methods for weed control, availability and cost of labor may be prohibitive in all but the smallest production situations.

INSECT CONTROL

Good cultural practices are the best insect control available. A healthy, actively growing yarrow plant is more resilient to insect attack. The ideal approach is a preventative program. Control insects early, when they are first detected; do not wait until a serious infestation occurs. Less chemical can be applied to spots as they develop than would be required to spray the entire crop. Aphids, leaf hoppers, spider mites and thrips are the most common insects encountered.

DISEASE CONTROL

Foliar fungal diseases, including powdery mildew, downy mildew and rust, are the most serious disease problem on yarrow. Powdery mildew is distinguished by white spots on both sides of the leaves. Downy mildew is distinguished by small yellow spots on the top of the leaves and white mold on the bottom. If mildew is a recurring problem, it might be wise to slightly increase the spacing between plants to improve air circulation around the foliage. Also, irrigating early in the day will lower the relative humidity in the micro-climate around the crop before nightfall, which will help reduce the incidence of foliar fungal diseases.

Rust is characterized by raised spots called pustules found on the undersides of leaves and stems. The pustules usually appear reddish in color, but may range from bright yellow to black. If the case is severe, the pustules will become enlarged and grow together, destroying leaves and occasionally the entire plant. Remove and destroy rust-infected leaves. At the end of the season, cut infected plants to the ground and remove all plant debris. Do not compost.

Another problem encountered by yarrow is stem rot, caused by *Rhizoctonia solani* and resulting in decay of the stem base. Fungicides and crop rotation help to alleviate the problem. Allowing the soil to dry between watering will help to retard the development of soil pathogens.

YIELDS

Higher plant densities (i.e. closer spacing) result in significantly higher yields per square foot of production space. Research with *Achillea* Coronation Gold showed that a density of one plant per square foot of production space yielded 46 stems per square foot, while a density of one plant per two square feet yielded 18 stems per square foot. The higher plant density beds had 45 percent more stems with a length of 20 inches or greater. In both yield and quality, closer spacing was better.

Yields will be low the first growing season; approximately five to seven stems per square foot can be expected. Stems will be short — between 10 and 20 inches. Production in the second and third years will range from 30 to 50 stems per square foot, with about 70 to 85 percent of the stems longer than 20 inches (*Achillea* Coronation Gold).

The high-density planting will require the beds to be dug and divided every three to five years. Stagger bed planting over a three-year period, digging and dividing one-third of the plants each year. This will have a smoothing effect on production and sales. The problem of low yields the first year after planting will be balanced by the high yields of the plants left undivided and in production.

Divide the plants in September. Cut the tops off to ground level, dig up the root clump and cut it into pieces containing three to five buds each. Plant the strongest pieces back into the production bed. It may be expected that each clump will yield four to five new plants, so the potential to increase the size of the production area exists.

Yields expressed here were produced under experienced care using drip irrigation with soluble fertilizer injected in the water. Soil type and weather conditions will affect the production level you may achieve.

HARVEST & POSTHARVEST REQUIREMENTS

Fresh Yarrow

Harvest when almost fully open. Fresh yarrow has a vase life of 10 to 14 days.

Dried/Preserved Yarrow

Yarrow is used extensively as a dried material. Of all the yarrows, the yellow cultivars seem to retain their color the best. Most whites turn a muddy beige, the colored pastels fade to an off-white and the reds, especially the scarlet, turn a blackish blue-red.

Harvest flowers when fully open. Flowers should be hung to dry in a dark space to avoid fading of the flower color.

Achillea is marketed fresh and dried, and serves as a filler flower in design work. The foliage by itself is unique in its airy, ferny appearance and is useful as an alternative to the standard foliage available.

REFERENCES

Armitage, A.M. 1992. *Field Studies of Achillea as a Cut Flower: Longevity, Spacing, and Cultivar Response.* Journal American Society Horticultural Science 117(1):65-67.

Armitage, A.M. 1992. *"Specialty Cut Flowers", Introduction to Floriculture,* 2nd ed. Roy A. Larson editor. Academic Press, Inc., New York. pp. 159-192.

Perry, Leonard P. 1989. *Perennial Cut Flowers.* Proc. 2nd Natl. Conf. on Specialty Cut Flowers, Athens GA p. 155-161.

Robelis, I.N. 1989. *Magic and Medicine of Plants.* Reader's Digest Assoc., Pleasantville, NY.

A-2 GLADIOLUS

The gladiolus has a global history. The gladiolus (glad) was captivating enough to prompt the creation of the American Gladiolus Society in Boston in 1910, and interest has continued to this date. Countless species grow across the world, from South Africa to the Mediterranean to West Asia.

Glads grow from two to six feet high, topped by a flower spike bearing a double row of trumpet-shaped florets. The flowers range from one to eight inches in diameter and may be ruffled and deeply cut, or simple and plain. The plant's sturdy, sword-shaped leaves inspired the plant's name, which comes from the Latin word for sword, *gladius*. The colors range from white and yellow to purple, smokey — even green shades. In general, glads are not fragrant.

Low cost and ease of culture are reasons glads are so popular today. They are relatively free from insects, have an extremely wide color range and a long blooming season. Also, they increase rapidly and are easy to carry over from year to year. Expert breeders and amateurs have devoted more than a century of hybridizing and selection to modify the plant to the colorful, floriferous varieties in demand today.

Today, glads are the most widely grown outdoor cut flower. Since 1935, greenhouse production has been virtually eliminated because of outdoor winter and spring production. Consumers have responded, finding uses for glads that range from fancy centerpieces to bridal bouquets.

VARIETIES TO GROW

The glads grown as cut flower crops belong to *G. x hortulanus*. Most varieties in this complex group of hybrids can be grown as commercial crops. Choose varieties by color for the product mix desired in your intended market.

CULTURAL REQUIREMENTS

Soil

Glads grow best in sandy loam, though almost any soil can be adapted. The key element in soil selection should be proper drainage; glads do not grow well in too-wet soil (puddles remain 24 hours after the soil is saturated). Too-wet, packed down soil hampers root growth, diverts moisture and locks up plant food. It also contributes to root rot.

If drainage is a problem, add organic matter such as leaves, spoiled hay, straw, manure or compost in late fall to ground that will be planted with glads the following spring. The addition of sand, in most cases, will decrease aeration and drainage. To be of benefit, large amounts of sand (several inches) must be added to the existing soil. Raising the beds three to six inches will also improve drainage.

The soil should have a pH of 6.0 to 6.5. Till the soil about two weeks before planting.

Planting

Glads grow from corms, produced by the storage of food at the base of the leaves. Unlike true bulbs, which are layered, corms are solid masses of tissue and are actually the base of the current year's stem, which grows from the point on the upper surface.

Each year, soon after foliage appears, a new corm develops on top of the old one, which shrivels and dies. Papery husks form around the corm, overlapping and facing the pointed tip. The husks are the bases of old leaves and protect the corm from mechanical injury, insect and disease infection, and water loss. Leave the papery tunic on the corm until just before planting, when it may be removed for treating with fungicides. One or more corms may form on an old corm.

Cormels (little corms) may develop around the base of the corm. Cormels are often used to propagate a glad cultivar. When planted, they will develop into small corms the following year.

Corms are graded into seven sizes, based on diameter in inches:

Jumbo — 2" and larger

No. 1 — 1½" and larger

No. 2 — 1¼" — 1½"

No. 3 — 1" — 1¼"

No. 4 — ¾" — 1"

No. 5 — ½" — ¾"

No. 6 — under ½"

Corms graded Jumbo, 1, 2 and 3 will produce marketable flowers the first year. Grades 4, 5 and 6 will develop to the larger sizes for flowering the following year.

Larger corms may flower earlier than the smaller corms, with a potential five-day difference between successive grades. The number of spikes produced per 100 corms and the number of florets per spike increase as the size of the corms increases. The planting of jumbo or number 1 grade corms will generally have a competitive advantage in quality of the spikes produced.

To prevent disease problems after planting, treat corms by dusting or dipping in fungicide. Soak the corms according to label instructions for concentration and timing.

Plant when the soil has warmed to a depth of six inches or when native deciduous trees begin to leaf out. Corms planted in cold soils are apt to rot before they begin to grow.

For cut flower use, plant glads in rows spaced 12 to 36 inches apart, depending on size of flowers desired, production system (bed or field row), equipment and space available. The spacing between corms, and their depth in the soil, will depend on corm size, soil type and quality desired. Generally, space the corms two to six inches apart (large corms spaced six inches) in trenches or individual holes. Large, show-quality flowers require more space, about two to four times the corm diameter. In light soils, plant large corms six to seven inches deep. In heavy soils, plant large corms about four inches deep. Plant small corms shallower. Deeper-planted corms flower later by a few days, but may support the spike with little or no additional support required. Place corms by hand, pointed side up, then cover mechanically.

Glads exposed to wind may require support to ensure tall, straight flower spikes. When the plants are eight inches tall, mound the soil around the base. Later, tie glads to wires extended the length of the row, or stake each plant individually. In either method, provide for some movement by the flower spike to prevent damage and breakage. Consider the labor required when you design the support system to be used.

After the first planting, plant at one- to two-week intervals to lengthen the bloom season. Days to bloom can vary from 60 to 120 days, depending on the variety and size of corm, with larger corms blooming earlier than smaller corms. Time the last planting to bloom before killing frost. In Kansas, the last planting is generally in mid to late July. Growers in more northern or southern locations would make their last planting earlier or later respectively. With planning, the blooming season can extend for several months.

Watering

Glads need plenty of water. Lack of water inhibits spike growth, flower development and corm growth. Watering at planting will help develop a good root system, which is especially important on late plantings in warmer weather when top growth is prone to get ahead of root growth. Water becomes essential when flower spikes begin to form and when florets begin to open. Provide at least one inch of water each week to ensure good growth, making sure the water soaks six to eight inches into the soil. Drip irrigation is recommended because it places the water on the ground where it is needed and not on the flowers or foliage.

Fertilization

Fertilizer can help produce large flowers on glads. Apply at the rate of one and a half to two pounds of actual nitrogen from a 1-1-1 ratio fertilizer per 1,000 square feet per crop. For example,

two pounds of actual nitrogen would be 10.0 lbs/1000 sq. ft. of
super phosphate (0-20-0), 5.0 lbs./1000 sq. ft. of potassium nitrate
(20-0-44), and 3.0 lbs./1000 sq. ft. of ammonium nitrate (33-0-0).
If following a single application plan, apply a slow-release nitrogen type at planting time. If a split application is desired, apply
one-third at planting, one-third at midseason and the balance
when flower spikes emerge. Keep fertilizers away from corms and
stems to prevent damage to the plants.

Weed Control

Growers must control weeds in glad production, as competition
with weeds reduces the quantity and quality of floral production.
A bed full of weeds also increases the time required to harvest,
raising labor costs. Several options are available to combat weed
growth: herbicides, barriers or mulches, hoeing and hand-weeding.

Due to limited production of many species of specialty cut flowers, only a few herbicides have been labeled for use. Treflan and
Dacthal have been effective pre-emergence herbicides for use with
glads. If weeds are already established, cultivate, hoe or pull them
by hand. Other herbicides that have been labeled for use with
glads are: XL (benefin and oryzalin), Ornamec and Fusilade (fluazifop-P-butyl), Betasan (bensulide), Pre-San (benzensulfonamide) and Pennant (metolachlor). Gallery has also been labeled
for use on glads but should only be used on corms larger than one
inch in diameter and only after the shoot has emerged above
ground. As always, it is critical to read the label on all chemicals
and apply only as directed. Chemical labels are subject to change
and should always be checked before purchase or use to be certain
the chemical is currently labeled for the intended use. It is illegal
to use a chemical in a manner inconsistent with its label.

Weed barriers and mulches prevent weed growth and have the
added benefit of restricting soil splash from rain and irrigation on
foliage and flowers. The greatest benefits from these materials
occur early in the growing season while the glads are becoming
established. Materials such as green hay and sawdust are

commonly used in the production of glads. Mulching creates a cooler growing environment that slows growth, lengthens the stem and flowerhead and adds distance between the buds. Mulch also provides a more consistent soil moisture level by reducing evaporation from the soil surface.

While hoeing and hand-weeding are excellent methods for weed control, availability and cost of labor may be prohibitive in all but the smallest production situations.

Insect Control

Good cultural practices are the best insect control available. A healthy, actively growing glad is more resilient to insect attack.

The ideal approach is a preventative program. Control insects early, when they are first detected; do not wait until a serious infestation occurs. Less chemical can be applied to spots as they develop than would be required to spray the entire crop. Several insects afflict glads: thrips, red spider mites, aphids and wireworms.

Thrips, tan to black in color and $\frac{1}{25}$ inch long, are the major insect pest of glads. They feed on sap from leaves and flowers abraded by their rasping mouth parts, leaving behind small, silvery flecks. Thrips also injure untreated glad corms while in storage. Treat corms with an insecticide before planting and after harvest to prevent thrip infestation. Throughout the season, monitor the glads for thrip infestation and control with insecticides as required.

Red spider mites are reddish-yellow or black and less than $\frac{1}{16}$ inch long. They attack foliage with their sucking mouth parts. Infestation is characterized by grayed foliage and webbing on the plants. Control will normally require three applications of an insecticide spaced about a week apart. Consult the label for specific recommendations.

Aphids are visible to the naked eye. They have sucking mouth parts and are most active on the young, growing parts of plants. Infestation is distinguished by crinkled and distorted foliage and leaf buds. Plants may have a sooty appearance. Aphids are also carriers of many viral diseases.

Wireworms injure corms in the field and sometimes eat the roots from other plants in the field. The pest is the larval stage of the click-beetle or snapping beetle. Mature larvae are slender, hard-shelled, dark brown or yellow worms, about an inch long. They are most troublesome in too-wet soil. Control by sterilizing the soil where practical.

Disease Control

White break produces white streaks or blotches on flowers. This is thought to be caused by a virus. Discard corms that produce such flowers.

Mosaic or sprekling virus, carried by aphids, produces light green streaks on young leaves and flecks or stripes on flowers. In some cases the plant will stunt or shorten. The problem is worse with late-season plantings and large corms. Plant large corms early and medium corms later in the season to help alleviate the problem. Rogue affected plants and remove from the field.

Bacterial leaf blight *(Bacterium gummisudans)* produces water-soaked, brown spots that expand vertically along the leaf, forming square or rectangular lesions. Under moist conditions a sticky film develops over the infected leaf. Control by spraying young stock at 10-day intervals. The blight does not infect the corm.

Scab *(Bacterium marginatum)* is characterized by circular depressions with raised margins on the corms. Rust-colored, dull brown or purple circular or elliptical spots will appear on the foliage near the base.

Fusarium yellows *(Fusarium orthoceras var. gladioli)* makes the tips of the leaves yellow and die back until the entire plant yellows. Infected corms show brown rot at the basal scar, spreading upward into the core and out to the nodes on the corms. The fungus lives for several years in the soil and infects corms planted there. Late infection of corms may not show at digging time, but corms may rot in storage or before flowering the next year. Control by following proper corm storage procedures. Several resistant varieties are 'Albania,' 'Alice Tiplady,' 'Apricot Glow,' 'Minuet,' 'W.H. Phipps,' 'Picardy,' 'Souvenir' and 'Spirit of St. Louis.'

Botrytis blight *(Botrytis gladioli)* is characterized by light brown spots surrounded by a darker ring. Foliage turns brown suddenly, making the infected field appear burned. Gray-brown mold often appears on affected tissue. Botrytis attacks the flower spike on the stem and at the base of the floret bract. Infected spikes rot after packing and are soft on arrival at their destination. The fungus also invades the corm, producing spongy rot of the entire corm or brown lesions on the sides. Control by proper storage and curing of corms (described under "corm storage") and by dusting foliage in the field. Rogue affected plants. Botrytis attacks all varieties of glads.

Curvularia is characterized by oval, tan to dark brown spots, each of which appears on both sides of the leaf. The spots grow from pinhead size to an inch in length in a few days, and black, powder-like spores develop in the dead areas. The edge of the spot is sunken below the green or yellow tissue around it. Not all varieties are susceptible. Control by spraying the foliage with fungicide.

Stemphylium leaf spot produces small yellow spots that show on both sides of the leaves, mostly near the leaf tips. They mature to round spots up to ⅛ inch in diameter with red or brown centers. Leaves of affected plants become yellow prematurely, and resulting corms are small. Many varieties of glads are susceptible.

Glads are susceptible to numerous corm rots, such as dry rot, neck rot, fusarium rot, penicillium rot and hard rot. Dry rot *(Sclerotinia gladioli)* affects plants at the soil surface and results in premature yellowing. Minute black sclerotia are usually present on the diseased leaf base. Diseased corms have circular, reddish-brown spots on the sides and lower half of the corm. Infected corms mummify in storage.

Rhizoctonia neck rot *(Rhizoctonia solani)* causes the plants from cormels to rot off at the base of the leaves. Corms will have horizontal stripes. No satisfactory control is known.

Fusarium rot *(Fusarium oxysporum var. gladioli)* occurs during the storage period. Affected corms have prominent, irregular concentric markings on the diseased area.

Penicillium rot *(Penicillium gladioli)* is also primarily a storage rot of corms, which at low temperatures develops as a green mold over the lesions.

Hard rot *(Septoria gladioli)* produces symptoms like those of dry rot, and probably cannot be distinguished from it unless a diagnostic isolation is made.

Control for these corm rots through proper storage techniques. If the problem continues, try planting on new, sterilized soil or rotating as much as possible.

Most of the diseases that affect glads can be controlled by selecting good planting sites and using clean corms. Follow the procedures outlined in the corm storage section to ensure a disease-free crop.

Corm Storage

Lift and store glad corms each fall to prevent disease problems while corms are in the ground. Corms are ready for digging six to eight weeks after blooming or when foliage begins to yellow and die back. If the tops are still healthy, delay digging to add to corm development, but make sure corms are dug before the first hard freeze. Corms that are dug too early will succumb to storage breakdown faster than those that have matured.

Dig corms when the soil is dry to make digging and cleaning easier. Break up the soil with a spade or digging fork and pull the plants by hand. Shake off loose soil. If the cormels are needed for future propagation, dig corms carefully and group by varieties immediately. Break off the plant as close to the corm as possible. Doing this by hand, rather than using shears or scissors, will leave a small hole in the husk on the top of the corm and allow moisture to escape faster in the drying process.

Put corms in a light, warm, airy place for two to three weeks to cure. It is important to dry corms as rapidly as possible to help prevent storage problems.

During drying time, a cork layer forms between the new corm and the old corm and roots. After the corms are cured, snap off the old corm by hand and discard it. This will leave a clean scar on the new corm. Undue delay in cleaning results in greater difficulty in removal. Remove the loose husks, leaving the wrapper husks intact. Also remove the small cormels and place in a labeled paper bag for winter storage.

Dust corms with an insecticide labeled for thrip control. Discard all diseased corms and place the rest in uncovered trays with screen or slat bottoms, arranged to allow air to circulate between them. Place no more than four layers of corms in each tray to prevent heating. Paper bags, mesh onion bags and nylon stockings are also used for winter storage. Keep the varieties labeled and separated because light-colored varieties multiply faster than dark colors.

Store corms in a dark, dry, well-ventilated place, with temperatures between 35°F and 45°F. Before planting the next season, go through the corms again and discard any diseased corms.

Proper storage, curing, drying, cleaning and dusting practices will prevent diseased corms.

HARVEST AND POSTHARVEST

Gladiolus spikes exhibit negative geotropism. This means that if the floral spikes are laid flat in storage or transport, the tips will curve upward. While Asian-style design work may call for spikes with natural curves, the market generally prefers straight spikes. Keep spikes upright in the field through use of stakes or supports to prevent the spikes from bending. Use tall containers that hold the stems upright during harvest, handling, packing, storage and transit.

Harvest Practices

Handling and harvest practices depend greatly on the intended market of the glads. Regional, national and international whole-sale markets require harvest when the basal (lowest) florets on the spike are just showing color. Local wholesale markets want spikes with more florets showing color and the basal florets partly opened. Local retail markets need the basal florets fully open to display their beauty to the consumer.

• Cut stems as long as possible.
• Keep at least four leaves on the plant to stimulate corm development.
• Keep the spikes vertical.

Postharvest Practices

The maturity of the spike at harvest will determine its storage time and vaselife. Less mature spikes store longer than more mature spikes. Glads harvested with closed florets can be stored upright and dry-wrapped in moisture-proof materials for one week at 36°F-40°F. This can be beneficial to growers who want to pack glads immediately after harvest and ship them up to a week later. Spikes with closed florets can also be stored upright in preservative for one to two weeks. Growers selling to local markets may prefer this storage method. More mature spikes (more open florets) will store a shorter time and have a shorter vaselife.

Glads are sensitive to fluoride in their holding water. Fluoridated city water may contain enough fluoride to damage glads. Growers using city water, well or pond water should test their water for fluoride. The city water treatment plant will have information on the fluoride content of city water. If the fluoride content is high (0.25 ppm or above), growers should either find an alternative water source or consider installing a reverse osmosis (RO) water system.

Store at 36°F-40°F (2°C-5°C) and 85 percent to 90 percent relative humidity.

PACKAGING AND PACKING

As discussed earlier, glads must be kept upright, even during packaging and packing. Buyers expect it. Growers selling directly to local wholesalers and retail florists will often transport and deliver glads in buckets of floral preservative. Glads intended for regional, national and international markets should be packed dry in special gladiolus hampers that keep the spikes upright.

Glads are normally placed into bunches of ten stems for wholesale and retail florist markets. Five-stem bunches are common in farmers markets. Many growers selling at farmers markets also offer individual stems of glads, allowing customers to create their own bouquets.

REFERENCE LIST

Nowak, Joanna and Ryszard M. Rudnicki. 1990. *Postharvest Handling and Storage of Cut Flowers, Florist Greens and Potted Plants.* Research Institute of Pomology and Floriculture, Skierniewice, Poland. Timber Press, Portland, Oregon.

Sacalis, John N. 1989. *Fresh (Cut) Flowers for Designs, Care and Handling, Retail and Consumer Care Information.* Ohio Florists' Association Publication. p. 60-63.

A-3 LIATRIS (GAYFEATHER)

Liatris is a flower with many aliases: blazing star, Kansas gayfeather, devil's colic, rattlesnake master, starwort, button snakeroot. Whatever its name, liatris has gained popularity as a cut flower crop for both greenhouse and outdoor production.

Liatris are erect, normally unbranched plants that grow from one to five feet tall. Liatris grow from round or oval, woody corms, each of which develops several flowering stems. Numerous, narrow leaves grow alternately on the stem, becoming shorter and thinner near the flower spike. The flower heads grow in several rows along the stem to form a wand-like spike up to 15 inches in height. The flowers on the spikes open from the top downward (basipetally). One variety, *L. aspera,* flowers from the bottom up. The purple varieties are in the greatest demand, though there is also interest in the rose-red and white varieties.

The corms sprout in spring, and blooms appear in late summer. Liatris will grow and produce flowers in poorer soil than most plants, and will endure heat, cold and drought. They grow in full sun.

Liatris belongs to the Compositae family. About 40 species of the hardy perennial grow across North America from southern Canada to northern Mexico, and east of the Rocky Mountains through Florida. *Liatris spicata, L. aspera* Michx. and *L. pycnostachya* Michx. are the major commercial species, often used as colorful accents in cut flower arrangements.

VARIETIES TO GROW

L. aspera
'Rough blazing star' — 6'; purple; blooms naturally in August.

L. gramnifolia
'Loose-flowered' or 'Button snakeroot' — 4'; purple; blooms
    naturally from August to October.

L. punctata
'Dotted blazing star' — 1'; purple; blooms naturally from August
    to October.

L. pycnostachya

'Eureka' — 3-6'; deep rose-purple; blooms naturally from August
   to September.

'Tall blazing star' — 3-5'; rose-purple; blooms naturally from
   August to September.

L. pycostachya alba

3-5'; white; blooms naturally from August to September.

L. scariosa

'September glory' — 4'; deep purple; blooms naturally from
   August to September.

'White spire' — 3'; white; blooms naturally from August to
   September.

L. spicata

'Gayfeather' — 6'; rose-purple; blooms naturally from August to
   September.

'Atlantic' — 2½'; rose-purple; blooms naturally from August to
   September.

'Kobold' — ¼' - ½'; rose-lavender; blooms naturally from July to
   August.

'Floristan violet' — 3'; purple; blooms naturally from July to
   September.

'Floristan white' — 3-4'; white; blooms naturally from July to
   September.

CULTURAL REQUIREMENTS

Soil

Liatris grow successfully in soils of a wide range of textures and
fertility levels. Native liatris plants will normally be found growing
on a slope and often on rocky ground. They prefer a well-drained
soil with a pH in the range of 6.5-7.0. The addition of several
inches of organic matter incorporated into the planting bed will
help provide the desired soil structure for commercial production.

Planting

Plant corms on six to eight inch centers in beds three to four feet wide and up to 120 feet long. The beds should be separated by walkways of a width sufficient for mowers or harvest equipment. Plant a maximum of four corms per square foot to avoid an erratic root system and to control diseases by allowing for adequate air circulation between stems. Plant corms one inch deep.

Corms from three-and-a-half to five inches in circumference produce the greatest number of flowering stems, when compared to smaller corms. Prepare corms for planting by soaking in a solution of four percent Pro-Gibb (g/l) and Ronilan (2g/l) for 40 to 60 minutes.

The number of flowering stems per corm decreases as the day length increases. Corm planting to bloom is about 70 to 90 days. In unusually warm conditions, such as corms planted later in the summer, planting to bloom may be as short as 50 days. The duration of the harvest period (10 to 15 days) appears to be the same regardless of the planting date. Flower harvest of *L. spicata* from a single planting may last three to four weeks.

Plant the first corms in early April and the last ones by late July to early August depending on local weather conditions. To ensure continuous harvest throughout the growing season, plant corms every 10 to 14 days in April and May, with 21 days between plantings in June and 28 days in July. This will extend the blooming season from late June through September. More frequent planting results in poor separation of blooming dates. Corms planted later in the summer flower more quickly on shorter stems.

Use a two-year planting rotation. The first year, sequentially plant the corms and do not dig them in the fall. The second year, sequentially plant additional corms, but do not plant during May. (The first-year planting that remains in the field will flower naturally in July.) During the fall, dig the corms that were planted in the first year and divide them. In the spring of the third year, sequentially plant the first-year corms, thus beginning the cycle over again. If the plants have not become over-crowded by the end of the second season you may decide not to dig them and then go ahead in the following spring and plant a third crop of staggered plantings, thus going into a three-year planting rotation.

Sometimes support is needed as the stems elongate, but use support only when necessary in windy areas. *L. pycnostachya* is a taller variety and needs careful supporting.

Watering

Water corms as needed for the first three weeks after planting to provide a moderately moist soil to help sprout the corms. Then you need to allow the soil to dry between waterings but not so much so as to stress the plant. Winds will dry out liatris, especially during rapid flower stem elongation. Leaves and elongating stems may wilt, causing leaf scorch, brown leaf tips, reduced flower size and a severe reduction in marketability of the crop.

Drip irrigation to supplement natural rainfall is recommended.

Fertilization

Most growers treat liatris as a medium nitrogen-requiring plant. Three weeks after planting corms, fertilize with a 20-20-20 fertilizer at 400 ppm nitrogen injected into the drip system every 10 days for four feedings or band a 1-1-1 ratio dry fertilizer at a rate of 1lb. actual nitrogen per 1,000 sq.ft. of production area. Do not provide additional fertilizer the remainder of the season.

Propagation

Liatris may be grown from cuttings, seeds or corms. Cuttings produce short flowers and are not widely used commercially. Growing liatris from seed requires specialized handling and is a long-term project.

Corm division is the most frequent propagation method used, as it attains consistent height, color, form and quality. Also, shoot development will be uniform and flower stems will be longer. Division is usually in the fall after stem die-back, though early spring division prior to shoot growth is possible.

Dig and divide the corms into divisions containing a single growing point. Treat them with a fungicide to prevent rotting and fungal disease problems during storage. Dry and store in slightly moist sphagnum peat moss at 28°F-30°F until planting next season. They should not be allowed to thaw and then refreeze. Do not allow them to dry out while in storage. Liatris corms require ten weeks of cold storage before replanting to promote sprouting and shoot elongation. After freezing, the corms may be held for up to two weeks at 40°F-45°F while awaiting planting.

Weed Control

Growers must control weeds in the field production of liatris, as competition with weeds reduces the quantity and quality of floral production. A bed full of weeds also increases the time required to harvest, raising labor costs. Several options are available to combat weed growth: herbicides, barriers or mulches, hoeing and hand-weeding.

Due to limited production of many species of specialty cut flowers, only a few herbicides are labeled for use. Fusilade (fluazifop-P-butyl), Lesco (fluazifop-p-butyl), Ornamec (fluazifop-p-butyl) and Acclaim (fenoxaprop-ethyl) have been labeled for use on *L. spicata*, gayfeather. Chemical labels change — read the label before purchasing or using any chemical to be sure it is currently registered for your intended use.

Weed barriers and mulches prevent weed growth and have the added benefit of restricting soil splash from rain and irrigation on foliage and flowers. The greatest benefits in weed control from these materials occur in the first growing season while the liatris plants are becoming established.

While hoeing and hand-weeding are excellent methods for weed control, availability and cost of labor may be prohibitive in all but the smallest production situations.

Insect Control

Good cultural practices are the best insect control available. A healthy, actively growing liatris plant is more resilient to insect attack. The ideal approach is a preventative program. Control insects early, when they are first detected; do not wait until a serious infestation occurs. Less chemical can be applied to spots as they develop than would be required to spray the entire crop.

Insect pests are of minor concern in Liatris plantings. Aphids, thrips and whiteflies may be occasional pests.

Disease Control

Diseases often reduce the quantity and quality of liatris flowers, and, in some cases, cause significant plant mortality. Some diseases, such as powdery mildew and rust, are perennial problems, while other diseases may be sporadic. The table lists some of the more common liatris diseases with their symptoms and control. Be careful using the table! Certain plant diseases are difficult to identify by field symptoms. Be sure to consult a plant pathologist for accurate disease diagnosis before applying any fungicides.

Liatris diseases can, for the most part, be controlled by a combination of sound cultural management and chemical control. Avoid overhead watering and keep plants adequately spaced for good air circulation. Overcrowding may result in plant losses from rust and powdery mildew and other foliar diseases. Water the plants early in the day to allow for good foliage drying before nightfall. Keep fields as weed-free as possible to avoid plant competition and to control insect problems. Rotate planting beds in the field each year to avoid build-up of soilborne fungal pathogens and nematodes.

Routine fungicide applications may be necessary to control powdery mildew on susceptible varieties of liatris. Control is much more effective if fungicides are applied before symptoms of mildew are apparent. Other fungal diseases may be controlled by curative fungicide applications beginning as soon as symptoms develop. Don't wait until plants are severely blighted to start applying fungicides. Be sure to diagnose the disease correctly and follow all instructions on the fungicide label.

Disease	Symptoms	Control
Leafspots		
Erysiphe cichoracearum	White, powdery growth on the surface of the leaves.	Provide good air circulation. Remove and destroy diseased plants.
Coleosporium lacinariae	Orange-yellow spots on the upper surface of the leaf.	
Puccinia poarum	Brick-red pustules or blisters form on the lower leaf surface.	
Other Leafspots		
Phyllosticta liatridis *Septoria liatridis*	Leaves may develop roughly circular spots.	Consult a diagnostic lab for proper identification.
Wilts		
Root-knot nematode (*Meloidogyne sp.*)	Stunted growth, yellowing, wilting of foliage. Roots may develop excessive galling.	Test for presence of root-knot nematode. Rotate planting location or fumigate soil.
Sclerotinia sclerotiorum Stem rot.	Sections of plant may yellow and die.	Provide good air circulation. Remove and destroy diseased plants.
Verticillium albo-atrum Wilt.	Leaves turn yellow and die. Infected plants are stunted or killed. A vascular discoloration may be present in the lower stem.	Remove infected plants. The fungus is soilborne, so if disease severity increases from year to year, rotate planting location.

Yields

Expect from 1.3 to 1.5 flower stems per corm the first season, three to four stems the second and third years, and then a decline in the number and quality of stems resulting from overcrowding. To avoid this decline, divide and transplant after the third season. Expect 10 percent of harvested stems to be unsaleable due to mechanical or cultural problems.

HARVEST AND POSTHARVEST

Harvest

Liatris provides a colorful spike form for floral design work. Its airiness provides a texture different from most flower spikes. Also, where most spike flowers open from the bottom up, liatris opens from the top down. Liatris can be stored up to two weeks at 36°F-40°F.

Fresh Market

Harvest practices:

Harvest for sale as a fresh cut flower when three to four florets have begun to open if stems will be placed into a floral preservative. If placing into plain water, harvest when the top half of florets have opened.

Cut stems so as to leave two to three inches below the cut to ensure future production. Or, cut at soil line but leave a third of the flowering stems on the corm cluster to facilitate new corm development. The idea is to leave sufficient leaf surface area for photosynthesis to sustain the vigor of the plant.

Standard bunch size for wholesale floral markets is 10 stems per bunch. Grade no.1 has all stems longer than 30 inches.

Refrigerated storage at 40°F (5°C) will decrease vase life.

The use of a preservative will dramatically increase vase life.

Dried and Preserved Market

Harvest practices:

Harvest when flower spike is fully open but before any florets become over-mature.

Dry hanging upside down. Or, dry upright to allow the florets to stand out more. Either way is a matter of personal preference.

REFERENCES

Bailey, L.H. 1925. *The Standard Cyclopedia of Horticulture.* The MacMillan Company.

Ball, Vic. 1991. *Ball Red Book.* 15th edition, Geo. J. Ball Publishing.

Healy, William E. *Producing Cut Flowers-Liatris.* Cooperative Extension Service, University of Maryland. Fact Sheet 467.

Nowak, Joanna and Ryszard M. Rudnicki. 1990. *Postharvest Handling and Storage of Cut Flowers,* Florist Greens, and Potted Plants. Timber Press.

Stimart, Dennis P.. 1991. *Strategies of Growing Fresh Cut Flowers of Liatris and Paeonia.* Proceedings of the Fourth National Conference on Specialty Cut Flowers, Association of Specialty Cut Flower Growers, Inc.

A-4 PEONY

"This peony was a large plant and surely cheered its owner for years."
.... Alice Harding

"June...the peony is the month's crown, the focus, the highlight of all that is beautiful in the garden picture."
.... James Kelway

The peony began its role as a favored flower centuries ago, and the curtain has not yet fallen on its performance. In mythology, the peony first enchanted Leto, mother of Apollo, who gave the plant to the physician Paeon to cure Pluto's wound from the Trojan War. The Chinese adopted the peony as the principle flower in the Chinese Imperial Palace Gardens, calling it 'Sho Yo', meaning "most beautiful." In the 8th century, its charm captivated the Japanese, who developed more than 300 cultivars. Much later, in the early 19th century, European gardens began to feature the peony. Today, gardeners throughout Europe, Asia and North America regard the peony as one of the easiest, most rewarding plants to grow. With its long-lasting, colorful blooms, the peony also enjoys popularity as a cut flower used in wedding bouquets and large floral arrangements.

Peonies grow from an underground crown and have either pointed or large and bulky roots. After the blooming season, stem buds, or "eyes," form at the base of the stems. These buds are the source of new stems in the spring. Flowers are terminal with one to three lateral buds. In Kansas, peonies bloom in May and June.

There are two groups of peonies: tree peonies and herbaceous peonies. Tree peonies grow to eye-level on woody stems with few branches. The stems of these peonies stay alive all winter, and they bloom early. Tree peonies are not used for cut flowers, though they are somewhat popular in gardens.

Herbaceous peonies are more commonly grown, and do well in a wide range of soil types and climates. Their bushy green, pink or red stems grow two to four feet tall and turn green by the time they are cut down in the fall. Each cultivar has leaves of a particular shade of green and a shape ranging from broad to grass-like. Flower colors include white, yellow, cream, pink, rose and deep red varieties. The flowers are grouped into five types according to the shape of the petals: single, Japanese, anemone, semi-double and double.

Single peonies have five or more broad petals in one or two rows surrounding a center of golden, pollen-bearing stamens. Japanese peonies have five or more petals and a center of feathery structures called staminodes. Anemone peonies have five or more petals in several rows with broad central petals. Semi-double peonies have five or more outer petals and a center of broad petals with pollen-bearing stamens intermixed. Bomb peonies have a row of outer guard petals surrounding a pompon tuft of dense petals. Double peonies have five or more outer petals with the central stamens and carpels transformed into petals that make up the main body of the large, full flower. All types are grown as cut flowers, though the double types are the most popular.

CULTIVARS TO GROW

For successful cut flowers, choose peonies with these characteristics:
• plant vigor and health
• ample stem production
• ability to imbibe water
• ability to hold up in storage
• ability to withstand shipping

Several sources across the country have suggested a list of peonies suitable for cut flower purposes. These are provided in the table below. All are double flowers unless otherwise indicated. The varieties in bold type are ones favored by the author.

Red

Early:

Convoy, Raspberry Ice, Red Rose, **Kansas, Red Charm, Richard Carvel,** Firebelle, Red Grace, Rosedale, Flame (single)

Midseason:

Big Ben, Howdy, **Paul M. Wild,** David Harem, **Karl Rosenfield, Red Comet, Felix Crousse,** Lora Dexheimer, Renato, **Felix Supreme,** Midnight Sun (Japanese), **Shawnee Chief,** Gerry, Mt. St. Helens

Late:

Old Faithful, **Philippe Rivoire**

Pink

Early:

Cytherea (semi-double), Fairy's Petticoat, **Monsieur Jules Elie,** Coral Charm (semi-double), June Rose, Princess Margaret, **Edulis Superba,** Mister Ed

Midseason:

Angel Cheeks, **Duchesse d'Orleans,** Nancy Nicholls, Sea Shell (single), Gay Paree, President Taft, Sweet 16, Largo (Japanese), Queen of Sheba, Top Brass, Mrs. F.D.R., **Raspberry Sundae,** Walter Faxon, Mrs. Livingston Farrand, Riene Hortense

Late:

Hansina Brand, Minuet, **Sarah Bernhardt,** Hermoine, Nick Shaylor, Vivid Rose, James Pillow

White

Early:

Festiva Maxima, Mme. de Verneville, Charlie's White, Duchesse de Nemours, Miss America (semi-double), 69A

Midseason:

Ann Cousins, Festiva Supreme, **Snow Mountain,** Lois Kelsey, Baroness Schroeder, Florence Nicholls, Marshmallow Puff, Bridal Icing, **Gardenia, Mother's Choice,** Bridal Shower, Gay Paree

Late:

Elsa Sass, Lullaby, Mrs. Frank Beach, Louise Marx (Japanese), **Mary E. Nicholls**

CULTURAL REQUIREMENTS

Soil

Peonies prefer a fertile clay loam with a well-drained subsoil. Optimum pH is 6.5. Good drainage is vital to avoid root rot and fungal diseases.

Plow the soil to a depth of one to three feet and allow it to settle before planting. A deeper-plowed soil will facilitate root growth, with a corresponding increase in the size of top and amount of bloom. Peonies are a perennial plant with a productive life of 25 years or more. It is therefore important to add as much organic matter to the soil as possible before planting. This preparation should be done as far in advance of planting as possible to allow the soil to settle and prevent the peonies from sinking after planting.

Planting

Plant in a location with full sunlight, away from the competitive effects of tree roots. A sheltered location is preferable, where the peonies will be protected from heavy winds. Choose a permanent location, as peonies should not be harvested for three years after transplanting.

Plant healthy roots of the best commercial varieties, and take care not to injure the root in any way. If buds accidentally break off, new ones will usually form, but they will be weaker. Examine roots for fungal growth and cut off rotted parts. Keep roots moist until they are planted in the ground; if roots are dry, soak them for several hours before planting. If planting is delayed, repack roots in the container, wetting the packing material thoroughly. They can keep for a week or two without damage. If roots must be kept longer, heal them in. Dig a trench long enough, wide enough and deep enough to hold the roots without crowding them and plant them about six inches apart. They will keep as long as a year without serious damage.

Peonies go dormant in late August, so plant between September 1 and the time the ground freezes. Planting in early autumn gives the soil ample time before frost to settle around the newly planted roots, making them less likely to heave during the winter. Stock dug the previous fall and kept in cold storage over winter may be planted in the spring. Such peonies will be less vigorous the first year because the root system will have had a shorter time to develop.

Plant spacing depends on cultivation method. For cross cultivation, plant spacing should be four feet every way. Peonies are more commonly planted in rows with a 24-inch to 36-inch spacing between plants and four feet between rows.

Dig each hole large enough to accommodate the root without crowding it. In heavy clay soil, plant so the buds are one to two inches below the soil surface. If the soil is light and friable, two to three inches is the proper depth. If the roots are planted too deep, a gnarly and much-branched stem develops between the roots and the shoots. These plants are predisposed to decay or develop galled overgrowth. Too-shallow planting increases the possibility of the root being displaced by frost during winter or early spring. Also, if the root is too near the surface, it may become exposed and rot rapidly or be injured by cultivation. Small divisions need extra care and should not be planted as deeply as standard divisions or one-year roots. Plant them no deeper than two inches.

Do not plant the root upside down. Fill in around the roots with soil until no voids are left below the plant or among the rows. Air pockets in the soil will dry the roots out, causing them to die. Firm the soil well and fill in until the soil just covers the roots and buds. Pour in about a gallon of water and let it settle, then fill in with loose soil, mounding it up a few inches for winter protection and to keep the roots from heaving. Normally, the mound will sink to proper level. If it does not, level it in the spring. As the peony grows older, the crown naturally pushes upward and has to be covered with soil.

Culture

After the ground is frozen, cover the plants with a mulch of leaves, wheat straw or other material to prevent the peonies from being heaved out of the ground through alternate freezing and thawing. This will not be necessary after the first winter, except in the case of tiny divisions or young seedlings, which should be mulched for several years. Do not use manure or the dead leaves and stems of the peony itself as a mulch.

Remove mulch on all peonies as soon as the shoots break through the ground in the spring. Young peony plants are particularly slow in shoot appearance and may be a week or two later than established plants. When the soil is sufficiently dry, shallow cultivate to break up the soil crust, being careful not to injure roots near the soil surface.

Disbudding, the removal of lateral flower buds growing in the leaf axles, should be done when the axillary buds are barely large enough to handle. Disbudding enhances the growth of the terminal flower bud because all the plant's resources are used to develop a single flower per stem. Removal of the terminal bud to promote lateral bud development or spray types is done with certain cultivars for particular markets. If quantity is desired, and smaller flowers with little stem length are acceptable, then lateral buds may be allowed to develop.

Peonies grown for cut flower use may not require staking in normal weather conditions, as the flowers are cut when in bud.

Watering

While the peony will withstand dryness of the soil to the point of drought without succumbing, a reasonable amount of moisture is essential for the best development. Peonies should have a liberal supply of water, especially while in bloom.

Fertilization

Before initiating a fertilizer program, always test the soil for nutrient content. The increased water requirement of cut flowers creates an increased requirement for fertilization. The application of fertilizer should coincide with crop needs.

One to two pounds of actual nitrogen per 1,000 square feet of production area per year of a 1-1-1 ratio fertilizer is adequate for plant growth and flower production. There are two approaches to timing of the fertilizer application. Both approaches apply one-half the annual amount of fertilizer at shoot emergence in the spring. One approach applies the second half after the plants go dormant in the fall. The second approach applies one-fourth of the annual amount just after flower harvest and the balance at dormancy in the fall.

Keep all fertilizers away from the crowns. Spread fertilizer over the area where the roots grow, six to 18 inches from the crown and thoroughly work it into the soil around the plants. Over-application of nitrogen should be avoided.

Weed Control

Growers must control weeds in the field production of peonies. Several options are available to combat weed growth: herbicides, barriers or mulches, and hoeing and hand-weeding.

Due to limited production of many species of specialty cut flowers, only a few herbicides are labeled for use. Acclaim (fenoxaprop-ethyl) and Dachthal (dimethyl tetrachloroterephthalate) have been registered for use on peonies. Chemical registrations/labels change — contact your local county extension agent for an update on herbicides currently labeled for peony production.

Weed barriers or mulches prevent weed growth and have the added benefit of restricting soil splash from rain and irrigation on foliage and flowers. The greatest benefits in weed control from these materials occur in the first growing season while the peony plants are becoming established. If a mulch is used over winter, be sure to remove it as soon as peony shoots start appearing to avoid diseases.

While hoeing and hand-weeding are excellent methods for weed control, availability and cost of labor may be prohibitive in all but the smallest production situations. Peonies develop a strong system of feeder roots near the surface of the soil, so the plant must be cultivated with great care to avoid injury to the shallow roots. Use the hoe with caution in keeping down the weeds. Do not cultivate deeper than two inches near the crown.

Insect Control

Good cultural practices are the best insect control available. A healthy, actively growing plant is more resilient to insect attack. The ideal approach is a preventative program. Control insects early, when they are first detected; do not wait until a serious infestation occurs. Less chemical can be applied to spots as they develop than would be required to spray the entire crop. While peonies are not subject to damage from major insect pests, several general feeders may require an occasional rescue spray treatment.

Thrips may be the most common insect pest of peonies. They may go undetected because of their small size ($\frac{1}{25}$ inch long). Also, the feeding damage of a few thrips may go unnoticed because of the large size and plentiful amount of tissue characterizing peony flowers. The cumulative damage of high thrip populations will be more noticeable; flowers and foliage will be covered with silvery flecks caused by the thrips' rasping-sucking mouthparts.

Rose chafers may be occasional pests of peonies. These beetles are readily visible ($\frac{1}{2}$ inch in length) and identifiable. They have tan-colored bodies and reddish-brown heads and thoraxes. Rose chafers emerge from the soil in June and early July, and feed on a wide range of plants including peonies. After mating, they deposit eggs in the soil, where the larvae feed and develop. The larvae themselves are not reported to be of economic importance.

Ants are attracted to peonies because of the sweet excretion on the flower buds created by the separation of the sepals covering the bud. The ants play no part in pollination of the peony flowers. After the excretion is gone, ants are no longer attracted to the buds. Peony flowers are commonly pollinated by two-winged insects belonging to the order *Diptera.*

Disease Control

Diseases often reduce the quantity and quality of peony flowers, and, in some cases, cause significant plant mortality. Some diseases, such as Botrytis blight and red spot, are perennial problems, while other diseases may be sporadic. The table lists some of the more common peony diseases with their symptoms and control. Certain plant diseases are difficult to identify by field symptoms. Be sure to consult a plant pathologist for accurate disease diagnosis before applying fungicides.

Peony diseases can, for the most part, be controlled by a combination of sound cultural management and chemical control. Use only clean, high-quality plant material. It may be advisable to treat the roots with a fungicide dust (captan or thiram) for direct planting in the field. If possible, sow the transplants on a slightly raised plant bed with drip irrigation. Avoid overhead watering and keep plants adequately spaced for good air circulation. Overcrowding may result in plant losses from red spot and other fungal and foliar blights. Water the plants early in the day to allow for good foliage drying before nightfall. Closely monitor plants for any signs of diseases or insect activity. Remember that insects may transmit virus diseases. Keep fields as weed-free as possible to control insect and virus problems. Rotate planting beds in the field when buildup of soilborne fungal pathogens and nematodes are a problem.

Routine fungicide applications may be necessary to control red spot on susceptible varieties of peony during most years. Control is much more effective if fungicides are applied before symptoms of red spot are apparent. Other fungal diseases may be controlled by curative fungicide applications beginning as soon as symptoms develop. Don't wait until plants are severely blighted to start applying fungicides. The table lists fungicides that have been labeled for control of specific disease problems. Chemical registrations change — read the label before purchasing or applying any chemical to be certain it is currently registered/labeled for your intended use. Be sure to diagnose the disease correctly and follow all instructions on the fungicide label.

PEONY DISEASES

Disease	Symptoms	Control
Leafspots & Blights		
Botrytis spp.	Blight. Sudden wilting of shoots. Brown or black rot can be seen at the base of stems, below ground. Grayish fungal growth is visible on stems just above soil line. Infected flowers turn brown, and large, irregular, brown areas develop on leaves. Fungal growth may also develop on infected plant parts.	Apply mancozeb, ferbam, or fixed coppers to soil and foliage in early spring and repeat it at 7- to 14-day intervals as necessary. Shorten intervals between applications during wet weather.
Phytophthora cactorum	Blight. Infected stems, leaves, blossoms and buds are brown and leathery. Black cankers form on stems and cause them to fall over.	Application of mancozeb to control Botrytis blight will also help prevent Phytophthora blight.
Cladosporium spp.	Red spot or measles. Small, dark red, circular spots on leaves. Spots coalesce to form blotches that are dark purple on lower leaf surface.	Application of mancozeb to control Botrytis blight will also help prevent other fungal leafspots.
Other Leafspots		
Alternaria sp. *Cercospora paeoniae* *Phyllosticta* spp. *Septoria paeoniae*		Application of mancozeb to control Botrytis blight will also help prevent other fungal leafspots.

Disease	Symptoms	Control
Rots & Wilts		
Verticillium albo-atrum	Wilt. During the bloom period, foliage and shoots may wilt, with the lower shoot remaining intact. An internal vascular discoloration may be present in the lower stem. Infected plants may be stunted or killed.	Remove infected plants. The fungus is soilborne, so replanting in the same area may result in redevelopment of wilt.
Other Root Rots & Wilts		
Fusarium sp. *Rhizoctonia solani* *Sclerotinia sclerotiorum* *Thielaviopsis basicola*	Several soil-borne fungi may damage the roots and crowns of peony. Look for stunted plants. Roots and crowns may exhibit brown to black lesions.	Avoid mechanical injury to roots and crowns during cultivation. Avoid poorly drained soils. Keep plants vigorous by proper irrigation and fertilization.
Nematodes		
Root nematodes *Meloidogyne* spp. *Rotylenchus buxophilus*	Plants are stunted and spindly and fail to bloom. Roots have numerous small galls.	Avoid planting in nematode infested soil or fumigate before planting.
Virus		
Peony ringspot	Greenish-yellow concentric bands, occasionally small, necrotic spots. Not a serious problem.	Rogue infected plants. Do not divide any plants showing virus symptoms. No chemical control is available.

Propagation

The easiest and most satisfactory method of propagation is by root division. Division of young roots helps increase stock quickly and produces plants that flower more freely. Young roots are straighter, smoother and easier to cut evenly. Two-year stock is best, though three-year stock may also be divided. Roots older than three years may also be successfully divided and grown; it is such roots which ordinarily are divided in private gardens. Because older peony roots are large and intertwined, it is difficult to divide them without much waste. A few cultivars have a way of growing in separate pieces, each piece with a small crown of its own. This may make division easier, but it prevents the development of a fine, large plant.

Lift and divide the roots after the plants go dormant. Before lifting, cut the leaves and stems off to the ground. Carefully dig around and under the plants, taking care not to break off the roots. Wash off soil. Use a sharp, sterilized knife to cut the roots into divisions containing two to five strong buds and a generous portion of fleshy root. Shorten roots to four- to six-inch stubs and remove the smaller, thread-like roots. Scarce or valuable cultivars may be cut into smaller pieces of one or two buds each. Such divisions should be placed in a cold frame for the first year. Too minute or too frequent division causes roots to lose vigor and delays bloom.

Dig up all roots. If a fleshy piece has broken off near the crown, it will often develop buds and form a crown of its own. The chance of the lower part of a root finger making any growth is very small. When dormant, peonies withstand considerable exposure and can be shipped long distances safely. Figures 20-1 and 20-2 illustrate a blade used for digging peony roots.

Figure 20-1: U-Blade Attachment for Digging Peony Roots

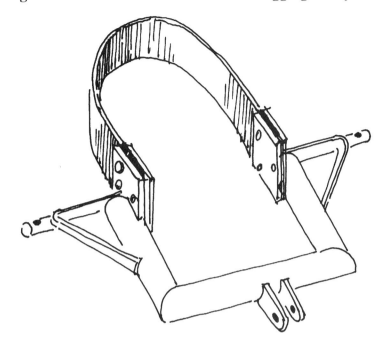

Figure 20-2: Digging Peony Roots With U-Blade Attachment

Harvest and Yields

Flowering stems are normally not harvested the first three years after planting. During this time, the buds are merely pinched off, leaving as much foliage (photosynthetic area) as possible on the plant to increase plant resources for growth. The fourth year, each plant can be expected to produce 15 to 30+ flower stems depending on variety. Only one-third of these should be harvested. The remaining flower buds should be pinched off to maximize leaf surface area and plant development. From the fifth year on, a mature, vigorous plant may produce 20 to 40+ flower stems, one-third to a half of which should be left unharvested to maintain the photosynthetic capacity of the plant.

An alternative harvest approach to preserving the photosynthetic capacity of the plant during the formative early years provides some cash flow. All flowers are harvested during the first three years, but only a few inches of stem are cut off with the flower. The stem is cut back to just below the first leaf. This first leaf is always very small and is usually located 2-3 inches below the flower. These very short stem flowers are not saleable as fresh cut flowers but can be sold and used as dried flowers. The price per flower is less than that for a long-stemmed fresh cut, but it does provide some cash flow to help with expenses during the first few years after planting.

Optimum productivity is reached the fifth year and may continue for more than 25 years. The length of the harvest season depends on spring temperatures. Warm spring temperatures shorten peony harvest, while cool spring temperatures lengthen harvest. Generally, the harvest season for commercial cut flower cultivars lasts 10 to 12 days, although each cultivar's harvest may be as short as two to four days. Late-season cultivars and very full double cultivars often fail to open under sudden hot temperatures.

The first step in harvesting is to pick the right stage of development. Follow these guidelines:

• peonies should be harvested in their soft bud stage.

- sepals should be completely separated
- colored surface petals should be exposed and beginning to separate slightly
- the bud when squeezed sideways should offer the resistance of a stale marshmallow.

Determining the ideal stage of maturity to harvest will take some practice. Depending on the cultivar, reds should be harvested when softer and more open than pinks and whites.

Harvest with the longest stems possible but always allow a minimum of two leaves to remain below the cut. Harvest at least twice a day, if not more, depending on temperatures. High temperatures (80°F and up) hasten flower development. Harvesting only once per day will result in some flowers being more mature than desirable and therefore unharvestable.

<u>Do</u> <u>not</u> immediately put freshly harvested stems in water; let the harvested stems sit at least 20 minutes. Flowers immediately placed in water may "blast," or open prematurely. Place the stems in water with a preservative solution for 15 to 30 minutes to rehydrate. Remove from water and be sure buds, stems and foliage are dry before sleeving and placing into cold storage. Store dry (out of water) by placing bunches horizontally on shelves in cold storage (32°F-36°F) for best results. Peonies handled and stored in this manner will keep four weeks without significantly reducing vaselife.

GRADING

In 1938, the United States Department of Agriculture published standards for grades of cut peonies in the bud (Effective April 1, 1938). These standards specify 12 stems to the bunch, though current USDA reports use five or 10 stems to the bunch. Peonies have also been graded into classes of light, medium and heavy with 10, eight and six stems per bunch, respectively. The heavy grade is composed of taller, thick-stemmed flowers while the light grade contains shorter, thin-stemmed flowers.

USDA Standards for Cut Peonies in the Bud

Numbers and letters in parentheses following grade terms indicate where such terms are defined under Definitions of Terms.

The tolerances for the standards are on a container basis. However, individual packages in any lot may vary from the specified tolerances as stated below, provided the averages for the entire lot, based on sample inspection, are within the tolerances specified.

For a tolerance of 10 percent or more, individual packages in any lot may contain not more than one and one-half times the tolerance specified, except that when the package contains 15 specimens or less, individual packages may contain not more than double the tolerance specified.

For a tolerance of less than 10 percent, individual packages in any lot may contain not more than double the tolerance specified, provided at least one specimen which does not meet the requirements shall be allowed in any one package.

U.S. No. 1 shall consist of peonies of similar varietal characteristics (1) which have fresh (2), strong (3), well-trimmed (1) and unbroken stems (6) which are fairly straight (7). The buds shall be well-shaped (8), fresh (2), firm (9) with calyxes normally expanded (10) but not overmature (11), free from puff balls (12), bull heads (13) and wood heads (14). The buds and stems shall be free from decay and freezing injury and from damage (15) caused by dirt or other foreign material, discoloration, moisture, disease, insects, mechanical or other means.

Each bud shall be not less than one inch in diameter (16) and, unless otherwise specified the overall length of bud and stem shall be not less than 24 inches but in no case shall the overall length be less than 20 inches.

Tolerances

In order to allow for variations other than size, incident to proper grading and handling, not more than a total of five percent, by count, of the peonies in any container may be below the requirements of this grade but not more than one-half percent shall be allowed for decay. In addition not more than a total of 10 percent, by count, of the peonies in any container may not met the specified size requirements, but not more than one-half of this amount, or five percent, shall be allowed for buds which are smaller than the minimum diameter required.

U.S. No. 2 shall consist of peonies of similar varietal characteristics (1), which have fresh, fairly well-trimmed (5) and unbroken stems (6) which are not badly curved or crooked. The buds shall be fresh (2), firm (9) with calyxes normally expanded (10) but not overmature (11), free from puff balls (12), bull heads (13) and wood heads (14). The buds and stems shall be free from decay and from damage (15) caused by freezing, and from serious damage (17) caused by dirt or other foreign material, discoloration, moisture, disease, insects, mechanical or other means.

Each bud shall be not less than seven-eighths inch in diameter (16), and unless otherwise specified the overall length of the bud and stem shall not be less than 20 inches but in no case shall the overall length be less than 18 inches.

Tolerances
In order to allow for variations other than size incident to proper grading and handling, not more than a total of 10 percent, by count, of the peonies in any container may be below the requirements of the grade, but of this amount not more than one-half of this tolerance, or five percent, may be allowed for defects causing serious damage (16) and not more than one-fifth of this amount, or one percent, shall be allowed for decay. In addition, not more than a total of 10 percent, by count, of the peonies in any container may not meet the specified size requirements but not more than one-half of this amount, or five percent, shall be allowed for buds which are smaller than the minimum diameter required.

Unclassified shall consist of peonies which have not been classified in accordance with the foregoing grades. The term "unclassified" is not a grade with the meaning of these standards but is provided as a designation to show that no definite grade has been applied to the lot.

Standards for Bunching

Cut peonies in the bud may be packed loose or bunched. When bunched, each bunch shall contain 12 peonies, having buds which are reasonably uniform in size and development and stems which are reasonably uniform in length. When bunched the peonies shall be arranged so that the buds form a flat surface across the top of the bunch. Each bunch shall be held intact by two rubber bands, one placed five to six inches below the base of the buds and the other three to four inches from the base of the stems.

It is recommended that a No. 30 rubber band doubled be used three to four inches from the base of the stems and a No. 18 rubber band not doubled be used five to six inches from the base of the buds.

In order to allow for variations incident to proper bunching, not more than five percent, by count, of the bunches in any container may not meet the requirements for bunching.

Definitions of Terms

As used in these standards:

1. "Similar varietal characteristics" means that the stems, foliage and buds of the peonies have the same general character of growth and color.

2. "Fresh" means that the buds and foliage are bright, not badly wilted, limp or flabby.

3. "Strong" means that the stem is fairly stiff and sturdy enough to hold the bud in a reasonably erect position.

4. "Well-trimmed" means that all lateral or side buds, and all foliage on the lowest six to eight inches of the stem have been neatly removed, but the foliage on the remainder of the stem has not been removed to the extent that the appearance of the peony is damaged.

5. "Fairly well-trimmed" means that all the lateral or side buds and all the foliage on the lowest six to eight inches of the stem has been neatly removed but the foliage on the remainder of the stem has not been removed to the extent that the appearance of the peony is seriously damaged.

6. "Stems" means the flower stalks with the attached foliage.

7. "Fairly straight" means that the stem is of normal growth and is not more than slightly curved or crooked.

8. "Well-shaped" means that the bud is symmetrical, not lopsided or otherwise deformed.

9. "Firm" means that the bud is fairly compact and yields slightly to moderate pressure of the fingers.

10. "Normally expanded" means that the calyxes have expanded to the extent that the true color of the outer petals is exposed. At this stage of development the two large calyxes and the outer petal at the top of the bud have developed to the extent that they will yield to slight pressure of the fingers.

11. "Overmature" means that the bud is soft and the outer petals have started to unfold.

12. "Puff ball" means a bud of poor substance which usually expands prematurely. The bud is usually long, soft on one side and feels soft to very soft in comparison with a normal bud of the same variety.

13. "Bull head" or "hard head" means a bud which is hard to very hard and which will not open or expand.

14. "Wood head" means a bud which is hard, usually flat, with the petals separated at the top and forming a small opening through which the interior of the bud can be seen.

15. "Damage" means any injury or defect which materially affects the appearance or shipping quality of the cut peonies. Inconspicuous anthracnose spots shall not be considered as damage.

16. "Diameter" means the greatest diameter measured through the center of the bud at right angles to a line running from the base to the top of the bud.

17. "Serious damage" means any injury which seriously affects the appearance or shipping quality of the peonies.

Some common mistakes often made by growers in marketing peonies:

1. Selection or suitability of varieties for commercial cutting. There seems to be only a limited number of varieties that respond favorably to commercial handling. Even those respond differently under varying cultural conditions, localities and seasons. The essential features of a good peony are:

    a. It must be a flower of good color and attractive form through all stages of development.

    b. A double flower is preferable; desirable fragrance is important.

    c. A free and reliable bloomer from year to year.

    d. Stiff, wiry, straight stems of uniform length (20 to 32 inches) and low-set foliage of good color and quality.

    e. Varieties which produce a single bud, or with a few laterals per stem are best. Less labor is required for disbudding.

    f. A good shipper, tolerant to abuse, and responsive to storage and water treatments.

2. Failure to recognize the proper stage of maturity for cutting. The proper stage of maturity varies greatly with different varieties.

3. The rapidity and condition with which the peonies are cut, graded and placed in storage.

4. Proper crating. Each crate should contain one variety and one grade. All crates should be well-filled and firm, but not

packed and overcrowded. Either extreme may prove expensive. Never mix different varieties or grades in the same crate if at all avoidable.

5. A mistake in quoting size — for example, quoting U.S. No. 1 and crating U.S. No. 1 with unclassified without distinctly indicating same. Packing and quoting accordingly is important.

Author's Comment:
It should be noted that the above USDA grades and standards prescribe that a bunch of peonies contain 12 flower stems. These standards became effective April 1, 1938. A long time ago. As mentioned earlier and worth repeating here, current USDA market reports use five or ten stems to the bunch. A number of other floriculture crops are currently marketed as ten stems to the bunch. In practice, the wholesale peony market appears to be adopting a 10-stem bunch as the standard unit of commerce.

AMERICAN PEONY SOCIETY

The American Peony Society was organized in 1903 to: "increase the general interest in the cultivation and use of the peony, to improve the methods of its cultivation, to increase its use as a decorative flower, to properly supervise the nomenclature of the different varieties and kinds of peonies, to encourage the introduction of improved seedlings and crosses, and to hold exhibitions with all members participating in the showing of their homegrown peonies."

American Peony Society
250 Interlachen Road
Hopkins, MN 55343

REFERENCES

Harding, Alice. 1985 (1917). *The Peony.* Waterstone & Co. Limited, London.

Honeywell, E. R.; Gaylord, F.C.; and Fawcett, K.J. 1940. *Peony Studies.* Indiana Agr. Exp. Sta. Bul. 444:47.

Rogers, Allan. 1995. *Peonies.* Timber Press, Inc. Portland, Oregon.

USDA. 1938. *United States Standards for Grades of Cut Peonies in the Bud.* Agricultural Marketing Service.

USDA. 1993. *Wholesale Ornamental Crops Report.* Agricultural Marketing Service.

Watson, L. and Dallwitz, M.J. 1995. *The Families of Flowering Plants: Descriptions and Illustrations.* URL http://muse.bio.cornell.edu/delta/

A-5 ANNUAL STATICE

Statice belongs to the genus *Limonium,* which consists of 300 species of mostly herbaceous perennials, some low shrubs and annuals. Native to the Mediterranean region, they grow in salt marshes and sea cliffs, and in semidesert and desert regions. The genus name comes from the Greek word *leimonion,* the name of an unidentified plant that grew in salt marshes.

Statice have large, leathery leaves and airy clusters of small, delicate flowers on nearly leafless, many-branched stems. The tiny flowers consist of two parts: an outer, papery envelope, the calyx, and an inner part called the corolla which is often a different color.

Statice need full sun and good drainage. They tolerate heat, drought and most of them, saline soils. Although there are many species available, this chapter will deal with the annual statice, *L. sinuatum.* The flowers make good filler flowers in arrangements, and keep good color even when dried.

CULTIVARS TO GROW

Many varieties of *L. sinuatum* are available, with colors ranging from white to pink, blue and deep purple.

'Excellent series' — a series of colors are available
'Turbo series' — a series of colors are available
'Fortress series' — a series of colors are available
'Blue river' — deep blue
'Bonduelli' — golden yellow
'Kempf's blue imp.' — dark blue
'Lavandin' — clear lavender
'Market grower's blue' — deep blue
'Midnight' — deep blue
'Surworowii' (rattail statice) — rose

CULTURAL REQUIREMENTS

Planting

Statice seed comes either clean (decorticated) or unclean (still imbedded in the dried flower heads). Clean seed can be sown more easily and precisely. Statice prefer sandy soil with a pH of 6 to 6.5. Use dolomite or limestone to adjust soil pH where necessary. Statice are deep rooting so till the soil as deep as possible. Raise the beds three to five inches high to improve drainage and reduce the risk of root rot diseases.

Grow two to three rows of statice plants per bed. Space the plants 12 to 14 inches between rows (alternate space), with 14 to 16 inches between plants. The plant density will be about 14,500 per acre with beds on 54-inch centers.

Taller varieties will need support to keep the flower stems straight. Plastic mesh materials as illustrated in Figures 5-6 and 5-7 of Chapter 5 (How to Plant) are ideal for this purpose.

Watering

Overhead watering is not recommended. It may damage the flowers, cause spotting on petals, splash soil onto the foliage and promote the spread of disease. Drip irrigation is recommended because it places the water on the ground where it is needed, not on the flowers or foliage. The foliage of annual statice grows in a rosette pattern clustered near the soil surface. Soil splashed onto the surface of the leaves will reduce the photosynthetic capacity of the plant.

Fertilization

Before initiating a fertilizer program, always test the soil for nutrient content. The increased water requirement of cut flowers creates an increased requirement for fertilization. The application of fertilizer should coincide with crop needs.

Fertilize statice to promote growth. Before planting, broadcast superphosphate at 500 pounds per acre, and apply nitrogen at 30 to 40 pounds per acre. Cultivate into the soil. Additional fertilizer can be added as needed through injection into drip lines or banded with a granular fertilizer.

Weed Control

Due to limited production of many species of specialty cut flowers, only a few herbicides are labeled for use. Oxidiazon, EPTC and DCPA have been labeled for use in statice production, although the use of EPTC requires mechanical incorporation which limits it usefulness in many plant procedures. Chemical registration/labels change — read the label before purchase or use to be sure the chemical is currently labeled for your intended use.

Weed barriers and mulches prevent weed growth and restrict soil splash on foliage and flowers from rain and irrigation. Plastic barriers can be successful in controlling weeds within annual statice crops.

Insect Control

Good cultural practices are the best insect control. A healthy, actively growing statice plant is more resilient to insect attack. The ideal approach is a preventative program. Control insects early, when they are first detected; do not wait until a serious infestation occurs. Less chemical can be applied to spots as they develop than would be required to spray the entire crop. Leafhoppers are a serious threat to the health and productivity of statice crops. The insect itself does little damage but it is the primary vector of aster yellows disease. Aster yellows disease will devastate a crop and has no cure. Leafhoppers must be controlled to prevent them from feeding on an infected plant and then spreading it to other plants in the surrounding area. A grower intending to produce annual statice should be familiar with the information on insect monitoring in Chapter 9 and the section on aster yellows in Chapter 10.

Lepidopterous larvae, such as armyworms, cutworms and loopers attack the tender terminal growth.

Sucking and rasping insects, such as aphids, mealy bugs and thrips usually cause minimal damage. Large populations of these insects rarely appear.

Mites, particularly spider mites, cause the most serious damage to statice. They may appear in large numbers on the underside of the leaves. Populations of these insects usually peak during flower harvest and large numbers migrate from the leaves to the flower spike.

Disease Control

Major diseases affecting statice are *Anthracnose, Cercospora* and *Botrytis.* Crown rots may be caused by *Collectotrichum, Rhizoctonia* and Southern blight *(Sclerotium rolfsii).* Use a preventative maintenance spray program which alternates combinations of fungicides, insecticides and acaricides every 10 to 14 days for statice until spray-on-demand practices are developed.

Aster yellows disease is the most serious of diseases affecting annual statice. See Chapter 10 for more information.

Harvest

The intended market will determine the height of the cut and stage of flower opening at harvest. For example, for the longest stems, the cut needs to be made close to the rosette of leaves. Only one cut per plant can be made with this method. To extend the growing season and increase the number of stems per plant, cut not at the rosette but above one of the large leaves on the flowering stem. New flowering shoots will emerge from axillary buds. The stem length of the first and later cuts will be shorter than the one-cut approach. Harvest when flowers are almost fully open (when 75 percent of the calyces show color).

Fresh statice is usually sold in 1-pound bunches, which contain approximately 10 stems. Dried statice is sold in bunches by weight (4 oz. bunches) and in bunches by stem number to retail buyers (10 stems). Statice preserved with glycerine is sold similar to dried statice.

Dried and Preserved Statice

The easiest method to preserve statice is to hang them upside down in bunches in a dark and hot dry place. This will take about two weeks to completely dry the stems. The air drying process is discussed in greater detail in Chapter 15.

Another method is to preserve the flowers with glycerin. The stems will be more pliable than dried statice. Place fresh stems in a water/glycerin/dye solution. This mixture will replace a portion of the water in the plant with glycerin and keep the stems in a soft pliable condition. The dye gives the stems a natural-looking green color. This process of preserving with glycerin and color-processing the stem is described in Chapters 15 and 16.

To prevent mold from forming, be sure the plant material is completely dry before placing into storage. Preserved plant materials being stored under warehouse conditions are subject to insect damage. Storage facilities should be screened to prevent insect entry and plant materials treated for insect pests and eggs which may be present. Insect control measures for stored floral products are discussed in Chapter 9.

REFERENCES

Armitage, Allan. 1994. *Specialty Cut Flowers*. Timber Press, Inc. Portland, Oregon.

Sacalis, John N.. Second Edition, 1993. *Cut Flowers, Prolonging Freshness, Postproduction Care and Handling*, second ed. Ball Publishing, Batavia, Illinois.

A-6 SUNFLOWERS

Sunflower, or *Helianthus,* is native to North America. It was domesticated by Native Americans, whose careful selection increased the seed size by approximately 1,000 percent over the last 3,000 years. They used sunflowers for food, dye and medicine, and extracted the oil for ceremonial body painting and pottery. Sunflowers are present in the mythic belief system of many tribes. The Hopi believe that when the sunflowers are numerous, it is a sign that there will be an abundant harvest. The Teton Dakota had a saying, "When the sunflowers were tall and in full bloom, the buffalos were fat and the meat good."

Early settlers grew sunflowers for food and garden decoration, and European explorers brought sunflowers along trade routes to Spain, Italy, Egypt, Afghanistan, India, China and Russia. The seeds yield a variety of products, ranging from snack food to soap, and the stems and heads may be made into paper or used for fuel. One English herbalist found a use for sunflower buds: he boiled and ate them with butter, vinegar and pepper, like artichokes. Recently, the sunflower has found yet another use: this time as a cut flower.

CULTIVARS TO GROW

Helianthus annuus (common sunflower, annual)
'Abensonne' — 7-8' tall; yellow flowers, bronze center.
'Autumn Beauty' — 5-7' tall; up to 4-5" wide flowers; mix of
    yellow, bronze, purple, bicolors.
'Full Sun' — gold-yellow flowers; 3-4' tall; pollenless; day-
    neutral.
'Gold Crest' — 3-4' tall; small, golden flowers.
'Italian White' — 5-7' tall; 5" wide flowers; creamy white
    flowers, black center.
'Lemon Queen' — 5' tall; 4-5" wide flowers; lemon-yellow
    flowers; brown center.
'Orange Sun' — 3½' tall; apricot-orange double flowers.
'Sunbright' — 5-6' tall; 4-5" wide flowers; golden-yellow flowers,
    dark brown center; pollenless.

'Sunburst Mixed' — 4' tall; 4" wide flowers; crimson, lemon, bronze and gold flowers.

'Sunrich Lemon' — yellow flowers, black center; pollenless; day-neutral.

'Sunspot' — 2' tall; 10-12" wide flowers; golden yellow flowers, golden brown center;

'Taiyo' — 5' tall; 6" wide flowers; gold-yellow ray flowers, black center.

'Valentine' — 5' tall; 6" wide flowers; lemon-yellow flowers; black center.

Helianthus debilis
— light pink to purple; 2-3" wide flowers; cucumber-shaped leaves

Helianthus decapetlus (wild perennial sunflower)
— double, cactus, other type flowers.

New cultivars are being produced each year. Check seed catalogs for listings of new cultivars to try.

CULTURAL REQUIREMENTS

Planting

Sunflowers adapt to a wide range of soil types and climates. They prefer to grow under high light intensities in a well-drained soil, though they also grow well in poor soil and under dry conditions. They prefer a near-neutral soil pH, in the range of 6.5 to 7.5.

Annual sunflowers are grown from seed sown directly in the field after threat of frost has passed. Plant seeds nine to 12 inches apart in the row and 18 to 36 inches between rows. The ideal planting depth is one and one-half to two and one-half inches. The soil temperature should be above 50°F four inches below the soil surface.

Sequential planting every two to four weeks is useful to provide continuous harvest and to take advantage of long terminal flower stems. Laterals are shorter and flowers are smaller after the terminal has been cut.

Most cultivars appear to be day-neutral or flower somewhat faster during short days. Warm temperatures result in faster flower development than cool temperatures. Temperatures below 50°F slow development significantly.

Watering

Sunflowers are drought-tolerant; their deep roots can extract water at depths of up to six feet. However, sunflowers do best when they are not stressed for water. Withholding water may reduce stem length and decrease flower diameter. The amount and frequency of water required will vary with the weather and maturity of the sunflower crop. Base the irrigation schedule on the soil moisture status in the root zone and irrigate to provide sufficient but not excessive water. Insufficient water will reduce crop production and quality, whereas a consistently saturated soil will reduce growth and promote the development of root rot. On average, a sunflower in active growth uses about 0.15 inches of water per day. A mature sunflower plant with a full leaf canopy under conditions of 95°F and low relative humidity may use 0.3 inches of water per day.

Fertilization

Germinating sunflower seed is sensitive to soluble salts from fertilizer applied in the row with the seed. No more than one-fourth pound of actual nitrogen and potash per 1,000 sq.ft of production area should be placed in the row in contact with the seed. Somewhat higher levels of phosphate can be placed with the seed at planting. Cold soils reduce availability and uptake of nutrients. During a cool, wet spring, some starter fertilizer placed with the seed or in bands two inches to the side and two inches below the seed can help produce vigorous seedlings.

Apply nitrogen at the rate of 2 to 2½ pounds of actual nitrogen per 1,000 sq.ft. Apply a small amount prior to planting. Apply the majority of the nitrogen as a sidedressing before the plants are one foot high. A small portion of the total amount of nitrogen may be applied as the terminal bud shows signs of forming the flower head.

NO POSTAGE
NECESSARY
IF MAILED
IN THE
UNITED STATES

MAIL

ES MOINES IA

AGAZINE

5-2415

TO OUR
UNDERGROUND ISSUE

ın publishes 10 issues a year, monthly except for January and July. Combined.
lude 7% GST). Foreign orders: $33.90 US$.

otassium (K_2O) only on the basis
indicate low phosphorus levels,
)00 sq.ft. of production area. If the
 gh levels of phosphorus, apply ½ to
sq.ft. Broadcast the phosphorus
s plowing or discing.

f potassium, apply two pounds of
medium levels of potassium
pounds of K_2O. Broadcast the
and before the sunflower plants

trachloroterephthalate
... (Dacthal®) and pendimethalin (Prowl®)
been labeled for sunflower production. Chemical registra-
tions/labels change — contact your county extension agent for an
update on herbicides currently labeled for sunflower production.

Insect Control

Good cultural practices are the best insect control available. A
healthy, actively growing sunflower plant is more resilient to
insect attack. The ideal approach is a preventative program.
Control insects early, when they are first detected; do not wait
until a serious infestation occurs. Less chemical can be applied to
spots as they develop than would be required to spray the entire
crop. As far back as 1936, 66 different species were recorded as
pests on sunflowers, although the occurrence of any specific pest
is sporadic.

In seed production, pests that feed within stem and head tissues
are of the greatest concern; they may structurally weaken plants,
disrupt nutrient flow and reduce or destroy seed. In cut flower
production, external feeders are of greater concern; the cut flower
market demands perfect or near-perfect flowers, and visible insect
damage reduces product value and marketability.

Currently, little is known about the impact of specific insect pests on sunflowers grown as cut flowers. As the industry builds, a database may emerge on the most important pests, their frequency of appearance and geographical range of occurrence. For now, it can only be speculated which pests will do the most damage.

Insect pests associated with sunflowers are either primary (they specifically feed on sunflowers) or secondary (they subsist on whatever plants are convenient).

Primary Feeders

Sunflower beetle — Overwintered adults (somewhat similar in appearance to Colorado potato beetles) feed on developing foliage and deposit eggs. Larvae (cream-colored and somewhat hump-backed in appearance) feed on foliage for an additional four to six weeks after which they enter the soil to pupate. Newly emerged adults feed on foliage in preparation for overwintering. There is one generation per season.

Sunflower bud moth, sunflower (head) moth and banded sunflower moth — Depending upon the specific species, one or all stages of development could be present at the same time during the growing season. The adult moths do no damage. The larvae may prevent head formation or feed on (or enter) the receptacle from where they tunnel into and destroy seeds. Flowers may become distorted, appear trashy due an accumulation of frass and webbing, or be destroyed by soft rot organisms often associated with head-feeding activities. Also, the mere presence of the larvae may be disturbing to consumers.

Sunflower maggot, sunflower midge, sunflower seed weevil, sunflower stem weevil, sunflower head-clipping weevil — These are considered to be infrequent in appearance and of minor concern when they appear. For all but the head-clipper, noticeable damage results from the cumulative activities of many individuals.

An individual female head-clipping weevil girdles the stem just below the head and then lays eggs on the head. The head eventually drops off. When head-clipping weevils occur, the number of clipped heads is minimal (one to three percent) in field situations.

Secondary Feeders

Caterpillars — Although generally sporadic in occurrence, several species of butterflies and moths may be found in great numbers. When they do occur, each female deposits many eggs on available foliage. The resulting larvae (caterpillars) may actively feed on sunflowers. Butterfly species include the painted lady (thistle caterpillar), silvery checkerspot and imported cabbage-worm. Moth species include the armyworm, beet armyworm, fall armyworm, cabbage looper, corn earworm, virgin tiger moth (woolly bear caterpillar), variegated cutworm, and webworms.

Grasshoppers — Many grasshoppers are general feeders. Three of the most common species found in Kansas are the two-striped, red-legged and differential grasshoppers. These occasionally reach outbreak population levels. Especially in dry years when natural vegetation is insufficient to support existing populations, grasshoppers will move great distances in search of food sources. Sunflower plantings may be totally destroyed.

Control

Because of their small size, insects may easily escape notice until substantial damage has occurred. While rescue spray treatments prevent additional damage, the quality of flowers and foliage cannot be restored, and their marketability may be decreased. Growers should closely monitor their plantings for insect pests. Scouting is a labor-intensive activity which, when started, must be faithfully conducted. A knowledge of the various pests (life stages, habits, damage potential, time of appearance) is essential. Refer to Chapter 9 for a more detailed discussion of insect monitoring and control practices.

Because the cut sunflower industry is so new, there is a lack of specifically registered insecticides. In the National Pesticide Information Retrieval System (NPIRS), which accesses approximately 23,000 current federally registered pesticide product labels, not one product is registered for sunflowers grown for ornamental purposes. However, various products have been registered for use on field crop sunflowers grown for oil or confectionery seed production. These materials include some formulations of the active ingredients *Bacillus thuringiensis* var. *kurstaki* (BioBit®, Condor®, Cutlass®, DiPel®, Larvo-BT®, Steward®, Vault®), carbaryl (Sevin®), chlorpyrifos (Lorsban 4E®), endosulfan (Thiodan®), esfenvalerate (Asana®), methidathion (Supracide®) and methyl parathion. Some of these materials are restricted-use products and legally for sale only to certified persons who may use the products themselves or directly supervise the use of the products by non-certified personnel. Under the broad umbrella of "field grown sunflowers," one could legally employ these materials on sunflowers grown for ornamental purposes.

Additional materials become available if one uses "ornamentals" as a catch-all to include sunflower plants grown for cut flowers: *Bacillus thuringiensis* var. *kurstaki* (same products as listed above), chlorpyrifos (Dursban® 4E, Pageant*DF, Acme® Dursban), cyfluthrin (Tempo® 2), fluvalinate (Mavrik®), rotenone (Rotacide® EC) and rotenone/pyrethrin (Pyrellin® EC).

As always, before purchasing or using any chemical, check the label to ensure that the product can legally be used on the target site and against the specific pest. Follow label instructions when mixing and applying materials.

Bird Control

Birds are not a problem if sunflowers are harvested as fresh cut flowers. If left to dry in the field as seed heads, sunflowers will be an attractive food source to birds. The seeds are readily accessible and high in nutritional value, and the flower head itself provides a perfect perch. Although many species of birds feed on sunflowers, migrating flocks of red-winged blackbirds do the most damage. Yellow-headed blackbirds and common grackles also cause significant losses.

Blackbirds often come to feed on the insects and weed seeds in a sunflower field before the crop is vulnerable to damage. Once the crop matures and the birds include the sunflower seed in their diets, efforts to move the birds fail. Although blackbirds are protected under the Migratory Bird Treaty Act, one section of the act provides that control of blackbirds damaging agricultural crops is legal without a special permit (check with your state wildlife office to be sure this section of the law is still in effect). A combination of cultural practices, mechanical and chemical harassment is most successful in controlling blackbirds.

Several cultural practices may be used to control blackbirds. First, do not plant sunflowers next to cattail sloughs, marsh areas or woodlots because blackbirds are likely to roost in such areas. Control weeds early to eliminate one food source from the field. Also, delay plowing-down the harvest stubble of other crops to create an alternate feeding area for harassed birds.

Use both mechanical and chemical harassment to frighten birds away from sunflower fields as soon as they are seen in the vicinity, regardless of the maturity of the crop. Use of rifles, automatic exploders and other electronic frightening devices work with varying degrees of success. Many of these may only be practical for large growers, as they can be expensive. Fright-producing repellents may also be available; check with the state wildlife office to see which are labeled for use in sunflower production. Controlling vertebrate pests is discussed in Chapter 11.

Disease Control

Diseases often reduce the quantity and quality of sunflowers and, in some cases, cause significant plant mortality. Diseases such as Sclerotinia head rot, Rhizopus head rot and rust are perennial problems, while other diseases may be sporadic. The table lists some of the more common sunflower diseases, their symptoms and control. Be careful using the table! Certain plant diseases are difficult to identify by field symptoms. Be sure to consult a plant pathologist for accurate disease diagnosis.

Unfortunately, there are no fungicides currently labeled for control of sunflower diseases. Nevertheless, many of these diseases can by suppressed or controlled by starting with clean seed, maintaining good cultural and sanitation practices during the growing season, rotating planting sites each year and controlling insects that feed on the seed.

Disease	Symptoms	Control
Sclerotinia Wilt, Stalk Rot and Head Rot		
Sclerotinia sclerotiorum	Sudden wilting of leaves. Root rot. Gray-green to brown canker at base of stem. Seed layer falls away, leaving a bleached, shredded skeleton interspersed with large sclerotia. Upon harvest, infected heads shatter.	No resistant hybrids are currently available. Plant in non-infested fields. Use clean seed. Prevent build-up of sclerotia in soil by monitoring the field for Sclerotinia diseases and rotating crops. No chemical is registered.
Downy Mildew		
Plasmopora halstedii	Dwarfed and yellowed (chlorotic) leaves. In humid weather, white cottony masses on the lower or upper leaf surfaces. Little, if any, seed produced.	Rotate crops. Destroy volunteer sunflowers early. Avoid poorly-drained fields. Delay planting until soil temperatures support rapid seed growth.
Phoma, Black Stem and Head Rot		
Phoma sp.	Large black lesions on stems. Lesions also on leaves, the back of the head and at the crown or base of the stalk. The leaf wilts, the petiole turns black and the stem lesions expand to form a large, shiny black patch with definite borders. Plants produce smaller heads and the stem may rot through.	No hybrids are immune, though some are more tolerant than others. Rotate crops to minimize the concentration of Phoma fungus in the soil. Control insects to reduce insect transmission of the fungus.

Disease	Symptoms	Control
Rust *Puccinia helianthi*	Cinnamon-colored spots on leaves, possibly on stems, petioles, bracts and back of the head in severe infestations. The spots eventually turn black.	Destroy volunteer plants early. Control wild annual sunflower around commercial fields. Avoid large concentrations of susceptible hybrids in one area. Avoid high rates of nitrogen fertilizer and high plant populations.
Rhizopus Head Rot *Rhizopus stolonifer*	Heads turn brown and mushy. Thread-like fungus develops on surface of head and within fleshy receptacle. Tiny, black structures form on fungus growth. Sometimes heads separate from stalk and drop off.	Head rod is usually associated with insect feeding to the seed. Insect control is important in preventing

Yields

Approximately 75 to 80 percent of the seeds planted will germinate, grow and produce acceptable flowers in a well-managed crop. The potential exists for significantly reduced yields of marketable flowers if the grower fails to adequately care for the plants.

One terminal flower and three to five axillary flowers may be harvested from each mature plant. The terminal flower will have the longest stem length. Axillary flowers may have stem lengths too short to be marketed through wholesale or retail florist market channels. Alternative markets such as farmers markets or sales in a dried form may need to be developed for these shorter stemmed flowers.

Harvest and Postharvest

Even if sunflowers look sturdy growing in the field, care must be exercised during harvest and handling. Before they are cut, they have the highest quality and vase life potential that they are ever going to have. After harvest, quality can only decrease.

Place into bunches containing either five or ten stems. Single stems are often offered for sale at farmers markets. Smaller flowered cultivars are often included in mixed bouquets.

Store at 36°F-41°F. Vase life is seven to 10 days and may be extended with preservatives.

Research at the University of California showed that pulsing sunflowers with a non-ionic detergent, Triton X-100, improved vase life. Longest vaselife was achieved with a one-hour pulse with 0.01% Triton X-100. The pre-storage Triton pulse worked in three ways: by increasing solution uptake during the one-hour pulse, minimizing weight loss during the dry storage period and significantly improving the uptake of water after dry storage.

REFERENCES

Jones, Rod, Serek Malgorzata and Michael S. Reid. *Detergents Increase the Vase Life of Cut Sunflowers (Helianthus Annus L.).* Cooperative Extension, University of California. April 1993.

McMullen, Marcia P., editor. *Sunflower Production and Pest Management.* Extension Bulletin 25 Revised. North Dakota State University. December, 1985.

Culture Profile, *Sunflower (Helianthus annuus).* The Cut Flower Quarterly, 1992.

A-7 ZINNIA

Zinnias are popular in flower gardens because of their colorful blooms and ability to withstand hot summer temperatures. Recently, new hybrid zinnias have attracted the attention of cut flower growers.

Zinnias' color spectrum ranges across the rainbow from crimson to dark purple. The solid colors are the most popular, though there is interest in the variegated forms. Zinnias also display great variety in shape and size, growing anywhere from three to 30 inches high. The three types of flowers — pompon, cactus and dahlia — all have flower diameters ranging from under two inches to more than four inches.

Native to Mexico, modern garden zinnias have been developed primarily from one species, *Zinnia elegans* Jacq., named in honor of Johann G. Zinn, professor of Botany at Gottingen. There are now 16 to 20 species, mostly annual, found in Mexico, Texas, New Mexico, Colorado and Chile. The other two species, *Z. angustifolia* and *Z. haageana,* are compact, have smaller flowers and are not really useful as cut flowers.

VARIETIES TO GROW

Z. elegans cultivars:

'Cactus-Flowered' (3,000-4,000/oz.) — 24"; mix of colors; quilled blooms.

'Candy Cane' — 17"; pink, rose and cerise stripes on white, gold blooms striped or flecked orange-scarlet; double and semi-double blooms.

'Cut-N-Come Again' — 24-36"; scarlet, pink, yellow, salmon, white, others; double blooms.

'Dahlia Flowered' (3,800/oz.) — 30"; mix of colors; double blooms.

'Lilliput' (4,800/oz.) — 18-24"; mix of colors; pompon blooms.

'Pumila' (4,000/oz.) — 24-30"; mix of colors; double blooms.

'Rose' — 20-22"; rose-pink with a touch of salmon; double and semi-double, dahlia-type blooms.

'Rose Pinwheel' —12"; pink, deep rose; daisy-like blooms.

'Ruffles' (2,700 to 3,100/oz.) — 24-30"; scarlet or mix of colors; double blooms.

'State Fair' (2,440/oz.) — 30-36"; mix of colors; double blooms.

'Sunbow' — 18-20"; range of colors; double blooms.

'Whirligig' — 20"; bicolored yellow-crimson, red-white, pink-white, cream-rose, bronze-red, others; double blooms.

'Yellow Marvel' — 15"; yellow; dahlia blooms.

CULTURAL REQUIREMENTS

Planting

Zinnias are grown from seeds (3,000-6,000 seeds/oz.), germinating in five to seven days at 75°F. Zinnias grow poorly and become chlorotic at temperatures below 60°F. Ideal soil temperature for zinnia production is greater than 70°F.

Zinnias are short-day plants for flower-bud initiation, which means that they initiate vegetative growth when the days are long (dark period 10 hours or less) and flower development when the days are short. Stem length and flower size increase with an increase in day length and temperature, the greatest profusion of blooms occurring when the days are less than 14 hours long (dark period longer than 10 hours).

Small plants can be produced in a greenhouse and transplanted to the field to gain an earlier harvest advantage. Make sure the germination medium is sterile, loose and well-drained and has a pH of about 6-6.5. Do not add a surfactant to the germination medium; it can cause reduced plant vigor and losses in seed germination. Light has no effect on germination. Plants will be ready to transplant into the field in three to four weeks.

Seed is most commonly planted directly in the field in May. Space plants six inches apart within the row and space the rows 12 inches apart. Schedule sowing dates according to the desired time of flowering. When soil temperature is above 70°F at planting, seeding to first harvest is six to seven weeks.

Zinnias produce one flower per stem. When this first flower is harvested, there will be a time lag until branches form, grow and produce new flowers. During this period no flowers will be available for sale. To overcome this, make successive plantings at intervals to provide a continuous harvest of blooms for sale.

Plant medium flower size varieties such as 'Pumila', 'Ruffles' and 'Cut-N-Come Again' in two seedings spaced two to three weeks apart, depending on soil temperature at seeding. Plant large-flower types like 'State Fair' in several successive plantings. Plant the second seeding two weeks after the first and plant the following seedings a week apart. Research in Kansas has shown that about seven to eight plantings are required to provide consistent production. The later plantings seem to have fewer disease problems late in the harvest season. This is most likely because the plants in the late-planted beds are younger and less dense, and therefore have greater air circulation around the foliage.

Watering

Overhead watering is not recommended. It may physically damage the flowers, cause spotting on the petals, splash soil onto the foliage and promote the spread of disease. Overhead watering will subject zinnias to powdery mildew, a foliar fungus disease. Drip irrigation is recommended because it places the water on the ground where it is needed and not on the flowers or foliage.

Fertilization

In general, one and one-half to two pounds of actual nitrogen per 1,000 square feet of production bed space per year from a 1-1-1 fertilizer is adequate. For example, two pounds of actual nitrogen would be 10.0 lbs./1000 sq. ft. of super phosphate (0-20-0), 5.0 lbs./1000 sq. ft. of potassium nitrate (20-0-44), and 3.0 lbs./1000 sq. ft. of ammonium nitrate (33-0-0). If following a single application plan, apply a slow-release nitrogen type at planting time. If a split application is desired, apply one-third at planting, one-third at midseason and the balance in late August. Keep fertilizer off of foliage and flowers to prevent damage to the plants.

If soil test results indicate adequate phosphorus and potassium, then ammonium nitrate should be used in place of the complete fertilizer. Apply a portion of the fertilizer at planting, some in late June and a final application about August 1. Sandy soils will require an additional fertilizer application (the same total amount spread over four applications).

Low levels of boron in the soil may cause terminal bud blasting and slow branch development. High levels of boron may delay flowering 12 to 15 days.

It is important to note that a plant grown as a cut flower requires more nitrogen than the same plant grown for its color display in the garden. During the harvest of cut flowers, the long stems, any attached foliage and all flowers are removed. Fertilizer, then, must promote not only flowering, but also the vegetative growth of new branches of marketable length. Traditional recommendations for balanced fertilizers or fertilizers that favor phosphorus and potassium over nitrogen do not necessarily apply for commercial cut flower production, as additional nitrogen is needed to promote new vegetative growth.

Weed Control

Surflan (oryzalin), XL (benefin and oryzalin), Dacthal (DCPA), Fusilade (fluazilop-P), Pre-San (benzene sulfonamide), Pennant (metolachlor) and Poast (sethoxydim) have been labeled for weed control with zinnias. Chemical registrations/labels change — read the label before purchasing or using any chemical to be sure it is currently labeled for your intended use.

Insect Control

Primary insect problems on zinnias are aphids, thrips, caterpillars and stem borers. Aphids are visible to the naked eye. They have sucking mouth parts and are most active on the young growing parts of plants. Infestation is characterized by crinkled and distorted foliage and leaf buds. Plants may have a sooty appearance. Aphids are also carriers of many viral diseases.

Thrips, tan to black in color and ⅟₂₅ inch long, feed on sap from young leaves and flowers abraded by their rasping mouth parts. Foliage becomes distorted and wrinkled, the undersides of leaves and petals covered with small, silvery streaks.

Stem borers may cause plants to wilt due to their tunneling up the stem and disrupting water movement within the plant.

Disease Control

Zinnia seedlings often suffer from damping-off diseases generated by fungi such as *Pythium sp., Phytophthora sp.* or *Rhizoctonia sp.* Zinnias are especially susceptible to powdery mildew *(Eryshiphae cichoracearum)* when days are warm and nights are cool and damp. Overhead watering will contribute to the problem. Powdery mildew is distinguished by white spots on both sides of the leaves and makes the plants unattractive and misshapen. It may cause defoliation in severe cases.

If mildew is a recurring problem, it might be wise to slightly increase the spacing between plants to improve air circulation around the foliage. Also, irrigating early in the day will lower the relative humidity in the micro-climate around the crop before nightfall, which will help reduce the incidence of foliar fungal diseases. Powdery mildew can also be controlled with sulfur dust or spray.

Grey mold *(Botrytis cinerea)* attacks zinnias in wet weather and affects the leaves. Again, increasing plant spacing and irrigating in the morning will help reduce grey mold.

Leaf blight *(Alternaria sp.)* is identified by reddish-brown spots on the upper leaf surface, often with grayish-white centers. The leaves may eventually become brown and dry and the stems girdled, prompting wilting of the plant. Brown spots also appear on the petals, causing them to darken and wither. The disease is carried on the seeds, and all seeds should be treated with a disinfectant. The soil should be sterilized or new soil used.

Tomato spotted wilt virus is characterized by chlorotic, yellowish rings on the leaves and may destroy the growing points of the plants. Destroy all infected plants.

Root rot *(Phytophthora cryptogea)* is distinguished by wilting of the plants and rotting at the soil line and outer layers of the main roots. Plants are easily pulled and the root surface sloughs off. Control by sterilizing the soil or by moving to new soil.

Cottony mold *(Sclerotinia sclerotiorum)* is characterized by rotting at the base of the plant, accompanied by a cottony, white mold. Control is the same as for wilt.

Curly top causes stunted growth with shortened internodes and chlorotic secondary shoots. The disease is most common near beet fields. It is caused by a virus, and is not usually serious.

Aster yellows may also infect zinnias. Initial symptoms may appear as vein clearing, which spreads until the entire leaf becomes chlorotic. As the plant develops, the yellowing may spread, or it may remain restricted to one side or one section of the plant while the rest of the plant appears healthy. Mature leaves generally do not change color, but any new growth will be yellowish-green. Infection early in the growing season will almost always cause stunting, shortened internodes and dwarfed, deformed or lopsided flower heads; with heavy infections, no flower production will occur. If leafhopper feeding occurs late in the season, the flowers will be deformed and will remain a yellowish-green no matter what the normal color of the variety may be. One outstanding symptom of aster yellows is adventitious shoot proliferation, appearing as a mass of leaves with a bushy or witches' broom effect. The leaves are yellowish-green and are smaller and thinner than normal. During the latter part of the season, the foliage on the plant may become reddened or bronzed. The root is also affected by aster yellows infection, being smaller than normal and predisposing the roots to field disease problems. See Chapters 9 and 10 for a more detailed discussion of aster yellows disease and leafhopper control.

Yields

Higher plant densities (i.e. closer spacing) result in higher yields per square foot of production space. Six, eight, 10 and 12-inch spacings were studied at the Horticulture Research Center in Manhattan, Kansas. The research showed that in all comparisons closer spacing produced more marketable stems per square foot of production space than wider spacings.

The 'Pumila,' 'Ruffles' and 'Cut-N-Come Again' varieties can be expected to yield an average of 3.1 stems per square foot per week beginning about August 15th from a June 1st seeding. 'State Fair' can be expected to yield about 1.3 stems. The June 1st seeding will yield its first stems early to mid July and recycle back into bloom in the middle of August. A May 15th seeding will begin to bloom seven to 10 days earlier.

Yields expressed here were produced under experienced care using drip irrigation with soluble fertilizer injected in the water. Soil type and weather conditions will affect the production level achieved. The only thing consistent about the weather is that it is never normal.

HARVEST AND POSTHARVEST REQUIREMENTS

Fresh Zinnias

Fresh zinnias are more durable than gerbera daisies and so provide a good substitute. The flowers are similar in shape and form, but zinnias do not suffer from bent neck or require special postharvest handling. Zinnias can be stored up to four days at 36-40°F without affecting vaselife. Vaselife is five to seven days and can be enhanced with preservatives. Cut stems as long as possible, leaving at least two sets of nodes to ensure future production.

Dried Zinnias

Zinnias can be successfully dried and lend themselves well to use in value-added activities. They come in a wide range of colors and sizes, and provide a standard, round flower design shape that few dried flowers do. Most colors dry well except the deep reds and scarlets, which usually turn an undesirable black-red.

The drying and preserving operation should not become an outlet for seconds or low-quality flowers, although undersized, otherwise perfect flowers are acceptable and may be desirable.

The surround-and-cover drying method (described below) preserves the flower shape best. Hanging zinnias upside down can cause the petals to reflex inward and lose the desired round, daisy shape. Drying upright, zinnia stems often lack the stem strength to support the flowers as they dry. The succulent nature of the flower prevents it from being preserved with glycerin.

Because most of the stem is removed in the surround-and-cover method, many short-stemmed cultivars that are unsuitable for the fresh cut flower market can be used for drying. To use these short-stemmed dried flowers in value-added activities, the designer will either attach an artificial stem or wire or glue the flower to the finished product.

Surround-and-Cover Method:

• Remove most of the stem, leaving about ½ to 1", because the flowers dry most efficiently in shallow containers.

• Choose a drying substance, such as silica gel. Do not choose something that will soil the flowers or be difficult to clean off the flowers.

• Place the flowers with stems removed on a thin layer (½ to ¾") of drying substance in a shallow container (3-4" deep).

• Carefully pour the drying substance over, around and through the petals to cover the flowers.

• Carefully remove the desiccant material when the flowers are completely dry. An air blower of some sort will aid in removing the desiccant from the fragile dried flowers.

• A polymer coating may be applied to the flowers to prevent them from absorbing moisture from the atmosphere.

Although there are many other market options, zinnias are very popular at farmers' markets. They seem to sell well where fresh local produce is sold directly to the public. The medium-sized and small button types are good additions to mixed fresh bouquets. The large 'State Fair' types seem to sell best as single item bunches of ten stems or mixed with other large flowers. Dried zinnias are used in a broad range of value-added or craft items. The flowers are easily applied with hot glue to wreaths and decorative items.

REFERENCES

Boyle, Thomas H. and Dennis P. Stimart. 1983. *Developmental Responses of Zinnia to Photoperiod.* J. Amer. Soc. Hort. Sci. 108(6):1053-1059.

Boyle, Thomas H., Dennis P. Stimart and Marla S. McIntosh. 1986. *Seasonal Variation in Vegetative and Reproductive Development in Zinnia elegans Jacq.* J. Amer. Soc. Hort. Sci. 111(2):260-266.

Healy, William E. 1990. *Producing Cut Flowers: Cut Zinnias. Horticulture Production Information Sheet.* University of Maryland Cooperative Extension Service.

A-8 WOODY ORNAMENTAL BRANCHES

Many varieties of woody plants can be grown for their shapely branches. Most woody cuts are perennial plants and require a permanent or semi-permanent position. This can be advantageous when planted in locations that would be awkward for other crops. For example, as a windbreak, along fences or roads, or on hillsides, where they prevent soil erosion.

Some are not suitable for outdoor production. Many are produced indoors or kept indoors during the colder months of the year.

Because there are so many varieties of woodies, cultural requirements can only be discussed in general. Specific and unique requirements of the most commonly grown woodies will be discussed separately after the general requirements.

GENERAL CULTURAL REQUIREMENTS

Planting

The mature size of woody plants varies greatly between species. Plant spacing will vary from rows spaced 12 or 15 feet apart, with the plants spaced three to four feet within the row to planting on 12- to 20-foot centers both within and between rows. Grass is often planted between rows to provide all-weather accessibility.

Watering

Plants should not become stressed for water during the spring and summer growing season or a decrease in vegetative growth will occur. An irrigation system with emitters at each individual plant is a common means of providing supplemental water to the crop.

Fertilization

Before initiating any fertilizer program, always test the soil for nutrient content. Watering for optimal vegetative growth of branches creates an increased requirement for fertilization.

The regeneration and growth of branches requires an adequate supply of nitrogen. A winter, spring and early summer application schedule will provide a consistent supply of nitrogen. Apply a pound of actual nitrogen per 1,000 sq.ft. of production area of a 1-1-1 ratio fertilizer. Adjust the rate or ratio of nutrients according to soil test results. To reduce the risk of freeze damage do not fertilize in late summer or early fall — allow growth to slow and harden off before frost.

Weed Control

Growers must control weeds in the production of woody ornamental branches, as competition with weeds reduces the quantity and quality of production. A bed full of weeds also increases the time required to harvest, raising labor costs. Several options are available to combat weed growth: herbicides, barriers or mulches, tractor-mounted cultivators, hoeing and hand-weeding.

Due to limited production of many species of these trees and shrubs, no herbicides are labeled for use on woody plants being grown for the production of decorative branches. Some herbicides are labeled for use in nursery tree and shrub production or landscape uses. Check labels to see if any may apply to your intended use.

Weed barriers and mulches prevent weed growth and have the added benefit of restricting soil splash from rain and irrigation on foliage, flowers or berries. The greatest benefits from these materials occur in the first few growing seasons while the plants are becoming established.

While hoeing and hand-weeding are excellent methods for weed control, availability and cost of labor may be prohibitive in all but the smallest production situations. Tractor attachments are available for cultivating up to and around individual plants.

Insect Control

Good cultural practices are the best insect control available. A healthy, actively growing plant is more resilient to insect attack. The ideal approach is a preventative program.

Control insects early, when they are first detected; do not wait until a serious infestation occurs. Less chemical can be applied to spots as they develop than would be required to spray the entire crop.

Stem borers are the primary insect of concern.

Disease Control

The best disease control is a healthy, actively growing tree or shrub. Do not allow plants to become stressed. Many woody ornamental plants which are pruned heavily each year are vulnerable to fungal infections. The best control is to carefully manage the growth of the plant to avoid environmental stresses. An example of a plant readily susceptible to disease from stress is Curly Willow which is highly susceptible to cankers when stressed for water.

WOODY PLANT SPECIES COMMONLY GROWN FOR DECORATIVE PURPOSES.
(stem form, bark characteristics, berries, flowers or seed pods)

Acer palmatum (Japanese Maple)

Acer rubrum (Red maple)

Aesculus hippocastanum (Horsechesnut)

Alnus incan (alder)

Althea

Amelanchier (serviceberry)

Betula (birch)

Buddlia davidii

Butterfly Bush

Buxus macrophylla

Buxus sempreviorns (English Boxwood)

Callicarpa (Beautyberry)

Carya (hickory)

Celastrus (Bittersweet)

Cercis canadensis (redbud)

Chaenomeles (Japanese Quince)

Chokecherry

Clethra
Cornus mas (cornelian cherry)
Cornus spp. (dogwood)
Corylus (hazelnut or filbert)
Crataegus (hawthorn)
Cytisus scoparius (scotch broom)
Daphne
Deutzia spp. (deutzia)
Ericas
Euonymus altatus
Exochorda
Flowering Almond
Flowering Quince
Forsythia
Fothergilla (fothergilla)
Hamamelis vernalis (Witch Hazel)
Hydrangea
Hypericum
Ilex (hollies)
Japanese Cherries
Kalmia latifolia (mountain laurel)
Kolkwitzia amabilis (beautybush)
Leonotis
Lonicera (honeysuckle)
Magnolia
Mahonia
Malus (apple/crabapple)
Nandina domestica
Ornamental Pear
Pernettya
Philadelphus spp. (Mockorange)
Pieris
Populus (poplar)
Prunus spp. (almond, cherry, peach,)
Pyracantha
Pyrus (pear)

Quercus (oak)
Rhus (sumac)
Ribes (Currant)
Salix discolor (Pussy Willow)
Salix torulosa (Curly Willow)
Salix (willows)
Sapium
Spiraea (spirea)
Symphoricarpus alba (Snowberries)
Syringa (lilac)
Viburnum
Wegelia
Wisteria (wisteria)

REFERENCES

Dirr, M.A. 1990. *Manual of Woody Landscape Plants: Their Identification, Ornamental Characteristics, Culture, Propagation and Uses.* 4th ed. Stipes Publishing Co., Champaign, IL.

Jenkins, D.F. 1991. *Woody Plants as Cut Flowers.* Proceedings of the 4th National Conference on Specialty Cut Flowers, Association of Specialty Cut Flower Growers, pp. 68-74.

Perry, D. 1990. *Woody Ornamentals as Cut Flowers.* Proceedings of the 3rd National Conference on Specialty Cut Flowers, Association of Specialty Cut Flower Growers, pp. 131-137.

Wyman, D. 1969. *Shrubs & Vines for American Gardens.* MacMillan Publishing Co., New York, NY.

APPENDIX B

LISTS, LISTS & MORE LISTS

B- 1   Organizations........................336

B- 2   State Flower Growers Associations 338

B- 3   State Florist Associations..............340

B- 4   Directories.......................341

B- 5   Reference Books 341

B- 6   Magazines, Bulletins & Newsletters......345

B- 7   Websites........................348

B- 8   Suppliers of General Materials..........349

B- 9   Cut Flower Seed Suppliers.............350

B-10   Suppliers of Plugs, Transplants & Bulbs...352

B-11   Plant Supplier Directories..............354

B-12   Suppliers of Soluble Organic Fertilizers...355

B-13   Synthetic, Organic & Biological Controls..355

B-14   Mulches.........................357

B-15   Mulch Removal Equipment 358

B-16   Irrigation Equipment 359

B-17   Subirrigation Equipment 359

B-18   Moisture Gauges & Meters 360

B-19   Frost Protection 360

B-20   Frost Protection-Fog. 360

B-21   Coverings & Windbreaks 360

B-22   Seeding & Planting Equipment 361

B-23   Hand-held Hoes 362

B-24   Wheel Hoes 362

B-25   Rear-tine Tillers/Walking Tractors 363

B-26   Multi-row Rototillers 363

B-27   Specialized Cultivators. 363

B-28   Flame Weeders. 363

B-29   Tool Carriers 364

B-30   Subsoilers 364

B-31   Bed Shapers. 364

B-32   Transplanting Equipment 365

B-33   Bird Control. 366

B-34   Deer Repellents 367

B-35   Electric Fences. 367

B-36   Pocket Gopher Control. 368

B-37   Refrigeration 368

B-38   Containers & Sleeves for Harvest,
          Holding & Packing 368

B-39   Labels 369

B-40   Suppliers of Fresh Flower Food
          & Preservatives 369

B-41   Glycol Preservatives. 370

B-42   Dyes for Color Processing 370

B-43   Freeze-drieds 370

B-44   Design Containers, Pots & Baskets 370

B-45   Florist Supplies 371

B-46   Display Fixtures. 373

B-47   Floral Design Schools 373

B-48   Cleaning Supplies 374

B-49   Office Systems. 374

B-50   Greenhouses. 375

B-51   Harvesting Equipment 376

The information presented in this appendix is provided as an aid in finding a source of supply or information useful in the daily operation of a specialty cut flower business. The lists of sources of supply were gathered from a variety of growers, trade show exhibitors and catalogs. No endorse-ment is intended or implied, nor is any criticism of similar companies or products not mentioned. In addition, other sources may be available as no list can be 100 percent complete.

APPENDIX B-1
ORGANIZATIONS

Alberta Market Gardeners Association
c/o ACDC - S, SS #4
Brooks, AB, Canada T1R 1E6
800-661-2642

American Association of Nurserymen
The national trade association of the nursery
industry includes multifaceted business
engaged in all aspects of growing and selling
landscape plants and related products.
American Association of Nurserymen
1250 I Street NW, Suite 500
Washington, DC 20005
202-789-2900/Fax: 202-789-1893
www.anla.org

American Floral Endowment
11 Glen-Ed Professional Park
Edwardsville, IL 62025
608-692-0045

American Floral Services, Inc.
The largest independent, international flowers-
by-wire company. Specializes in providing
educational classes, publications, software and
business services for retail florists in North
America.
American Floral Services
P.O. Box 12309
Oklahoma City, OK 73157-2309
405-947-3373/Fax: 405-943-7131
www.afs.com

American Institute of Floral Designers
A non-profit organization promoting the art of
floral design as a professional career.
American Institute of Floral Designers
720 Light Street
Baltimore, MD 21230
410-752-3318/Fax: 410-752-8295
www.aifd.org

Association of Specialty Cut Flower Growers
(ASCFG) A national network of commercial
field growers. Their basic purpose is to provide
cultural, technical, and marketing information
to member growers.
Association of Specialty Cut Flower Growers
M.P.O. Box 268
Oberlin, OH 44074-0268
440-774-2887/Fax: 440-774-2435
www.ascfg.org

Bedding Plants International
Serves growers of greenhouse crops and
members of related industries.
Bedding Plants International
525 SW 5th Street, Suite A
Des Moines, IA 50309-4501
800-647-7742
www.bpint.org

Canadian Agri-Marketing Association
1235 17th Avenue SW, Suite 206
Calgary, AB, Canada T2T OC2
403-541-0911
isabel@mcphersonmanagement.com

Canadian Horticultural Council-Prairie Region
P.O. Box 98
#40 Elizabeth Street
Okotoks, AB, Canada T0L 1T0
403-938-6643/Fax: 403-938-5441

Dried & Herb Growers Association
Box 75147
Ritchie Postal Outlet
Edmonton, AB, Canada T6E 6KI

Floral Marketing Association
A division of the Produce Marketing
Association serving floral mass marketers and
their suppliers. Publishes the annual *FMA
Membership Directory & Buyers Guide* and a
monthly newsletter, *Floraline.*
Floral Marketing Association
1500 Casho Mill Road
P.O. Box 6036
Newark, DE 19714-6036
302-738-7100/Fax:302-731-2409
www.pma.com

Floral Trade Council
A coalition of fresh flower growers and wholesalers committed to building an environment
of fair trade for the domestic fresh flower
industry.
Floral Trade Council
P.O. Box 228
Haslett, MI 48840
517-339-9765/Fax: 517-339-1393
willcinmi@aol.com

Flowers Canada
7856 Fifth Line South R.R. #4
Milton, ON, Canada L9T 2X8
905-875-0707
www.flowerscanada.ca

FTD Association
A retail florist association providing training,
quality assurance, research and government
relations services.
FTD Association
29200 Northwestern Highway
Southfield, MI 48034-1099
800-788-9000, press 3/Fax: 810-948-6420
www.ftdassociation.org

Herb Growing & Marketing Network
Publishes *The Herbal Connection* and *The
Herbal Green Pages* and sponsors seminars.
Herb Growing & Marketing Network
P.O. Box 245
Silver Springs, PA 17575-0245
717-393-3295/Fax: 717-393-9261
email: HERBWORLD@
aol.com;http:/www.herhnet.com/

International Cut Flower Growers Association
A trade association for growers of fresh
cut roses.
International Cut Flower Growers Association
P.O. Box 99
Haslett, MI 48840
517-339-9544/Fax: 517-339-3760
www.rosesinc.org

International Freeze Dry Floral Association
88 Midridge Close SE
Calgary, AB, Canada T2X 1G1

Manitoba Natural Products Marketing Council
401 York Avenue, Suite 915
Winnipeg, MB, Canada R3C 0P8
204-945-4495/Fax: 204-945-6134
gmackenzie@dgr.gov.mb.ca

Perennial Plant Association (PPA)
A network of professional growers, retailers,
designers, educators and others who work with
perennials.
Perennial Plant Association
3383 Schirtzinger Road
Hilliard, OH 43026
614-771-8431/Fax: 614-876-5238

Saskatchewan Herb Research Centre
Department of Plant Science
University of Saskatchewan
51 Campus Drive
Saskatoon, SK, Canada S7N 5A8
306-966-5868/Fax: 306-966-8106
www.vsaskica/agriculture/plantsci/index.html

Society of American Florists
A national trade association chartered to serve
all retailers, wholesalers and growers. A source
of technical information, marketing support
and lobbying efforts on behalf of the U.S. cut
flower industry.
Society of American Florists
1601 Duke Street
Alexandria, VA 22314
800-336-4743/Fax: 703-836-8705
www.afs.com

United Flower Growers (Co-op Association)
They have floral auctions four days a week:
Mon, Tue, Thr. and some Fridays. No set standards for drieds/herbs. They do have certain
amount of stems per bunch, also information
on statice.
United Flower Growers
4085 Marine Way
Burnaby, BC, Canada V5J 5E2
604-430-2211/Fax: 604-430-3858

Wholesale Florists & Floral Suppliers
of America
A non-profit trade association whose purpose
is to preserve and strengthen the wholesale
florist position.
Wholesale Florists & Floral Suppliers
of America
147 Old Solomons Island Road, Suite 302
Annapolis, MD 21401
410-573-0400/Fax: 410-573-5001
www.wffsa.org

APPENDIX B-2
STATE FLOWER GROWERS
ASSOCIATIONS

Most states have a greenhouse growers
association or similar commercial floriculture
group. For information contact your State
Extension Specialist for Floriculture at the
Land Grant University in your state. Their
office will usually be found in the Department
of Horticulture.

Alabama Nurserymen's Association
Greenway Plants, Inc.
8170 Alabama High 9
Anniston, AL 36207
256-236-2233/Fax: 256-236-7218

Arkansas Greenhouse Growers Association
91 Snugg Circle
Mayflower, AR 72106
501-4705-0329

California Association of Flower
Growers & Shippers
2175 De La Cruz Blvd., Suite 1
Santa Clara, CA 95050
408-496-6187
pclinton@norcalflowers.org

California Cut Flower Commission
2339 Gold Meadow Way, Ste. 101
Gold River, CA 95670

Colorado Greenhouse Growers Association
7475 Dakin Street, Suite 540
Denver, CO 80221-6919
303-427-8132
www.cgga.org

Florida Nurserymen & Growers Association
1533 Park Center Drive
Orlando, FL 32835
407-295-7994
www.fnga.org

Georgia Flower Growers Association
P.O. Box 2945
LaGrange, CA 30241
706-845-0704
www.gaflowergrowers.org

Hawaii Tropical Flower Council
P.O. Box 4306
Hilo, HI 96720
808-959-3535

Society of Iowa Florists & Growers
48428 290th Avenue
Rolfe, IA 50581
712-848-3251

Kansas Greenhouse Growers Association
Dept. of Horticulture
Throckmorton Hall
Kansas State University
Manhattan, KS 66506
816-898-1807

Maine Florist & Growers Association
93 Water Street
Skowhegan, ME 04976
207-924-7102/800-531-0821

Michigan Floral Association
P.O. Box 24065
Lansing, MI 48909
517-394-2900/Fax: 517-394-3011

Minnesota Commercial Flowers Growers
Dept. of Hort. Science, University of MN
1970 Folwell Avenue
St. Paul, MN 55108
612-624-0736

New Hampshire Plant Growers' Association
56 Leavitt Road
Hampton, NH 03842
603-862-1074

North Carolina Commercial Flower Growers
Association
P.O. Box 52276
Raleigh, NC 27612
919-779-4618

Ohio Florists' Association
2130 Stella Court, Suite 200
Columbus, OH 43215
614-487-1117
www.ofa.org

Oklahoma Greenhouse Growers Association
400 North Portland
Oklahoma City, OK 73107
405-942-5276
ohic@ionet.net

Oregon Flower Growers Association
3626 N. Leverman
Portland, OR 97217
503-289-1500/Fax: 503-285-9833

Pennsylvania Flower Growers
8482 Red Haven Street
Fogelsville, PA 18051

South Carolina Greenhouse Growers
Stacy's Greenhouses
2121 Quarry Road
York, SC 29745
800-426-7980
timb@stacysgreenhouses.com

Tennessee Flower Growers Association
Dept. of Horticulture
2431 Center Drive, Room 252
University of Tennessee
Knoxville, TN 37996
865-974-1840

APPENDIX B-3 STATE FLORIST ASSOCIATIONS

Arkansas Florists Association
205 N. Springfield
P.O. Box 7
Plumberville, AR 72127
501-354-1160

California State Florist Association
1521 I Street
Sacramento, CA 95814
916-448-5266
www.cgfa.org

Connecticut Florists' Association
590 Main Street
Monroe, CT 06468
203-268-9000
ctflorists@aol.com

Illinois State Florists Association
1231 N. LaSalle Street
Ottawa, IL 61350
815-434-4732
www.illinoisflorist.org

State Florists of Assoc. of Indiana
317-996-2241

Society of Iowa Florists & Growers
48428 290th Avenue
Rolfe, IA 50581
712-848-3251

Kansas State Florists Association
204 N. Main
Hutchinson, KS 67501
316-662-6624

Louisiana State Florists Association
P.O. Box 15006
Baton Rouge, LA 70895
225-389-3129

Michigan Floral Association
P.O. Box 24065
Lansing, MI 48909
517-394-2900

Montana State Florists Association
P.O. Box 1456
Great Falls, MT 59403
406-452-6489

Nebraska Florists Society
1024 E. 14th Street
Fremont, NE 68025
402-721-0984

New York State Flower Industries
P.O. Box 440
Palatine Bridge, NY 13428
718-268-7717

North Central Florists Association
P.O. Box 46324
Eden Prairie, MN 55344
952-934-4505

Ohio Florists' Association
2130 Stella Court, Suite 200
Columbus, OH 43215
614-487-1117
www.ofa.org

Oklahoma State Florists Association
CS Box A0085
Oklahoma City, OK 73162
405-359-1112

Oregon Flower Growers
3624 N. Leverman
Portland, OR 97217
503-289-1500

Pennsylvania Flower Growers
8482 Redhaven Street
Fogelsville, PA 18051
814-726-3779

Rhode Island Florists Association
599 Broad Street
Cumberland, RI 02864
401-726-4643

Texas State Florists Association
P.O. Box 140255
Austin, TX 78714
512-834-0361
www.tsfa.org

Professional Florists Assoc. of Wisconsin
614 West Brown Deer Road
Milwaukee, WI 53217-1622
414-258-0804

APPENDIX B-4
DIRECTORIES

A membership directory and buyers guide is available from:
Association of Specialty Cut Flower Growers (ASCFG)
M.P.O. Box 268
Oberlin, OH 44074-0268
440-774-2887/Fax: 440-774-2435

Floral Membership Directory & Resource Guide (on disk)
($45 for PMA members) Training, programs and materials
Floral Marketing Division of the Produce Marketing Association
P.O. Box 6036
Newark, DE 19714-6036
302-738-7100
www.pma.com

A membership directory of wholesale florists and florist suppliers is available from
WF & FSA
147 Old Solmen's Island Road, Suite 302
Annapolis, MD 21401
703-242-7000
www.wffsa.org

APPENDIX B-5
REFERENCE BOOKS

Alberta Supernaturals by Buck Godwin, $8, including postage.
Olds College Bookstore
Olds College
Olds, AB, Canada TOM 1PO

Ball Culture Guide: The Encyclopedia of Seed Germination by Jim Nau, $49.95.
Ball Publishing
P.O. Box 9
Batavia, IL 60510-0009
630-208-9080
www.ballpublishing.com

Ball Field Guide to Diseases of Greenhouse Ornamentals by Margery L. Daughtrey and A.R. Chase, $66.95.
Ball Publishing
P.O. Box 9
Batavia, IL 60510-0009
630-208-9080
www.ballpublishing.com

Ball Floriculture Dictionary by Veronica Hoyos de Martens and M.L. Nydia Palma de Villarreal. Includes English-Spanish/Spanish-English with Spanish definitions. $29.95.
Ball Publishing
P.O. Box 9
Batavia, IL 60510-0009
630-208-9080
www.ballpublishing.com

Ball Perennial Manual:
Propagation and Production by Jim Nau,
$64.95.
Ball Publishing
P.O. Box 9
Batavia, IL 60510-0009
630-208-9080
www.ballpublishing.com

Ball Pest & Disease Manual by Charles C.
Powell and Richard K. Lindquist, $64.95.
Ball Publishing
P.O. Box 9
Batavia, IL 60510-0009
630-208-9080
www.ballpublishing.com

Ball Red Book, Vic Ball, editor. 16th edition.
The basic book on greenhouse growing written
for growers, $71.95.
Ball Publishing
P.O. Box 9
Batavia, IL 60510-0009
630-208-9080
www.ballpublishing.com

Care and Handling of Flowers and Plants by
C.L. Holstead, 1985. The Society of American
Florists (2 volumes).

Commercial Flower Forcing by A. Laurie,
D.C. Kiplinger, and K.S. Nelson.
McGraw-Hill, Inc.
1221 Avenue of the Americas
New York, NY 10020
800-262-4729

The Commercial Storage of Fruits, Vegetables,
and Florist and Nursery Stocks, Ag Handbook
66, 1990, $7.
USDA Agricultural Research
U.S. Government Printing Office
1305 SW. 1st
Portland, OR 97201
503-725-2300

Competitive Advantage by Michael E. Porter.
How to create and sustain a competitive
advantage.
Simon and Schuster
100 Front Street
Riverside, NJ 08075
ISBN 0684841460
800-223-2348

The Complete Book of Cut Flower Care by
M.J. Vaughan, 1988.
Timber Press
Portland, OR
503-227-2878

Control of Diseases on Commercial Outdoor
Flowers by Mary K. Hausbeck. North Central
Regional Extension Publication #491. $10
Publications Office
Cooperative Extension Service
Michigan State University
Room 10-B Agriculture Hall
East Lansing, MI 48824-1039
517-355-0240

Diseases and Pests of Ornamental Plants by
Pascal P. Pirone. Wiley-Interscience.

Diseases of Annuals and Perennials: A Ball Guide Identification and Control by A.R. Chase, Margery Daughtery and Gary W. Simone, 1995, $59.95
Ball Publishing
P.O. Box 9
Batavia, IL 60510-0009
708-208-9080
www.ballpublishing.com

Dried Fresh Flowers from Your Garden by Elizabeth Bullivant. A book written for hobbyists, $31.95.
Pelham Books/Stephen Greene Press
London, UK

Dry Kiln Operator's Manual, Agriculture Handbook #188. Useful for designing facilities for drying flowers.
Forest Service
U.S. Department of Agriculture

The Encyclopedia of Everlastings, The Complete Guide to Growing, Preserving, and Arranging Dried Flowers by Barbara Radcliffe. A book written for hobbyists.
Rogers; Weidenfeld & Nicholson

Everlasting Flowers for Pleasure and Profit by Jeannette Verhelst, $11.
Jeannette Verhelst
Box 178
Radville, SK, Canada, S0C 2G0

Floral & Nursery Times
P.O. Box 8470
Northfield, IL 60093
847-784-9797

From a Grower's Perspective: The Business of Growing Specialty Cut Flowers, proceedings of the 5th National Conference on Specialty Cut Flowers; 1992. Burlington, Vermont.
ASCFG
M.P.O. Box 268
Oberlin, OH 44074-0268
440-774-2887
www.ascfg.org

From a Grower's Perspective: The Business of Growing Specialty Cut Flowers, proceedings of the 6th National Conference on Specialty Cut Flowers; 1993. Overland Park, Kansas.
ASCFG
M.P.O. Box 268
Oberlin, OH 44074-0268
440-774-2887
www.ascfg.org

From a Grower's Perspective: The Business of Growing Specialty Cut Flowers, proceedings of the 7th National Conference on Specialty Cut Flowers; 1994. San Jose, CA.
ASCFG
M.P.O. Box 268
Oberlin, OH 44074-0268
440-774-2887
www.ascfg.org

Handling, Precooling, and Temperature Management of Cut Flower Crops for Truck Transportation by Roger E. Rij, James F. Thompson & Delbert S. Farham, 1979.
USDA-SEA AAT-W-5.

Holland Bulb Forcers Guide
by A.A. DeHertogh.
Ball Publishing
ISBN 90-9008455X
P.O. Box 9
Batavia, IL 60510-0009
630-208-9080
www.ballpublishing.com

Identification of Insects and Related Pests of Horticultural Plants-A Pictorial Guide, Ohio Florists Association; $25. Color pictures. #303
Ohio Florists Association
2130 Stella Ct.
Columbus, OH 43215-1033
614-487-1117
www.ofa.org

Kieft's Growing Manual by Kieft Bloemzaden BV; Blokker, Holland, $10. For annual, biennial, and perennial cutflowers and ornamental grasses grown from seed.
ASCFG
M.P.O. Box 268
Oberlin, OH 44074-0268
440-774-2887

Manual of Herbaceous Ornamental Plants by Steven M. Still.
Stipes Publishing Co.
202 West University
Champaign, IL 61820
217-356-8391

Manual of Woody Landscape Plants: Their Identification, Ornamental Characteristics, Culture, Propagation, and Uses by Michael A. Dirr.
Stipes Publishing Co.
202 West University
Champaign, IL 61820
217-356-8391

Ornamental Grasses by R. Grounds, Van Nostrand Reinhold, 1979.

Ornamental Grasses and Grasslike Plants by A.J. Oakes, Van Nostrand Reinhold, 1990, ISBN 0-442-23931-9; $68.95 approx.

Ornamental Grasses, The Amber Wave by Carole Ottesen; $29.95.
McGraw-Hill, Inc.
1221 Avenue of the Americas
New York, NY 10020
212-512-2000

Preserving Flowers & Foliage With Glycols & Dyes, a manual for the commercial producer by Mark Koch. 1995.
Robert Koch Industries
4770 Harback Road
Bennett, CO 80102
303-644-3763/Fax: 303-644-3045

Refrigeration and Controlled Atmosphere Storage for Horticultural Crops, Northeast Regional Agricultural Engineering Service, 123NRES, #22, $8.00
Cooperative Extension
152 Riley-Robb Hall
Cornell University
Ithaca, NY 14853
607-255-2080

Rodale's Illustrated Encyclopedia of Herbs
Rodale Press
33 East Minor Street
Emmaus, PA 18098-0099
610-967-8706

Specialty Cut Flowers by A. Armitage, 1994. The latest research based information on cut flower crops.
Timber Press
133 SW Second Avenue, Suite 540
Portland, OR 97204
503-277-2878

USDA-ARS Agricultural Handbook #66 by Fran Kolpack.
USDA-ARS-PQDI-HCQL
Building 002, Room 113
Beltsville, MD 20705
301-261-0025

Sources of Books

American Botanist Bookseller
P.O. Box 532
Chillicothe, IL 61253
309-274-5254

American Horticultural Society
Catalog of Garden Books
7931 East Boulevard Drive
Alexandria, VA 22308
800-777-7931
www.ahs.org

American Nurseryman Horticultural
Books, Videos &Software
77 W. Washington Street, Suite 2100
Chicago, IL 60602
800-621-5727 ext. 1

Ball Publishing
P.O. Box 9
Batavia, IL 60510-0009
630-208-9080
www.ballpublishing.com

Botanic Garden Crafters
Devonian Botanic Garden
University of Alberta
Hwy 60
Devon, AB, Canada
780-987-3054
www.discoveredmonton.com/devonion

Capability's Books
2379 Highway 46
Deer Park, WI 54007
800-247-8154

Rodale Inc.
33 East Minor Street
Emmaus, PA 18098-0099
610-967-8706
www.rodale.com

Storey Publishing
AICA Storey Book
105 Schoolhouse Road
Pownal, VT 05261
800-451-3522
www.storey.com

Timber Press
133 SW Second Avenue Ste. 450
Portland, OR 97204
503-227-2878
www.timberpress.com

APPENDIX B-6 MAGAZINES, BULLETINS AND NEWSLETTERS

Acres, U.S A.
P.O. Box 91299
Austin, TX 78709
512-892-4400
www.acaresusa.com

American Nurseryman
American Nurseryman's Publishing Co.
77 W. Washington Street, Ste. 2100
Chicago, IL 60602-2904
800-621-5727
www.amerinursery.com

American Vegetable Grower
This magazine offers articles on practices very
well suited to the field cut flower grower.
Meister Publishing Co.
37733 Euclid Avenue
Willoughby, OH 44094
440-942-2000
www.meisterpro.com

Back in Thyme
A bimonthly newsletter about heirloom flow-
ers, herbs and prairie plants.
Back in Thyme Publications
P.O. Box 963
Tonganoxie, KS 66086-0963
913-845-9309

The Business of Herbs
Northwind Publications
439 Ponderosa Way
Jemez Springs, NM 87025-8036
505-829-3448
herbbiz@aol.com

Canadian Florist Greenhouse & Nursery-Craft
Canada Section
Canadian magazine that has articles on pricing,
marketing, advertisements, classifieds.
Horticulture Publications Ltd.
3265 South Millway
Mississauga, ON, Canada LSL 2R3
905-820-3885/Fax: 905-820-3497
www.canadianflorist.com

Center for Alternative Plant & Animal Products
1970 Folwell Avenue
St. Paul, MN 55108
612-624-4217
www.capap.coafes.umn.edu

Center-Pivot-Irrigated Dry Edible Beans
(MF-999)
Department of Agricultural Economics
Manhattan, KS
785-532-6001

Commercial Outdoor Cuts For the South
Central United States
John Dole and Bear Creek Farms Inc.
1123 N. Manning
Stillwater, OK 74075
405-372-1493

Country Folks Grower
P.O. Box 121
Palatine Bridge, NY 13428
518-673-3237

Cut & Dried
222 Argyle Avenue
Delhi, ON, Canada N4B 2Y2
800-265-2827 ext. 249
www.annexweb.com

Cut Flowers: Production
C. Kopolow, May 1991, 16 pages.
Send a self-addressed gummed label to:
Agri-Topics
National Agricultural Library, Room 111
10301 Baltimore Blvd.
Beltsville, MD 20705
301-504-5755

Dying and Preserving Flowers and Foliages
Mark Koch.
Robert Koch Industries
4770 Harback Road
Bennett, CO 80102
303-644-3763/Fax: 303-644-3045

FloraCulture International
P.O. Box 9
Batavia, IL 60510
630-208-9080
www.growertalks.com

Floral & Nursery Times
P.O. Box 8470
Northfield, IL 60093
847-784-9797

Floral Management
1601 Duke Street
Alexandria, VA 22314
800-336-4743
www.afs.com

Floral Mass Marketing
205 W. Wacker Drive, Suite 1040
Chicago, IL 60606
800-732-4581
www.flowersnews.com

Floral Retailing
This is a free monthly publication. Covers all aspects of the supermarket floral department.
Vance Publishiing
10901 W. 84th Terrace
Lenexa, KS 66214
800-255-5113

The Florist
33031 Schoolcraft Road
Livonia, MI 48150-1618
800-383-4383
www.ftdassociation.org

Florist & Grower
1296 Hamilton Street
Springfield, OR 97477
541-686-9561

Florist Review
This magazine keeps you in touch with the retail trade.
Florist Publishing Co.
36410 SW Plass
Topeka, KS 66611
785-266-0888
www.floristsreview.com

Flowers &
Published monthly by Teleflora for retailers in "the business of flowers".
Teleflora
P.O. Box 16029
N. Hollywood, CA 91615-9871
800-321-2665

Forcing Flower Bulbs
Includes information on growing bulbs for cut-flowers.
International Flower Bulb Center
P.O. Box 172
Parklaan 5
2180 AD Hillegom
The Netherlands
718-693-5400/718-693-7780

GMPro Magazine
P.O. Box 1868
Fort Worth, TX 76101
800-433-5612
www.greenbeam.com

Greenhouse Business
P.O. Box 698
Park Ridge, IL 60068-0698
847-870-1576

Greenhouse Canada
222 Argyle Avenue
Delhi, ON, Canada N4B 2Y2
519-582-2521
www.annexweb.com

Greenhouse Product News
380 E. Northwest Highway
Des Plaines, IL 60016
800-220-7851
www.onhort.com

GrowerTalks
P.O. Box 9
Batavia, IL 60510
630-208-9080
www.ballpublishing.com

Growing Edge
P.O. Box 1027
Corvallis, OR 97339
541-757-8477
www.growingedge.com

Growing for Market
Lynn Byczynski; editor. A monthly journal of news and ideas for market gardeners. Articles on crop culture, handling, marketing, merchandising and profiles of successful growers provide subscribers with timely information and ideas, $24.
Growing for Market
P.O. Box 3747
Lawrence, KS 66046
Phone/FAX: 913-841-2559

The Herbal Connection and
The Herbal Green Pages
Maureen Rogers
P.O. Box 245
Silver Spring, PA 17575-0245
717-393-3295
www.herbworld.com

HortIdeas
750 Black Lick Road
Gravel Switch, KY 40328
606-332-7606
www.users.mis.net/~gwill

Irrigation Management Series
Cooperative Extension Service
Kansas State University

NMProMagazine
P.O. Box 1868
Fort Worth, TX 76101
800-433-5612
www.greenbeam.com

Peonies
J. MacLean and S. Whitmore, n.d., 4 pages.
Send a self-addressed gummed label to:
Agri-Topics
National Agricultural Library, Room 111
10301 Baltimore Blvd.
Beltsville, MD 20705
301-344-3355

Small Farm Center News
#1 Shields Avenue
University of California
Davis, CA 95616
530-752-8136
www.sfc.ucdavis.edu

Small Farm Today
3903 W. Ridge Trail Road
Clark, MO 65243
573-687-3525
www.smallfarmtoday.com

Small-Scale Agriculture Today
Ag Box 2244
Washington, DC 20250-2244
202-401-1805

Successful Farming
1716 Locust Street LS 442
Des Moines, IA 50309
515-284-2802
www.agriculture.com

Super Floral
10901 W. 84th Terrace, Suite 200
Lenexa, KS 66214
800-255-5113
www.superfloral.com

The USDA issues bi-weekly reports on cut-flower prices in various centers across the country. Available from:
Federal-State Market News
630 Sansome Street, Rm. 727
San Francisco, CA 94111

APPENDIX B-7 WEBSITES

Aggiehorticulture (Texas)
http://128.194.43.18/
http://aggie-horticulture.tamu.edu/

Aphis
http://www.aphis.usda.gov/

Entomology Index of Internet Resources
http://www.public.iastate.edu/
~entomology/Resourcelist.html

Flora-Source
http://www.flora-source.com

Grower Talks and Floriculture Home Page
http://www.growertalks.com

Information Services for Agriculture
Home Page
http://www.aginfo.com

Society of American Florists
http://www.safnow.org

Texas Plant Disease Handbook
http://cygnus.tamu.edu

Weather Forecasts-Local and National
http://www.mit.edu:8001/usa.html

APPENDIX B-8
SUPPLIERS OF
GENERAL MATERIALS

All Hort Systems, Inc.
P.O. Box 21554
Oklahoma City, OK 73156
800-242-3980/Fax: 405-751-4307

American Plant Products
9200 Northwest 10th Street
Oklahoma City, OK 73127
405-787-4833/Fax: 405-789-2352
www.americanplant.com

B.W.I. Springfield
P.O. Box 2208
Springfield, MO 65801
417-881-3003/Fax: 417-881-7055

Ball Seed Company
622 Town Road
West Chicago, IL 60185-2698
630-231-3500/Fax: 630-231-8918
www.ballseed.com

Dakota Plastics
P.O. Box 52
Watertown, SD 57201
605-886-6851

Gard'N-Wise Distributors
1515 E. 29th Street N.
Wichita, KS 67219
316-838-1474/Fax: 316-838-6104
www.gardnwise.com

Gempler's
Crop Management Supplies
P.O. Box 328
Belleville, WI 53508
800-382-8473/Fax: 800-551-1128
www.gemplers.com

Fred C. Gloeckner & Co.
600 Mamaroneck Avenue
Harrison, NY 10528
914-698-2300/Fax: 914-698-0848

Hummert International
4500 Earth City Expwy
Earth City, MO 63045
314-506-4500
www.hummert.com

ITML Texan Inc.
501 Precision Drive
Waco, TX 76710
254-751-1300

Henry F. Michell Co.
P.O. Box 60160
King of Prussia, PA 19406-0160
610-265-4200/Fax: 610-265-4208

Minnesota Distributing & Mfg. Inc.
1500 Jackson Street, NE
Minneapolis, MN 55413
612-781-6068/Fax: 612-781-8693

National Nursery Products
4950 Wells Drive
Roeland Park, KS 66205
913-362-0503/Fax:913-362-2569

Novartis Seed Co.
5300 Katrine
Downers Grove, IL 60515-4095
800-323-7253/Fax: 708-969-6373
www.novartis.com

Professional Turf Specialties
Lees Summit, MO 64004
816-257-2527

TENAX Corp
4800 E. Monument Street
Baltimore, MD 21205
800-356-8495/Fax: 301-725-0146
www.tenax.com

Tobin/Standard Seed Co.
931 West 8th Street
Kansas City, MO 64101
816-842-3838/Fax: 816-842-9809

United Greenhouse Systems
708 Washington Street
Edgerton, WI 53534
800-433-6834/Fax: 608-884-6137

Westcan Seed
P.O. Box 5466 Station A
Calgary AB Canada T2H 1X8
403-279-5168/Fax: 403-236-0854

Westgro Horticultural Supplies, Inc.
1557 Hastings Crescent SE
Calgary, AB, Canada T2G 4C8
403-287-3988 or 800-661-2991
Fax: 403-243-7470

Wheeler Mktg
487 S. Park Blvd.
Glen Ellyn, IL 60137
630-790-3600/Fax: 630-858-4100

APPENDIX B-9
CUT FLOWER SEED SUPPLIERS

Alberta Nurseries & Seeds Ltd.
Box 20
Bowden, AB, Canada T0M 0K0
403-224-3544/Fax: 403-224-2455
www.gardenersweb.com

W. Atlee Burpee Co.
300 Park Avenue
Warminster, PA 18991-0001
215-674-4900/800-888-1447/Fax: 800-487-5530
www.burpee.com

Ball Seed Co.
622 Town Road
West Chicago, IL 60185-2698
630-231-3500/Fax: 630-231-3605
www.ballseed.com

Ball Superior
59 Bramalea Road, Suite 200
Brampton, ON, Canada L6T 2W4
416-278-5201

Dacha Barinka
46232 Strathcona Road
Chilliwack, BC, Canada V2P 3T2
604-792-0957

Dominion Seed House
Box 2500
Georgetown, ON, Canada L7G 5L6
905-873-3037/Fax: 800-282-5746
www.dominionseed-house.com

Express Seed Co.
300 Artino Drive
Oberlin, OH 44074
800-221-3838/Fax: 216-774-2728
www.expressseed.com

Gardens North
5984 Third Line Road North
RR #3
North Gower, ON, Canada K0A 2T0
613-489-0065

Germania Seed Co.
5978 N.W. Hwy
Chicago, IL 60631
773-631-6631/Fax: 773-631-4449
www.germaniaseed.com

Harris Seeds
P.O. Box 24966
Rochester, NY 14624
800-544-7938
www.harrisseeds.com

JVK
P.O. Box 910
1894 Seventh Street
St. Catharines, ON, Canada L2R 6Z4
905-641-5599/Fax: 905-684-6260
www.jvk.net

Jelitto Perennial Seeds
125 Chenoweth Ln.
Louisville, KY 40207
502-895-0807/Fax: 502-895-3934
www.jelitto.com

Johnny's Select Seeds
Foss Hill Road
Albion, ME 04910-9731
207-437-4301/Fax: 207-437-2165
www.johnnyseeds.com

Leen de Mos
P.O . Box 54-2690 AB's
Gravenzade
The Netherlands

McFayden Seed Co. Ltd.
30-9th Street, Suite 200
Brandon, MB, Canada R7A 6N4
www.mcfayden.com

Modena Seed Company, Inc.
5727 Mission Street
San Francisco, CA 94112
415-585-2324/Fax: 415-585-6820

Novartis Seed Co.
5300 Katrine
Downers Grove, IL 60515
630-969-6300/Fax: 630-969-6373
www.novartis.com

OSC Seeds
P.O. Box 7
Waterloo, ON, Canada N2J 3Z6
519-886-0557/Fax: 519-886-0605
www.oscseeds.com

Park Seed-Wholesale
Cokesbury Road, Hwy 254
Greenwood, SC 29647-0001
800-845-3366/Fax: 803-223-6999
www.parkwholesale.com

Penn State Seed Company
Rt 309, Box 390
Dallas, PA 18612
570-675-8585
pennseed@epix.net

Rawlinson Garden Seed
1979 Rt. 2
Sheffieldd, NB, Canada E3A 8H9
506-446-3882/Fax: 506-357-2256

Richters
357 Hwy 47
Goodwood, ON, Canada L0C 1A0
905-640-6677/Fax: 905-640-6641
email: orderdesk@richters.com
www.richters.com

Stirling Perennials
18638 Kent Bridge Road
Morpeth, ON, Canada N0P 1X0
519-674-0571

Stokes
39 James Street
P.O. Box 10
St. Catharines, ON, Canada L2R 6R6
905-688-4300/Fax: 905-684-8411
www.stokeseeds.com

Stokes Seeds Inc.
P.O. Box 548
Buffalo, NY 14240-0548
800-263-7233/Fax: 716-695-9649
www.stokeseeds.com

Westcan Seed
P.O. Box 5466 Station A
Calgary AB Canada T2H 1X8
403-279-5168/Fax: 403-236-0854

APPENDIX B-10 SUPPLIERS OF PLUGS, TRANSPLANTS & BULBS

Ball Seed Company
622 Town Road
West Chicago, IL 60185-2698
630-231-3500/Fax: 630-231-8918
www.ballseed.com

Ball Superior
59 Bramalea Road, Suite 200
Brampton, ON, Canada L6T 2W4
905-791-3995
www.ballseed.com

Leo Berbee Bulb Co Inc.
P.O. Box 670
Marysville, OH 43040
937-642-0511

Bluebird Nursery, Inc.
P.O. Box 460, 519 Bryan Street
Clarkson, NE 68629
800-356-9164/Fax: 402-892-3738
www.bluebirdnursery.com

Bradbury Farms
19810 W. Bradbury Road
Turlock, CA 95380
209-668-7584/Fax: 209-668-7928
bradbury@sonnet.com

Brent & Becky's Bulbs
7463 Heath Trail
Gloucester, VA 23061
804-693-3966/Fax: 804-693-9436
www.brentandbeckys.com

Caprice Farm Nursery
15425 SW Pleasant Hill Rd
Sherwood, OR 97140
503-625-7241
www.capricefarm.com

Corn Hill Nursery Ltd
RR 5, Route 890
Petitcodiac, NB, Canada EOA 2H0

Doornbosch Bulb Co.
132 South St
Hackensack, NJ 07601
800-992-2852/Fax: 201-489-6809

Eagle Lake Nurseries Ltd
Box 2340
Strathmore, AB, Canada T1P 1K3
403-934-3622
www.eaglelakenurseries.com

Paul Ecke Ranch
P.O. Box 230488
Encinitas, CA 92023
800-468-3253
www.eckeranch.com

Florasource Ltd.
714-498-1131/Fax: 714-498-1196

Fred C. Gloeckner & Co.
600 Mamaroneck Avenue
Harrison, NY 10528
914-698-2300/Fax: 914-698-0848

A.M. Grootendorst, Inc. Nurseries
2450 Red Arrow Highway
P.O. Box 787
Benton Harbor, MI 49023
616-422-2411

Headstart Cut Flower Plugs
4860 Monterey Road
Gilroy, CA 95020
408-842-3030/Fax: 408-842-3224
www.headstartnursery.com

Heschke Gardens
11583 77th St S
Hastings, MN 55033
651-459-8381

Homestead Nurseries Ltd
33973 Cyril Street
Abbotsford, BC, Canada BQS 2E8
604-854-6601

Jackson & Perkins
P.O. Box 9100
Medford, OR 97501
541-864-2000/Fax: 541-776-2155
www.jacksonandperkins.com

Links Greenhouse
N9905 Link Road
Portage, WI 53901
608-742-6758

McFayden Seed Co. Ltd.
30-9th Street, Suite 200
Brandon, MB, Canada R7A 6N4
www.mcfayden.com

Mount Arbor Nurseries
P.O. Box129
Shenandoah, IA 51601
712-246-4250

Pepieniere Charlevoix
391 Boulevard Maillou
La Malbaie, Quebec, Canada G5A 1M6
418-439-4646

Piroche Plants Inc
20542 McNeil Rd
Pitt Meadows, BC, Canada V3Y 1Z1
604-465-7101

M. Putzer Hornby Nursery Ltd
7314 Sixth Line
Hornby, ON, Canada L0P 1E0
905-878-7226

L.J. Rambo Wholesale Nurseries
10495 Baldwin Rd
Bridgman, MI 49106
616-465-6771

Reath's Nursery
County Road 577 N-195
Vulcan, MI 49892
906-563-9777
www.reathsnursery.com

Sarcoxie Nurseries
1510 Joplin St
Sarcoxie, MO 64862
417-548-3512

Sheridan Nurseries
RR4 Tenth Line
Georgetown, ON, Canada L7G 4S7
905-873-1475

Sherman Nursery Co
P.O. Box 579
Charles City, IA 50616-0579
800-747-5980/Fax: 515-228-5980
www.sales@shermannursery.com

Stuifbergen Bulb Export Co.
1645 SE Decker Street
Lees Summit, MO 64063
816-524-0840/Fax: 816-524-0978

Stutzman Greenhouse
6709 W Hwy 61
Hutchinson, KS 67501
800-279-4505/Fax: 316-662-4211
www.stutzmans.com

Sunbay Farms
Watsonville, CA
831-724-7577/Fax 831-724-5829

Sunny Border Nursery
Box 483
Kensington, CT 06037
860-828-0321
www.sunnyborder.com

T & T Seeds Ltd.
Box 1710
Winnipeg, MB, Canada R3C #P6

Vandenberg Bulb Company
49 Black Meadow Road
Chester, NY 10918-0532
914-469-9161/Fax: 914-469-2015

Van Noort Bulb Co. Ltd.
417 Winona Road N.
Stoney Creek, ON, Canada L8E 5E4
905-643-2152/Fax: 905-643-1844
or
22264 Highway 10 North
Langley, BC, Canada V3A 6H4
604-888-6555/Fax: 604-888-7640

Andre Viette Farm and Nursery
P.O. Box 1109
Fisherville, VA 22939
540-943-2315
www.viette.com

Walters Gardens
Box 137
Zeeland, MI 49464
616-772-4697

The Waushara Gardens
N5491 5th Drive
Plainfield, WI 54966
715-335-4462

Westcan Seed
Box 5466 Station A.
Calgary AB, Canada T2H 1X8
403-279-5168/Fax: 403-236-0854

APPENDIX B-11 PLANT SUPPLIER DIRECTORIES

Anderson Horticultural Library
3675 Arboretum Drive, P.O. Box 39
Chanhassen, MN 55317-0039
612-443-2440
www.arboretum.umn.edu

Directory of North American Nurseries
http://plantinfo.umn,edu

Gardening by Mail
P.O. Box 1338
Sebastopol, CA 95473
707-829-9189
www.virtualgarden.com

Gardener's Source Guide
P.O. Box 206
Gowanda, NY 14070-0206

GMPro Buyers' Guide
P.O. Box 1868
Fort Worth, TX 76101
612-443-2440

The Herbal Green Pages $45
P.O. Box 245
Silver Spring, PA 17575
717-393-3295
www.herbworld.com

Plant Source Journal
606 110th Avenue NE, Suite 301
Bellevue, WA 98004
425-454-7733
www.psj.linnaeus.com

SAF Buyer Guide
1601 Duke Street
Alexandria, VA 22314-3406
800-336-4743

APPENDIX B-12
SUPPLIERS OF SOLUBLE, ORGANIC FERTILIZERS

American Meat Protein (AMPC)
2621 E. Mamie Eisenhower Drive
Boone, IA 50036
515-432-8021
www.americanprotein.com

ARBICO
P.O. Box 4247 CRB
Tucson, AZ 85738-1247
800-827-2847/Fax: 520-825-2038
www.arbico@aol.com

ATTRA
Box 3657
Fayetteville, AR 72702
800-346-9140
(Request the Information Package "Organic Fertilizers" for sources.)
www.attra.org

California Spray Dry Company
P.O. Box 5035
Stockton, CA 95205
209-948-0209

ENP Inc.
P.O. Box 618
Mendota, IL 61342
800-255-4906/Fax: 815-538-6981
www.fertilegrower.com

APPENDIX B-13
SYNTHETIC, ORGANIC & BIOLOGICAL CONTROLS

American Insectaries
30805 Rodriquez Road
Escondido, CA 92036
760-751-1436
www.betterbugs.com

Applied Bionomics
11074 West Soanich Road
Sidney, BC, Canada V8L 5P5
250-656-2123

ARBICO
P.O. Box 4247
Tucson AZ 85738-1247
520-825-9785/Fax: 520-825-2038
www.aribico@aol.com

ATTRA
Box 3657
Fayetteville, AR 72702
800-346-9140
(Request the Information Package "Integrated Pest Management" for sources.)
www.attra.org

BioLogic Company
P.O. Box 177-BG
Willow Hill, PA 17271
717-349-2789
www.biologicco.com

Brinkman B.V.
The Netherlands
31-174811333

FMC Corp. Chemical Group
1735 Market Street
Philadelphia, PA 19103
215-299-6661/Fax: 215-299-6256
www.chem.fmc.com

Gerhart Inc.
North Ridgeville, OH
216-327-8056

Great Lakes IPM
10220 Church Road, NE
Vestaburg, MI 48891
517-268-5693 or 517-268-5911
www.greatlakesipm.com

Hydro-Gardens, Inc.
P.O. Box 25845
Colorado Springs, CO 80936
719-495-2266/Fax: 719-531-0506
www.hydro-gardens.com

IPM Laboratories Inc.
P.O. Box 300
Locke, NY 13092-0300
315-497-2063/Fax: 315-497-3129
www.ipmlab.com

JRM Chemical Inc.
15663 Neo Parkway
Cleveland, OH 44128
800-962-4010
www.soilmoist.com

Kentucky Garden Supply
731 Red Mile Road
Lexington KY 40504
859-254-1355

Koppert B.V.
The Netherlands
31-189140444

Necessary Organics
8906 Wentworth Avenue South
Minneapolis, MN 55420
952-881-5535
www.intagra.com or www.concerngarden.com

Novartis
P.O. Box 2430
Oxnard, CA 93034
805-986-8265/Fax: 805-986-8267
www.novartisflowers.com

Organic Control Inc. /ORCON
5132 Venice Blvd.
Los Angles, CA 90019
323-937-7444/Fax: 323-937-0123

Phero Tech Inc.
7572 Progress Way
Delta, BC, Canada V4G 1E9
604-940-9944/Fax: 604-940-9433
www.pherotech.com

Praxis
2723 116th Avenue
Allegan, MI 49010
616-673-2793
praxis@allegan.net
www.praxis-ibc.com

Research Organics Inc.
4353 E. 49th
Cleveland, OH 44125
216-883-8025/Fax: 216-883-1576
www.resorg.com

Richters
357 Hwy 47
Goodwood, ON, Canada LOC IAO
905-640-6677
www.richters.com

Valent BioSciences Corp.
870 Technology Way
Libertyville, IL 60064
800-323-9597/Fax: 708-937-3679

Whitmire Research Laboratories
3568 Tree Court Industrial Blvd.
St. Louis, MO 63122
800-325-3668/Fax: 314-225-3739
www.wmmg.com

APPENDIX B-14
MULCHES

AEP Industries Inc.
125 Phillips Avenue
South Hackensack, NJ 07606
201-641-6600/Fax: 201-807-2447
www.aepinc.com

Ben Meadows Co.
3589 Broad Street
Atlanta, GA 30341
770-662-5771

Buckeye Tractor Co.
P.O. Box 123
Columbus Grove, OH 45830
800-526-6791/Fax: 419-659-2082

Carolina Seeds
P.O. Box 2658
Boon, NC 28607
828-297-7333/Fax: 828-297-3888
www.carolinaseeds.com

Chesmore Seed Co.
P.O. Box 8368
5030 Hwy. 36
St Joseph, MO 64508
816-279-0865/Fax: 816-232-6134

Control Plastics Inc.
37625 Sycamore Street
Newark, CA 94560
800-600-2010/Fax: 510-742-0093
cplastics@pacbell.net

Delhi Foundry and Farm Machinery Ltd.
171 King Street
West Delhi, ON, Canada N4B 1X9
519-582-2770/Fax: 519-582-4442
www.delhifoundry.com

Excelsior Plastics
201 S. McCleary Rd
Excelsior Springs, MO 64024
816-499-3648

Forestry Suppliers
P.O. Box 8397
Jackson, MS 39284-8397
800-647-5368
www.forestry-suppliers.com

Harmony Farm Supply
3244 Hwy. 116 No
Sebastopol, CA 95472
707-823-9125/Fax: 707-823-1734
www.harmonyfarm.com

Holland Transplanter Co.
P.O. Box 1527
Holland, MI 49422-1527
616-392-3579/Fax: 616-392-7996
www.transplanter.com

Hummert International
4500 Earth City Expressway
Earth City, MO 63045
314-506-4500
www.hummert.com

Mechanical Transplanter Co.
1150 S. Central Street
Holland, MI 49423-5230
800-757-5268/Fax: 616-396-3619
www.mechanicaltransplanter.com

Peaceful Valley Farm Supply
P.O. Box 2209
Grass Valley, CA 95945
530-272-4769
www.growerorganic.com

Rochelle Plastic Films Inc.
P.O. Box 606
Hwy. 38 West
Rochelle, IL 61068
815-562-7848/Fax: 815-562-7849

Tenax Geotenax Corp.
4800 E. Monument Street
Baltimore, MD 21205
800-356-8495/Fax: 410-522-7015
www.tenax.com

Tredegar Industries Inc.
1100 Boulder Pkwy.
Richmond, VA 23225
804-330-1223/Fax: 804-330-1201
www.tredegar.com

Tyco Plastics
18901 E. Railroad St
City Of Industry, CA 91748
800-654-8110/Fax: 626-912-6872
www.tycoplastics.com

APPENDIX B-15 MULCH REMOVAL EQUIPMENT

Buckeye Tractor Co.
P.O. Box 123
Columbus Grove, OH 45830
800-526-6791/Fax: 419-659-2082

Holland Transplanter Co.
P.O. Box 1527
Holland, MI 49422-1527
616-392-3579/Fax: 616-392-7996
www.transplanter.com

Market Farm Implement
257 Fawn Hill Road
Friedens, PA 15541
814-443-1931
www.marketfarm.com

Mechanical Transplanter Co.
1150 S. Central Street
Holland, MI 49423-5230
800-757-5268/Fax: 616-396-3619
www.mechanicaltransplanter.com

Rain-Flo Irrigation
884 Center Church Road
East Earl, PA 17519
717-445-6976/Fax: 717-445-8304

Reddick Fumigants Inc.
P.O. Box 391
Williamston, NC 27892
800-358-8837/Fax: 919-792-4615
vlily@williamstonnc.com

APPENDIX B-16 IRRIGATION EQUIPMENT

Agro Dynamics
10 Alivn Ct.
East Brunswick, NJ 08816
800-872-2476/Fax: 908-257-9770
www.agrodynamics@ecoscience.com

American Plant Products
9200 NW 10th
Oklahoma City, OK 73127
405-787-4833/Fax: 405-789-2352
www.americanplant.com

Antelco Micro Irrigation
878 Waterway Place
Longwood, FL 32750
407-331-0699/Fax: 407-331-0169
www.antelco.com

Chapin Watermatics Inc.
P.O. Box 490
740 Water Street
Watertown, NY 13601-0490
315-782-1170/Fax: 315-782-1490
www.chapindrip.com

Chesmore Seed Co.
P.O. Box 8368
5030 Hwy 36
St Joseph, MO 64508
816-279-0865/Fax: 816-232-6134

Dramm Corp.
P.O. Box 1960
Manitowoc, WI 54221-1960
920-684-0227/Fax: 920-684-4499
www.dramm.com

Hydro-Gardens Inc.
P.O. Box 25845
Colorado Springs, CO 80936
800-634-6362/Fax: 719-531-0506
www.hydro-gardens.com

Market Farm Implement
257 Fawn HollowRoad
Friedens, PA 15541
814-443-1931
www.marketfarm.com

Michigan Orchard Supply
07078-73½ Street
South Haven, MI 49090
800-637-6426/Fax: 616-637-7419

Rain-Flo Irrigation
884 Center Church Road
East Earl, PA 17519
717-445-6976/Fax: 717-445-8304

Roberts Irrigation Products Inc.
700 Rancheros Drive
San Marcos, CA 92069-3007
760-744-4511/Fax: 760-744-0914
www.robertsirrigation.com

T-Systems International Inc.
7545 Carroll Road
San Diego, CA 92121
800-765-1860/Fax: 619-578-2344
www.tsystemsinternational.com

Trickle- Eez Co.
3550 Chambersburg Road
Biglerville, PA 17307-9542
717-337-3030/Fax: 717-337-1785
www.trickl-eez.com

APPENDIX B-17 SUBIRRIGATION EQUIPMENT

Bouldin & Lawson Inc.
P.O. Box 7177
McMinnville, TN 37110-7177
800-443-6398/Fax: 615-668-3209
www.bouldinlawson.com

Larchmont Engineering and Irrigation Inc.
11 Larchmont Lane
Lexington, MA 02173
978-250-1260

Tico Mfg. Inc.
Rt. 13, Box 173
Williamstown, NY 13493
315-964-2214/Fax:0315-964-2299

APPENDIX B-18
MOISTURE GAUGES
AND METERS

Automata Inc.
104 New Mohawk Road, Suite A
Nevada City, CA 95959
800-994-0380
www.automata-inc.com

Larchmont Engineering and Irrigation Inc.
11 Larchmont Lane
Lexington, MA 02173
978-250-1260

Spectrum Technologies Inc.
23839 W. Andrew Road
Plainfield, IL 60544
815-436-4440/Fax: 815-436-4460
www.specmeters.com

APPENDIX B-19
FROST PROTECTION

AGTROL Chemical Products
7322 Southwest Freeway, Suite 1400
Houston, TX 77074
713-995-0111/Fax: 713-995-9505
www.agtrol.com

Chesmore Seed Co.
P.O. Box 8368
5030 Hwy 36
St Joseph, MO 64508
816-279-0865/Fax: 816-232-6134

ENP Inc.
Box 618
Mendota, IL 61342
800-255-4906/Fax: 815-538-6981

APPENDIX B-20
FROST PROTECTION-
FOG

Antelco Micro Irrigation
878 Waterway Place
Longwood, FL 32750
407-331-0699/Fax: 407-331-0169
www.antelco.com

APPENDIX B-21
COVERINGS AND
WINDBREAKS

American Agrifabrics
1282 Old Alpharetta Road
Alpharetta, GA 30202
770-663-7600/Fax: 770-663-7690

Ken-Bar Inc.
P.O. Box 504
Reading, MA 01867-0704
617-944-0003/Fax: 617-944-1055

Market Farm Implement
257 Fawn Hollow Road
Friedens, PA 15541
814-443-1931
www.marketfarm.com

Mechanical Transplanter Co.
1150 S. Central Street
Holland, MI 49423-5230
800-757-5268/Fax: 616-396-3619
www.mechanicaltransplanter.com

Rain-Flo Irrigation
884 Center Church Road
East Earl, PA 17519
717-445-6976/Fax: 717-445-8304

Stokes Seed Inc.
39 James Street
St Catharines, ON, Canada L2R 6R6
800-263-7233/Fax: 716-695-9649
www.stokeseeds.com

Structures Unlimited Inc.
2122 Whitfield Park Avenue
Sarasota, FL 34243
800-541-8129/Fax: 941-756-9860

Tenax Corp.
4800 E. Monument Street
Baltimore, MD 21205
800-356-8495/Fax: 410-522-7015
www.tenax.com

Tyco Plastics
18901 E. Rail Road Street
City of Industry, CA 91748
800-654-8119/Fax: 626-912-6872
www.tycoplastics.com

APPENDIX B-22
SEEDING AND PLANTING
EQUIPMENT

Delhi Foundry and Farm Machinery Ltd.
171 King Street
West Delhi, ON, Canada N4B 1X9
519-582-2770/Fax: 519-582-4442
www.delhifoundry.com

Earthway Products
P.O. Box 547
Briston, IN 46507
800-464-3960

Gearmore Inc.
13740 Magnolia Avenue
Chino, CA 91710
909-548-4848/Fax: 909-548-4747

KPR Inc.
P.O. Box 608
Wendell, ID 83355-0608
208-536-6601/Fax: 208-536-6695
www.kprincorp.com

Market Farm Implement
257 Fawn Hollow Road
Friedens, PA 15541
814-443-1931
www.marketfarm.com

McConnell Manufacturing Co., Inc.
P.O. Box 269
Prattsburgh, NY 14873-0269
607-522-3701/Fax: 607-522-4100

Rain-Flo Irrigation
884 Center Church Road
East Earl, PA 17519
717-445-6976/Fax: 717-445-8304

Rispens Seeds Inc.
P.O. Box 310
Beecher, IL 60401
708-474-0241/Fax: 708-474-4127
www.rispensseeds.com

Siegers Seed Co.
8265 Felch Street
Zeeland, MI 49464
800-962-4999/Fax: 616-772-0333
www.siegers.com

Solex Corp.
P.O. Box 490
Dixon, CA 95620
707-678-5533/Fax: 800-248-6651
www.solexcorp.com

Timm Enterprises Ltd.
P.O. Box 157
Oakville, On, Canada L6J 4Z5
905-878-4244/Fax: 905-878-7888

Triangle M Equipment Ltd.
309 N. Polk
Morocco, IN 47963
219-285-2377/Fax: 219-285-6115

APPENDIX B-23
HAND-HELD HOES

Gardener's Supply Company
Wholesale Department
128 Intervale Road
Burlington, VT 05401
802-660-3506
www.gardeners.com

Langenbach
P.O. Box 453
Blairstown, NJ 07825
973-875-1475

Smith-Hawkins
35 Corte Madera
Mill Valley, CA 94941
415-381-1800
www.smmithandhawkins.com

APPENDIX B-24
WHEEL HOES

Dalton, Cooper and Gates Corp.
215 N. Main Street
Freeport, NY 11520
516-378-2190

Johnny's Selected Seeds
Foss Hill Road
Albion, ME 04910
207-437-9294
www.johnnyseeds.com

Market Farm Implement
257 Fawn Hollow Road
Friedens, PA 15541
814-443-1931
www.marketfarm.com

Peaceful Valley Farm Supply
P.O. Box 2209
Grass Valley, CA 95945
530-272-4769
www.growerorganic.com

Smallholding Supplies
Burcott, Wells, Somerset
BA5 1NQ Great Britain
Tel: 011-0749-72127

Smith-Hawkins
35 Corte Madera
Mill Valley, CA 94941
415-381-1800
www.smithandhawkins.com

Valley Oak Tool Company
P.O. Box 1225
Chico, CA 95927
530-342-6188

APPENDIX B-25
REAR-TINE TILLERS/
WALKING TRACTORS

BCS
P.O. Box 1739
Matthews, NC 28106
704-846-1040

Ferrari Tractor, C.I.E.
P.O. Box 1045
Gridley, CA 95948
530-846-6401
www.approtechag.com

Gravley
1 Gravely Lane
Clemons, NC 27012
336-766-4721

Mainline of North America
81 US Rt 40
London, OH 43140
740-852-9733

APPENDIX B-26
MULTI-ROW ROTOTILLERS

Market Farm Implement
257 Fawn Hollow Road
Friedens, PA 15541
814-443-1931
www.marketfarm.com

Mitchell Equipment, Inc.
10784 Industrial Parkway
Marysville, OH 43040
614-873-4620
www.multivator.com

Timm Enterprises, Ltd.
P.O. Box 157
Oakville, ON Canada L6J 4Z5
905-878-4244/Fax: 905-878-7888

APPENDIX B-27
SPECIALIZED
CULTIVATORS

Bezzerides Brothers, Inc.
P.O. Box 211
Orosi, CA 93647
209-528-3011
http://bezweb.lightspeed.net/~bezzbros

Budding Weeder Co.
7015 Hammond
Dutton, MI 49316
616-698-8613

Bush-Hog/Lilliston
P.O. Box 1039
Selma, AL 36702-1039
334-874-2700
www.bushhog.com

Friday Tractor, Inc.
69226 CR 687
Hartford, MI 49057

Lely Agricultural Implements-USA
P.O. Box 1060
Wilson, NC 27894-1060
252-291-7050

Market Farm Implement
257 Fawn Hollow Road
Friedens, PA 15541
814-443-1931
www.marketfarm.com

APPENDIX B-28
FLAME WEEDERS

Flame Engineering, Inc.
P.O. Box 577
LaCrosse, KS 67548
800-255-2469
www.flameeng.com

Thermal Weed Control Systems, Inc.
N1940 State Hwy 95
Neillsville, WI 54456
715-743-4163

APPENDIX B-29
TOOL CARRIERS

Market Farm Implement
257 Fawn Hollow Road
Friedens, PA 15541
814-443-1931
www.marketfarm.com

Roeters Farm Equipment, Inc.
565 120th Street
Grant, MI 49327
231-834-7888

TLW Steel Fabricators
15638 Sixty-Eighth
Coopersville, MI 49404
616-837-7163

APPENDIX B-30
SUBSOILERS

The Ferguson Mfg. Co., Inc.
P.O. Box 1098
Suffolk, VA 23434
757-539-3409

Guy Farm Equip. Co.
14213 Washington Street
Wood Stock, IL 60098
815-338-0600

Indiana Berry & Plant
5218 W. 500 South
Huntingburg, IN 47542
812-683-3055
www.inberry.com

Lely Corporation
Box 1060
Wilson, NC 27893
252-261-7050

Strohm Brothers Inc.
Route One
West Union, IL 62477
217-279-3306

APPENDIX B-31
BED SHAPERS

Buckeye Tractor Co.
P.O. Box 123
Columbus Grove, OH 45830
800-526-6791/Fax: 419-659-2082

Chesmore Seed Co.
P.O. Box 8368
5030 Hwy 36
St Joseph, MO 64508
816-279-0865/Fax: 816-232-6134

Delhi Foundry and Farm Machinery Ltd.
171 King Street
West Delhi, ON Canada N4B 1X9
519-582-2770/Fax: 519-582-4442
www.delhifoundry.com

Gearmore Inc.
13740 Magnolia Avenue
Chino, CA 91710
909-548-4848/Fax: 909-548-4747

Holland Transplanter Co.
P.O. Box 1527
Holland, MI 49422-1527
616-392-3579/Fax: 616-392-7996
www.transplanter.com

KPR Inc.
P.O. Box 608
Wendell, ID 83355-0608
208-536-6601/Fax: 208-536-6695
www.kprinc.com

Larchmont Engineering and Irrigation Inc.
11 Larchmont Lane
Lexington, MA 02173
978-250-1260

Market Farm Implement
257 Farm Hollow Road
Friedens, PA 15541
814-443-1931
www.marketfarm.com

Mechanical Transplanter Co.
1150 S. Central Street
Holland, MI 49423-5230
800-757-5268/Fax: 616-396-3619
www.mechanicaltransplanter.com

Rain-Flo Irrigation
884 Center Church Road
East Earl, PA 17519
717-445-6976/Fax: 717-445-8304

Reddick Fumigants Inc.
P.O. Box 391
Williamston, NC 27892
800-358-8837/Fax: 919-792-4615

Solex Corp.
P.O. Box 490
Dixon, CA 95620
707-678-5533/Fax: 800-248-6651
www.solexcorp.com

Triangle M Equipment Ltd.
309 N. Polk
Morocco, IN 47963
219-285-2377/Fax: 219-285-6115

Unverferth Mfg Co Inc.
Box 357
Kalida, OH 45853
800-322-6301/Fax: 419-532-2468
www.4unverferth.com

Weening Bros. Mfg. Inc.
585 Wist Road, RR1
Kettleby, ON, Canada L0G 1J0
905-775-3839/Fax: 905-775-8769

APPENDIX B-32 TRANSPLANTING EQUIPMENT

Ellis Manufacturing Co.
Box 930219
Verona, WI 53593
608-845-6472

Holland Transplanters Co.
P.O. Box 1527
Holland, MI 49422-1527
616-392-3579/Fax: 616-392-7996
www.transplanter.com

Market Farm Implement
257 Fawn Hollow Road
Friedens, PA 15541
814-443-1931
www.marketfarm.com

Mechanical Transplanter
1150 S. Central Street
Holland, MI 49423-5230
800-757-5268/Fax: 616-396-3619
www.mechanicaltransplanter.com

Powell Manufacturing Co.
P.O. Drawer 707
Bennetsville, SC 29512
843-479-6231

Speedling Inc.
Box 7220
Sun City, FL 33586
813-645-3221/Fax: 813-645-8123
www.speedling.com

APPENDIX B-33
BIRD CONTROL

Aquatic Eco-Systems, Inc.
1767 Benbow Court
Apopka, FL 32703
800-422-3939/Fax: 407-886-6787
www.aquaticeco.com

Aurum Aquaculture Ltd.
P.O. Box 2042
Bothell, WA 98041
206-488-5999/Fax: 206-487-2511

Avitrol Corporation
7644 East 46th Street
Tulsa, OK 74145
800-633-5069
www.avitrol.com

Bird-X
300 N. Elizabeth Street
Chicago, IL 60607
312-226-2473/Fax: 312-648-0319
www.bird-x.com

Cropking
P.O. Box 310
Medina, OH 44258
800-321-5656/Fax: 216-722-3958

J.T. Eaton & Co., Inc.
1393 East Highland Road
Twinsburg, OH 44087
800-321-3421/Fax: 216-425-8353
www.jteaton.com

Modern Agri-Products
3770 Aldergrove Road
Ferndale, WA 98248
206-366-4343

Nixalite of America Inc.
1025 16th Avenue
P.O. Box 727
East Moline, IL 61244
800-624-1189/Fax: 800-624-1196
www.nixalite.com

Reed-Joseph International
P.O. Box 894
Greensville, MS 38702
800-647-5554
www.reedjoseph.com

Specialty Ag Equipment, Inc.
P.O. Box 1227
Reedley, CA 93654
209-638-3631

Stoneco Inc.
P.O. Box 765
Trinidad, CO 81082
800-833-2264/Fax: 719-846-7700

The Tanglefoot Co.
314 Straight Avenue SW
Grand Rapids, MI 49504
616-459-4139/Fax: 616-459-4140
www.tanglefoot.com

Tenax Geotenax Corp.
4800 E. Monument Street
Baltimore, MD 21205
800-356-8495/Fax: 410-522-7015
www.tenax.com

Weitech Inc.
601 N. Larch Street
Sisters, OR 97759
800-343-2659/Fax: 503-549-8154
www.weitech.com

Wildlife Control Technology Inc.
2501 North Sunnyside #103
Fresno, CA 93727
800-235-0262
www.wildlife-control.com

APPENDIX B-34
DEER REPELLENTS

Dazon B.V.
P.O. Box 5502
Maastricht 6202 XA
Netherlands
011-31-43-620876/Fax: 011-31-43-635373

J.C. Ehrlich Chemical Co.
Magic Circle)
500 Spring Ridge Drive
Wyomissing, PA 19612
800-488-9495
www.jcehrlich.com

FLR Inc.
P.O. Box 108
Midnight, MS 39115
662-247-1257/Fax: 662-247-1715

Gustafson Inc.
P.O. Box 660065
Dallas, TX 75266-0065
800-527-4781
www.gustafson.com

Intagra Inc.
8906 Wentworth Avenue So.
Minneapolis, MN 55420
800-468-2472
www.intagra.com or www.concern.com

Reed-Joseph International Co.
P.O. Box 984
Greenville, MS, 38702
800-647-5554/Fax: 601-335-8850
www.reedjoseph.com

Tenax Geotenax Corp.
4800 E. Monument Street
Baltimore, MD 21205
800-356-8495/Fax: 410-522-7015
www.tenax.com

APPENDIX B-35
ELECTRIC FENCES

McBee Agri-Supply Inc.
16151 Old Hwy 63 N.
Sturgeon, MO 65284
573-696-2517
www.mcbcattle@aol.com

K-Fence Systems
RR 1, Box 195
Zumbro Falls, MN 55991
507-753-2943
www.info@kfence.com

Kiwi Fence Systems Inc.
121 Kiwi Road
Waynesburg, PA 15370
724-627-5640
www.kiwifence.com

Live Wire Products Inc.
1127 "E" Street
Marysville, CA 95901
800-272-9045/Fax: 530-743-0609

APPENDIX B-36 POCKET GOPHER CONTROL

Bonide Products Inc.
2 Wurz Avenue
Yorkville, NY 13495
315-736-8231
www.bonideproducts.com

Elston Manufacturing, Inc.
706 North Weber
Sioux Falls, SD 57103
800-845-1385
www.elstonmfg.com

F.B.N. Plastics
225 N "L" Street
Tulare, CA 93274
559-688-7269/Fax: 559-688-7275
www.blkwholetrap.com

LiphaTech Inc.
3600 W. Elm Street
Milwaukee, WI 53209
800-558-1003/Fax: 414-351-184
www.liphatech@execpc.com

P-W Manufacturing Co.
610 High Street
Henryetta, OK 74437
918-652-4981/Fax: 918-652-9770

Val-A Company
700-710 West Root Street
Chicago, IL 60609
800-621-0277

Van Diest Supply Co.
800 N. Washington
Abilene, KS 67410
800-448-2664
3290 Anderson Road
Garden City, KS 67846
800-282-2254

Wilco Distributors Inc.
P.O. Box 291
Lompoc, CA 93438-0291
805-735-2476/Fax: 805-735-3629

APPENDIX B-37 REFRIGERATION

Atmost Refrigeration
793 Rt 66
Hudson, NY 12534
518-828-2180
www.rtfmanufacturing.com

Bush Refrigeration
17 Admiral Wilson Blvd.
Camden, NJ 08109
800-220-2874
www.bushrefrigeration.com

SRC Refrigeration
6615 Nineteen Mile Road
Sterling Heights, MI 48314-2117
800-521-0398/Fax: 810-254-0485
www.srcrefrigeration.com

APPENDIX B-38 CONTAINERS AND SLEEVES FOR HARVEST, HOLDING AND PACKING

A-Roo Company, Inc.
P.O. Box 360050
Strongsville, OH 44136
440-238-8850
www.a-roo.com

Atlas Plastics, Inc.
640 Dell Road
Carlstadt, NJ 07072
201-440-1570

Control Plastics Inc.
37625 Sycamore Street
Newark, CA 94560
800-600-2010/Fax: 510-742-0093
cplastics@pacbell.net

Design Packaging Company
2834 West Chicago Avenue
Chicago, IL 60622-4494
773-486-8100 or 800-321-7659
www.designpackagingco.com

Epic Products Inc.
17390 Mt. Hermmann
Fountain Valley, CA 92708
714-641-8194/Fax: 714-641-8217

Moore Paper Boxes, Inc.
2916 Boulder Avenue
Dayton, OH 45414
937-278-7327

Sambrailo Paper Company
P.O. Box 50090
Watsonville, CA 95077-0390
831-424-0952
www.sambrailo.com

Smithers Oasis
919 Marvin Avenue
Kent, OH 44240
800-321-8286
www.smithersoasis.com

APPENDIX B-39
LABELS

Economy Label Sales
515 Carswell Avenue
Holy Hill, FL 32117
800-874-4465/Fax: 800-356-7650
www.economylabel.com

APPENDIX B-40
SUPPLIERS OF FRESH
FLOWER FOOD AND
PRESERVATIVES

Floralife Inc.
120 Tower Drive
Burr Ridge, IL 60521
630-325-8587

Gard Environmental Group
250 Williams Street
Carpentersville, IL 60110
847-836-7700/Fax: 847-836-7711

The John Henry Co.
P.O. Box 17099
Lansing, MI 48901-7099
517-323-9000
www.jhc.com

Robert Koch Industries Inc.
4770 N. Harback Road
Bennett, CO 80102-8834
303-644-3763/Fax: 303-644-3045
www.kochcolor.com

Pokon & Chrysal USA
3063 NW 107th Avenue
Miami, FL 33172
800-247-9725
www.pokonchrysalusa.com

SEGO International, Inc.
P.O. Box 3526
Portland, OR 97208
503-796-0133/Fax: 503-222-4178
www.segointernational.com

Smithers-Oasis Co.
919 Marvin Avenue
P.O. Box 118
Kent, OH 44240
800-321-8286
www.smithersoasis.com

Westcan Seeds
Bay 5466 Station A
Calgary AB, Canada T2H 1X8
403-279-5168/Fax: 403-236-0854

APPENDIX B-41
GLYCOL PRESERVATIVES

Robert Koch Industries Inc.
4770 N. Harback Road
Bennett, CO 80102-8834
303-644-3763/Fax: 303-644-3045
www.kochcolor.com

SEGO International, Inc.
P.O. Box 3526
Portland, OR 97208
503-796-0133/Fax: 503-222-4178
www.segointernational.com

APPENDIX B-42
DYES FOR COLOR
PROCESSING

Robert Koch Industries Inc.
4770 N. Harback Road
Bennett, CO 80102-8834
303-644-3763/Fax: 303-644-3045
www.kochcolor.com

SEGO International, Inc.
P.O. Box 3526
Portland, OR 97208
503-796-0133/Fax: 503-222-4178
www.segointernational.com

APPENDIX B-43
FREEZE-DRIEDS

A Delicate Frost
817 W. Douglas
Wichita, KS 67213
316-263-4140

Gardiners Freeze-Dried Flowers
4745 Calumet Drive
Knoxville, TN 37919
615-523-1109

Westcan Seed
Bay 5466 Station A
Calgary, AB, Canada T2H 1X8
403-279-5168/Fax: 403-236-0854

APPENDIX B-44
DESIGN CONTAINERS,
POTS & BASKETS

Art-Ful Floral Container
P.O. Box 971
Bedford, IN 47421
812-275-2438

Keith Avery Imports, Inc.
34 Clinton Street
Batavia, NY 14020
800-272-3727/Fax: 313-295-0521
www.willowspecialties.com

The Basket Affair
525 NW Saltzman
Portland, OR 97229
800-243-2992

Baskets Unlimited
4826 S. Sante Fe Avenue
Vernon, CA 90058
323-581-0111

Bennington Potters
324 County Street
P.O. Box 199
Bennington, VT 0520
802-447-7531

Brass Baron
10151 Pacific Mesa Blvd. # 104
San Diego, CA 92121
800-536-0987
www.brassbaron.com

Country Basket and Furniture
14512-G Lee Road
Chantilly, VA 22021-1636
703-818-9173
www.basketsimports.com

Diamond-Line Containers
708 Killian Road
Akron, OH 44319
216-644-9993

Formart Containers
P.O. Box 46
Cedarburg, WI 53012
262-377-3737

Hampton Brass
197 W. Queen Street
Hampton, VA 23669
800-368-4080

Indiana Glass
4460 Lake Forest Drive
Cincinnati, OH 45242
513-563-6789
www.landcastercolony.com

Jacks Baskets
5634 Mission Blvd.
Ontario, CA 91762-4652
909-988-7035

Mainly Baskets
1535 NE Expressway
Atlanta, GA 30329
404-634-7664

Pete Garcia Co.
5154 Peachtree Industrial Blvd.
Atlanta, GA 30341
800-241-3733

Texas Basket Co.
P.O. Box 1110
Jacksonville, TX 75766
903-586-8014
www.texasbasket.com

Whole Year Trading Co., Inc.
117 White Oak Lane
Old Bridge, NJ 08857
800-238-6694/Fax: 908-679-4411

Wholesale Basket Co.
3265 SW 100th
Portland, OR 97225
503-292-0437

APPENDIX B-45 FLORIST SUPPLIES

Avatar's World
106 E. Hurd Road
Edgerton, WI 53534
800-884-4730/Fax: 608-884-6920
www.avatarsworld.com

Best Buy Floral Supply
5715-6th Street SW
Cedar Rapids, IA 52404
800-553-8497
www.bestbuyfloral.com

C.F. Sales Company
42030 Koppernick
Canton, MI 48137
734-453-6797
www.cfsales.com

Chace Candles
4208 Balloon Park Road
Albuquerque, NM 87109
505-344-3413

Create-A-Card Inc.
16 Brasswood Road
St. James, NY 11780
631-584-2273
creatacardinc.com

Creative Candles
P.O. Box 412514
Kansas City, MO 64141
816-474-9711
www.creativecandles.com

Dakota Plastics
P.O. Box 52
Watertown, SD 57201
605-886-6851

Design Master Color Tool, Inc.
P.O. Box 601
Boulder, CO 80306
800-525-2644/Fax: 303-443-5217

Designer Dispatch
P.O. Box 250
Appletree Lane
Plumsteadville, PA 18949
215-766-2901/Fax: 215-766-2872

Fiberex, Inc.
4032 Parkway Drive
Florence, AL 35630
800-243-3455/Fax: 256-767-7606
www.fiberex.com

Florists Supply Ltd.
35 Airport Road
Winnipeg, MB, Canada R3C 2Z4
204-632-1210

Flowers, Inc. Balloons
325 Cleveland Road
Bogart, GA 30622
800-241-2094/Fax: 800-880-9759
www.flowersincballoon.com

Pete Garcia Company
5154 Peachtree Industrial Blvd.
Atlanta, GA 30341
404-458-8888

Glitter Wrap
701 Ford Road
Rockaway, NJ 07866
973-625-4200

Highland Supply Corporation
1111 6th Street
Highland, IL 62249
800-HSC-FOIL(472-3645)/Fax: 800-553-2948
www.highlandsupply.com

Insta-Foam (Flexible Products)
2050 N. Broadway
Joliet, IL 60435
815-741-6800
www.flexibleproducts.com

Princess Ribbon
3320 Tait Terr.
Norfolk, VA 23513
757-853-5500

Regenboog Dried Flowers, Inc.
1861 W. Oak Parkway
Marietta, GA 30062
800-537-7647/Fax: 404-424-2869
www.regenboog.com

Ribbon Narrow Sales
2500 Lemoine Avenue, Suite 401
Ft. Lee, NJ 07024
201-302-0233

San Francisco Candle
20929 Cabot Blvd.
Hayward, CA 94545
510-785-2582

Smithers-Oasis USA
P.O. Box 118
Kent, OH 44240
800-321-8286

APPENDIX B-46
DISPLAY FIXTURES

ACI The Display People
828 E. Edna Place
Covina, CA 91723
626-331-7677
www.acidisplay.com

APPENDIX B-47
FLORAL DESIGN
SCHOOLS

American Floral Art School
529 South Wabash, Suite 610
Chicago, IL 60605-1679
312-922-9328

Arizona School of Floral Design
713 N. 16th Street
Phoenix, AZ 85006
602-258-7875

Bannow Floral School
11189 Hall Road
Utica, MI 48087
810-254-9646/Fax: 810-254-5655

Benz School of Floral Design
Box 9909
College Station, TX 77842
979-845-1699
aggie>horticulture.tamv.edu<benz>

Canadian Institute of Floral Design
4025 Young Street, Suite 204
Toronto ON, Canada M2P 2E3
416-733-9968
cifd@indirect.com

Design Master
P.O. Box 601
Boulder, CO 80306
800-525-2644/Fax: 303-443-5217
enfo@dmcolor.com
www.dmcolor.com

Devonian Botanic Garden
University of Alberta
Edmonton, AB, Canada T6G 2E1
780-987-3054/Fax: 780-987-4141
www.discoveredmonton.>devonian

Elvamay School of Floral Design
410 W. Amerige Avenue
Fullerton, CA 92632
714-525-8464

Hixson's School of Floral Design
14125 Detroit Avenue
Lakewood, OH 44107
216-521-9277

Kansas School of Floral Design
826 Iowa
Lawrence, KS 66044
785-843-1400

Kishwaukee College
Department of Horticulture
21193 Malta Road
Malta, IL 60150
815-825-2086
http://kish.cc.il.us

Olds College
4500 50th Street
Olds, AB, Canada T4H 1R6
403-556-8240
www.oldscollege.ab.ca

Rittners School of Floral Design
345 Marlborough Street
Boston, MA 02115
617-267-3824
stevrt@tiac.net
www.floralschool.com

Shelton School of Floral Design
8426 Winkler Drive
Houston, TX 77017
713-644-4151

South Florida School of Floral Design
1612 S. Dixie Hwy.
Lake Worth, FL 33460
561-585-9491
floridaconnect@webtv.net
www.floralinstruction.com

Southern California School of Floral Design
2964 E. Yorba Linda Blvd.
Fullerton, CA 92631
714-776-7445/Fax: 714-776-7485

Trim Int'l Floral School, Ltd.
15290 E. 6th Avenue, Suite 290
Aurora, CO 80041
800-786-2640/303-388-7377/
Fax: 303-360-0371

APPENDIX B-48
CLEANING SUPPLIES

Dillon Floral Corp.
P.O. Box 180
Bloomsburg, PA 17815
570-784-5770/Fax: 570-387-8135
www.dillonfloral.com

Floralife, Inc.
120 Tower Drive
Burr Ridge, IL 60521
630-325-8587/Fax: 630-325-4924

Forestry Suppliers Inc.
P.O. Box 8397
Jackson, MS 39284-8397
800-647-5368/Fax: 800-543-4203
fsi@forestry-supplier.com
www.forestry-supplier.com

Plant Marvel Labs, Inc.
371 East 16th Street
Chicago Heights, IL 60411
708-757-7500/Fax: 708-757-5224
www.plantmarvel.com

APPENDIX B-49
OFFICE SYSTEMS

ADS Florists Systems
P.O. Box 13686
Roanoke, VA 24036
800-672-4422

Floral Office Systems, Inc.s
1503 Farmerville Hwy
Ruston, LA 71270
318-251-2146

APPENDIX B-50 GREENHOUSES

AgraTech
2131 Piedmont Way
Pittsburg, CA 94565-5071
925-432-3399
www.agra-tech.com

Atlas Greenhouse Sys, Inc.
Hwy 82 East, P.O. 558
Alapaha, GA 31622
800-346-9902/Fax: 912-532-4600
atlasgrn@surfsouth.com
www.atlasgreenhouse.com

Conley's Mfg.
4344 Mission Blvd.
Pomona, CA 91763
909-627-0981

Growell Greenhouses
791 Coleman Road
Cheshire, CT 06410
203-272-8147

Janco Greenhouses
9390 Davis Avenue
Laurel, MD 20723
800-323-6933
janco@jancoinc.com
www.jancinc.com

Ludy Greenhouse Mfg. Corp.
P.O. Box 141
New Madison, OH 45346
937-996-1921
www.ludy.com

National Greenhouse
6 Industrial Drive
Pana, IL 62557
800-826-9314
www.nexuscorp.com

Nexus Greenhouses
10983 Leroy
Northglenn, CO 80233
800-228-9639
www.nexuscorp.com

Oregon Valley Greenhouses
P.O. Box 220
Aurora, OR 97002
503-678-2700
ivans@ovg.com
ovg.com

Rough Brothers
5513 Vine Street
Cincinnati, OH 45217
800-543-7351
www.roughbros.com

Structures Unlimited Inc.
2122 Whitfield Park Avenue
Sarasota, FL 34243
800-541-8129/Fax: 941-756-9860
strucunltd@aol.com

Stuppy Greenhouse Mfg.
P.O. Box 12456
North Kansas City, MO 64116
800-877-5025
greenhouse@stuppy.com
www.stuppy.com

X.S. Smith
Old Deal Road
Eatontown, NJ 07724
800-631-2226
xssmith46@aol.com
www.xssmith.com

APPENDIX B-51
HARVESTING EQUIPMENT

Willamette Exporting, Inc.
7330 SW 86th Avenue
Portland, OR 97223
503-246-2671/Fax: 503-246-8675
wex@europa.com

INDEX

Acaricides, 303

Acclaim, 105-107, 249, 271, 283

Achillea, 42, 48, 57, 189, 218, 243, 245-249, 251-252

   ageratum, 246

   clypeolata, 247

   clypeolata x taygeata, 247

   'Coronation Gold', 247, 251

   filipendulina, 57, 247

   millefolium, 57, 105, 121, 247

   millefolium x Achillea clypeolata, 247

   ptarmica, 121, 246, 248

   taygeata, 121, 248

Acidity, 81, 83, 88

Activity chain, 6, 10

Agapanthus, 189

Ageratum

   houstonianum, 38, 105

Agrobacterium, 135

Air circulation, 67, 134, 139-140, 144, 163, 201-204, 212-213, 215-216, 226-227, 250, 269, 272, 285, 320, 322

Alberta Supernaturals, 154, 342

Algae, 77-78, 176

Alkalinity, 32, 81, 83, 189-190

Allium, 45, 189

   cepa, 143

Alstroemeria, 167, 189

Alternaria, 136, 286, 322

Amaranthus retroflexus, 143

Amblyseius

   californicus, 121

   lyseius cucumeris, 121

   iroquois, 121

   mekenziei, 121

Ambrosia, 207

Ammi majus, 38

Ammobium herb, 48

Ammonium nitrate, 88, 93, 258, 320-321

Ammonium sulfate, 88

Anemone coronaria, 45

Anethium graveolens, 143

Angle braces (ing), 182-183

Animal, 31, 107, 118, 136, 146, 149, 153, 158-159, 220, 347

Annual, 38, 40-42, 55, 66, 90, 92

Anthracnose, 295, 303

Antirrhinum, 105, 189

   majus, 39

Ants, 284

Aphid, 113-115, 121, 127, 136, 250, 259-260, 272, 302, 321

Aphidius matricariae, 121

Aphidoletes aphidimyza, 121

Apple, 207, 331

Aquilegia, 189

Ariana, 50

Artemisia, 48, 207

   albula, 105

   ludoviciana, 42

Asclepias

   incarnata, 42

   nivea, 143

   tuberosa, 42, 57

Aster, 39, 166, 190, 346

   ericoides, 43, 57

   novae angliae, 57

   novi belgii, 43, 57

Aster leafhoppers, 128

Aster yellows, 39, 41, 43, 128, 137, 141-143, 302-303, 323

Astilbe, 43, 166, 189

   x arendsii, 57, 105

Avatar's World, 183

Avena sativa, 143

Baby's breath, 40, 44, 49, 106, 143

Bachelor's button, 105, 143, 166

Bacillus

   lentimorbus, 119

   popilliae, 119

   thuringiensis, 119, 312

Bacteria, 78, 117, 135-137, 139, 167, 176, 219, 221, 229-230, 235, 260

Bacterial control, 221, 229-230

Bacterial leaf blight, 260

Bactericide, 220-221, 239

Bacteriostat, 220-221

Bactimos, 119

Bactur, 119

Baiting, 149, 151

Balloon flower, 45

Basket, 207, 335, 370-371

Bast fibers (raffia, jute, hemp), 207

Bat guano, 89

Beautyberry, 46, 330

Beautybush, 331

Bed preparation, 6, 59, 145

Bed Shapers, 4, 367

Bedder, 45, 60

Bedding plants, 55

Bee balm, 122

Beetle, 113, 115, 118, 284

   Black Carpet, 131

   Carpete, 131

   Click, 260

   Cigarette, 131

   Colorado Potato, 119, 310

   Japanese, 119

   Lady, 120-123

   Predatory, 122-123

   Snapping, 260

   Sunflower, 310

   Warehouse, 131

Bells of Ireland, 41, 49, 52

Benefin, 258, 321

Bensulide, 258

Benzensulfonamide, 258

Berry (ies), 46-47, 207

Betasan, 105-107, 258

Bettina, 50

Biennial, 38, 40, 55-56, 345

Biobit, 119, 312

Biological control, 114, 117, 119, 123, 133, 333, 355

Biorational control, 117

Biosafe, 119

BioVector, 119

Bird control, 312, 334, 366

Bittersweet, 46, 52, 69, 330

Black-eyed Susan, 106, 144

Black lichen, 208

Blanket flower, 143

Blazing star, 44-45, 122, 267-268

Bleach, 139, 151, 176, 314

   Bleaching, 212, 233-235

Bleeding heart, 106

Blight (s), 136, 260-261, 272, 285-286, 303, 322

Blue lace, 123

Bone meal

   Raw, 89

   Steamed, 89

Botrytis, 168, 202, 208, 303

   Blight, 136, 261, 285-286

   cinera, 322

   gladioli, 261

Bouquet (s), 14, 21-22, 24, 27, 51, 254, 265, 277, 316, 326

Bouvardia, 189

Boxwood, 218, 330

Brandy, 50

Brassica

   campestris, 121, 143

   hirta, 121

Bridal pink, 50

Bridal white, 50

Brigadoon, 50

Broadcast application, 92, 301, 309

Brokers, 28

Broom bloom, 218

Buck Godwin mouse trap, 155

Buckwheat, 122

Buddleia, 51, 53

Bulb (s), 45-46, 75, 135-136, 151, 255, 333, 343, 347, 352-354

Bull head (s), 292-293, 295

Bunch size, 7, 192, 215-216, 221, 223, 227, 274, 291, 294, 297, 303-304, 316, 326

Bunching, 191-195, 213-216

Bundle (s), 24, 184-185

Buttercup, 122

Butterfly flower, 42

Buxus

   macrophylla, 330

   sempreviorns, 330

Calcium, 77, 84, 88, 189, 235

   Carbonate, 83

   Hypochlorite, 233

   Nitrate, 88, 93, 248

Calendula, 105, 166

   officinalis, 143

Callicarpa, 46, 330

Callistephus chinensis, 39

Calyxes, 292-293, 295

Campanula, 189

Candia, 50

Canker (s), 136, 286, 314, 330

Canterbury bells, 53

Capsicum (peppers), 48

Carbaryl, 312

Carbohydrates, 90, 196

Carnation, 143, 189, 192, 233-235

Carnival, 50

Carrot, 122, 143

Carthamus tinctorius (safflower), 48

Caryopteris incana, 39

Caspia, 49, 218

Caterpillar (s), 113, 115, 118-119, 128, 311, 321

Catharanthus roseus, 143

Celastrus, 46

Celosia, 207 (see Cockscomb)

   argentea, 39

   cristata, 48

   Feather, 39

   Plume, 39, 51

   Wheat, 39

Centaurea, 189

   americana, 39

   cyanus, 39, 105, 143

Cercis, 46, 330

Cercospora, 303

   paeoniae, 286

Cerise Queen, 57, 247

Chaenomeles, 46, 330

Chenopodium album, 121

Chewing mouthparts insects, 115

China Aster, 39

Chinese Lantern, 41, 51

Chlorosis, 129, 141

Chlorpyrifos, 312

Choosing a site, 8, 11, 31

Chrysanthemum

   coccineum, 121

   frutescens, 143

   parthenium, 48

   x superbum, 43, 105

Chrysoperia carnea, 121

Cladosporium, 286

Clarkia amoena, 39

Classified ads, 22

Cleaning Supplies, 335, 374

Cloth of Gold, 57

Cockscomb, 39, 48, 51, 166

   Feather celosia, 39

   Plume celosia, 39, 51

   Wheat celosia, 39

Coffeeberry, 123

Cold storage temperature, 7

Cold-air drainage, 31, 33

Cole, Janet, 97

Coleosporium lacinariae, 273

Collectotrichum, 303

Color processing, 160, 233, 240, 304, 335, 370

Computer sales, 26

Conductivity meter, 84

Cone flower, 43, 106, 141-143, 167

Conservation, 123, 125

Consolida

   ambigua, 39, 105

   orientalis, 39

   regalis, 48

Container
  Cleaning system, 177, 194
  Display, 18-19
  Harvest, 170-172, 175-179
  Pesticide, 102, 130-131
  Preserving, 219
  Sanitation, 176
  Storage, 194
Containers & Sleeves for Harvest Holding &
  Packing, 335, 368
Control measure (s), 114, 124-125, 130, 132,
  135, 138, 147, 151-152, 304
Copper, 286
  Sulfate, 78
Coreopsis lanceolata, 143
Coriander, 121
Coriandrum sativum, 121
Corm, 45, 135-136, 244, 255-264, 267, 269-
  271, 274
Cormel (s), 255, 262-263
Corn spurry, 123
Cornelian cherry, 331
Cornflower, 39, 53, 143, 166
Cornus, 47
  mas, 331
Coronation Gold, 42, 57, 247, 251
Corporate gifts, 21
Cosmos, 40, 66, 105, 143
  bipinnatus, 40, 105, 143
Cost of access, 32
Cost-structure, 8, 10, 13
Cotoneaster, 122
Cotton seed, 89
Covered harvest trailer, 168-169, 181
Covered sales area, 17-18
Coverings & Windbreaks, 334, 360
Craft fair (s), 20, 22, 29
Craft store (s), 26, 28
Crescent, 24
Crop determination, 28
Crown gall, 135
Cucurbita pepo, 143

Cultivator, 334, 363
  Tractor-mounted, 100, 329
Currant, 332
Customer Service, 9, 21
Cut Flower Seed Suppliers, 333, 350
Cutworm (s), 113, 302, 311
Cyfluthrin, 312
Dacthal, 105-107, 249, 258, 321
Dahlia, 45, 56, 105, 166, 318-319
Daisy, 121, 143, 239, 318, 324-325
  Painted, 121
  Shasta, 43, 105
Damping-off, 139, 322
Dandelion, 123
Daucus, 189
  carota, 48, 122, 143
Decorative bark, 207
Deer, 146, 156-158, 334, 367
Deer Repellents, 157, 334, 367
Delphinium, 57, 166, 189, 346
  elatum, 106
  x cultorum, 143
Design Containers Pots & Baskets, 335, 370
Diammonium phosphate, 93
Dianthus
  barbatus, 40, 143
  caryophyllus, 143
Diazinon, 127
Dicentra, 189
  eximia, 106
Diethylene glycol, 217
Dill, 143
Dipel, 119, 128, 312
Diptera, 285
Directories, 333, 341, 354
Disc hiller, 60-61
Disease, 134-145
  Foliar, 67, 72, 79
  Control, 3, 6, 8, 70, 110-111, 113, 115-116,
    134, 136-138, 144-145, 163, 250, 260, 272,
    285, 303, 313, 322, 330
  Triangle, 137-138

Display fixtures, 15, 20, 335, 373

Distortion, 129, 137

Dogwood, 47-48, 331

Dole, John, 97

Dolomite, 301

Dolomitic limestone, 84

Doom, 119

Dried blood, 89

Dried flower, 48-50

    Transport system, 180

Driftwood, 207

Drip line, 6, 33, 96, 249, 301

Drip tape, 75

Drying, 41, 48, 50, 118, 151, 166, 175, 186-187, 208-213, 215-217, 226-227, 231, 263, 272, 285, 304, 325, 344, 350

    Dessicant drying, 231

    Facility, 186, 211-212, 215-216

    Freeze drying, 209, 231, 337, 373

    Sheds, 209, 211-212, 215

    Time, 212-213, 215-216, 263

Dusty miller, 53, 106

Dye (ing) 233-240

    Container, 235

    Dyebath, 237-239

    For color processing, 335, 370

    Immersion, 236-239

    Requirement, 235, 238

    Systemic, 234-236

Echinacea purpurea, 43, 57, 141

Echinops, 48, 53

    bannaticus, 43, 57

    exaltatus, 43

    ritro, 43

    sphaerocephalus, 43

Economic damage, 147

Electric fences, 157, 334, 367

Electro-conductivity, 84, 86

Electromagnetic radiation, 231

Emulsifiable concentrate, 129

Endosulfan, 312

English Boxwood, 330

Eremurus, 189

Ericas, 330

Eriogonum, 122

Erwinia, 135

Eryngium, 48, 122

    alpinum, 122

    amethystinum, 44

    planum, 44, 57

Eryngo, 44

Erysiphe cichoracearum, 273

Eschscholzia californica, 143

Esfenvalerate, 312

Ethylene gas, 188, 202

Ethylene glycol, 217

Eucalyptus, 47-48, 207, 218-219, 224-228

Eustoma grandiflorum, 40

Evaporation, 59, 108, 111, 201, 209, 212, 225, 259

Excelsior, 207

Extended indecision, 4, 6-7, 161, 165

Fagopyrum lentum, 122

False cypress, 46

False Queen Anne's lace, 38

Farmers market (s), 12, 16-17, 20, 29, 45, 55, 166, 192, 265, 315-316, 326

Fence (ing), 31, 68, 124, 156-158, 328, 334, 367

Fennel, 122

Fenoxaprop, 249, 271, 283

Ferbam, 286

Fern, 42, 52, 207, 247, 252

Fernleaf yarrow, 42

Fertigation, 93, 95-98, 111

Fertilizer, 58, 60-61, 81-97, 108

    Bat guano, 89

    Cattle, 89

    Chicken, 89

    Diammonium phosphate, 93

    Horse, 89

    Injectors, 94-96

    Inorganic, 87-88

    Integrated, 97

Phosphorus, 82-83, 88-89, 92, 97, 249, 309, 321

Potassium, 82-83, 88-89, 93, 97, 230, 249, 258, 309, 320-321

Sheep, 89

Sulfate of potash, 88

Swine, 89

Urea, 86-88, 93

Urea formaldehyde, 86

Field drainage, 31

Field production, 2, 55, 99, 141, 249, 271, 283, 343

Filler, 38, 44, 51-53, 244, 252, 300

Filter (s), 77-78, 95

Fire and Ice, 50

Flame retardants, 211

Flame weeders (ing), 100, 334, 363

Flax, 49, 52, 207

Floral Design Schools, 335, 373

Floriculture, 2, 252, 265, 297, 338, 343, 348, 351

Florist Supplies, 335, 371

Floss Flower, 38

Flowering crabapple, 47

Flowering onion, 45

Flowering quince, 331

Fluazifop-P- butyl, 258, 271

Fluazilop-P, 249, 321

Fluvalinate, 312

Focal, 51-53, 244

Foeniculum vulgare, 122

Forsythia, 47, 330

Fothergilla, 331

Freesia, 167, 189

Freeze drieds, 335, 370

Fresh flowers, 38-48

Friday flowers, 27

Friendship Gardens, 29

Frost Protection, 334, 360

Frost Protection-Fog, 334, 360

Fruit (s), 2, 17, 41, 46, 188, 207, 232, 343

Fumigants, 150, 216, 361, 368

Fungi (Fungus), 135-136, 139, 260-261, 273, 280, 287, 314-315

Disease, 79, 136, 140, 168, 198, 250, 271-272, 280, 285, 320, 322, 330

Gnat, 119, 121

Fungicide, 104, 136, 138-140, 157, 250, 255-256, 261, 271-273, 285-286, 303, 314

Leafspot, 67, 136, 139-140, 273, 286

Pathogens, 136, 272, 285

Fusarium, 136, 139, 287

Yellows, 260

Rot, 261-262

Fusilade, 105-107, 249, 258, 271, 321

Gaillardia pulchella, 143

Gaultheria, 47

Gayfeather, 44-45, 167, 243, 266-268, 271

Geotropism, 263

Gerbera, 190, 324

Gibberellic acid, 55-56

Gladiola, 106

Gladiolus, 45, 52-53, 56, 106, 167, 189-190, 192, 243, 253-254, 263, 265

Gladiolus x hortulanus, 143

Globe amaranth, 40, 49, 53

Globe thistle, 43, 48, 53, 167

Glycerin, 217-230

Glycol, 217-218, 221, 229-230

Gnatrol, 119

Godetia, 39, 189

Godwin, Buck, 154-155, 342

Goldenrod, 45, 52, 123, 167

Gomphrena, 207

globosa, 40, 49

haageana, 40

Gopher (s), 146-150, 334, 368

Gopher trap, 148

Gourds, 52, 207

Grace, 39, 93

Grade (s), 12, 77, 192, 194-195, 244, 256, 274, 291-294, 296-298

Grading, 26-28, 133, 161, 168-169, 179, 182, 244, 291-293

Grain, 49, 113, 131-132, 147, 149, 151-152, 183, 207, 216

Grape, 48, 69

Grapevine wreath, 207

Grass, harvest, 183-186

Grasshoppers, 113, 119, 311

Greenhouses, 139, 209, 211, 335, 375

Greenshield, 220-221

Grocery stores, 17, 26, 154

Groundwater contamination, 101

Guillotine cutters, 191

Gypsophila, 189
   elegans, 40, 106
   paniculata, 44, 49, 57, 143
   perfecta, 49

Gypsum, 88

Hamamelis vernalis, 331

Hand-weeding, 99, 249, 258-259, 271, 283-284, 329

Hard rot, 261-262

Hardpan, 58

Harvest, 160-204
   Handling, 236, 264
   Labor, 15, 111, 161, 165
   System, 161, 166, 173, 180, 183, 187, 204, 240
   Trailer, 168-169, 181, 185-186, 197

Hawthorne, 52

Heather, 167

Helianthus, 106, 306-307, 316
   annuus, 40, 143, 306, 316
   debilis, 307
   decapetlus, 307

Helichrysum
   angustifolium, 122
   bracteatum, 49, 106, 143

Helipterum manglesii, 49

Hemipteran predators, 121-123

Hemp sesbania, 123

Herbaceous perennial, 90, 300

Herbicide, 6, 32, 64, 99-102, 104-107, 130, 135, 249, 258, 271, 283, 302, 309, 329

Non-selective, 104
Post-emergent, 104
Pre-emergent, 104
Systemic, 104

Heterorhabditis, 119

Hippodamia convergens, 121

Hoe (ing), 99, 249, 258-259, 271, 283-284, 329
   Hand-held, 334, 362
   Wheel, 334, 362

Holly, 44, 47, 122, 167

Hollyhock, 167

Honeysuckle, 331

Hop, 30, 33, 47, 250, 297, 306

Hopi, 306

How to plant, 3, 8, 36, 58, 301

Hozon siphon proportioner, 94

Humulus, 47

Hurd, John, 183

Hydrangea, 47, 49, 53, 207, 331

Hydrogen peroxide, 233

Hydroxyquinoline citrate, 220-221

Hymenopteran parasitoid, 121-123

Iberis
   amara, 41
   sempervireas, 49

Identifying insects, 114, 124

Ilex, 47, 331

Immersion, 212, 218, 229-230, 232-234, 236, 239

Injectors, 94-96, 170-171

Inputs, 5, 9, 31, 70, 76, 131

Insect
   Control, 8, 70, 111, 113-114, 117, 127, 133, 250, 259, 272, 284, 302, 304, 309, 315, 321, 329
   Monitoring, 114, 142, 302, 311

Insecticidal soap, 116, 126-128

Insecticide, 104, 115-119, 124, 126-127, 129-130, 133, 143, 259, 263, 303, 311
   Botanical, 126-127
   Grub killer, 119

Insecticidal soap, 126-128
Refined light oil spray, 127
Systemic, 129, 143
Insurance, 131
Integrated fertilizer and irrigation management
system, 97
Integrated pest management, 97, 114, 358
Interior decorator, 22, 207
Internet, 26, 350
Iris, 106, 167, 192, 233, 346
Iron, 77-78, 110
Irrigation, 71-80, 93-97, 101, 248-249
Equipment, 333, 359
Management, 71, 97, 349
Subirrigation equipment, 334, 359
Trickle, 72-76, 78-80
Juniper, 218
Kansas State University, 1-2, 168, 217, 220,
225, 339, 349
Kelp, 89
Kelthane, 128
Knotweed, 122
Koch, Mark, 1, 225, 232, 345, 348
Kolkwitzia amabilis, 331
Labor
Cost, 4, 7, 92-93, 99, 111, 113, 161, 165,
170, 172, 180, 231, 249, 258, 271, 329
Cutting costs, 163
Direct costs, 6-7, 20
Efficiency, 7, 31, 58-59
Management, 4, 162
Selection, 162
Labor Model, Stevens, 3, 161, 164, 195
Lace cosmos, 40
Lacewings, 120-121
Lamb's ear, 53
Lambsquarter, 121
Lantana camara, 122
Larkspur, 39, 48, 53, 105, 143, 167, 346
Larvae, 113, 118-120, 122-123, 208, 216, 260,
284, 302, 310-312
Lath drying rack system, 186-187

Lath holder, 185
Lathed bundles, 185
Latifolia, 49, 218, 331
Lattice wall display, 19
Lavandula, 49, 106
Lavatera, 189
Lavender, 40, 49, 53, 106, 167
Lavender cotton, 123
Leafhoppers, 39, 113-116, 128, 136-137, 142-
143, 302, 323
Leafspots, 67, 136, 139-140, 273, 286
Lemon leaf, 47
Lepidium, 49, 218
Leptosphaeria, 136
Lesco, 271
Liatris, 44, 53, 56, 167, 192, 243, 266-268,
270-272, 274-275
aspera, 267
gramnifolia, 267
punctata, 267
pycnostachya, 122, 267-268, 270
pycostachya alba, 268
scariosa, 268
spicata, 45, 267-269, 271
Lichen, black, 208
Light
Exposure to, 211-212
Solution uptake, 227-229
Ligustrum, 122
Lilac, 39, 48, 53, 247-248, 332
Lilium, 46, 106
Lily, 46, 106, 167, 189
Lime, 77, 83
Limestone, 84, 301
Limonium, 41, 44, 189, 213, 300
caspicum, 49
latifolia, 49
latifolium, 44, 57, 106
perezii, 44, 57
sinuatum, 41, 49, 106, 141, 143, 300
suworowii, 49
tataricum, 44, 49, 57

Linkages, 9-10, 111, 133, 145, 180, 187, 232

Lisianthus, 40, 167

Lonicera, 331

Love-in-a-Mist, 41, 49, 143, 167

Lunaria, 49

Lysimachia, 189
 clethroides, 57

Macrosteles quarilineatus Forbes, 142

Magazines Bulletins & Newsletters, 333, 345

Magnesium sulfate, 88

Magnolia leaves, 52

Mail order, 22, 25-26, 207

Malathion, 127-128

Mallus, 47

Mancozeb, 286

Manure (s), 89, 107, 255, 282

Marginal burn, 129

Marguerite daisy, 143, 239

Marigold, 51-52, 106, 143-144, 167

Marina, 50

Marjoram, 207

Marketing, 11-34

Material safety data sheet, 236

Mavrik, 128, 312

Mechanical cultivation, 60, 99-100

Meloidogyne, 273, 287

Mentha spicata, 122

Mercedes, 50, 208

Merchandising, 20, 349 (see Marketing)

Mesurol bait, 128

Metaldehyde bait, 128

Methidathion, 312

Methyl parathion, 312

Metoclachor, 105-107

Michigan State University, 136, 344

Microbial insects, 117-119, 124

Micronutrient, 83

Mildew
 Downy, 250, 314
 Powdery, 44, 67, 136, 140, 250, 272, 320, 322

Milkweed pods, 52

Milky spore, 119

Millet, 207

Mini pumpkin, 52

Mites, 113, 115-116, 120-121, 123, 128, 250, 259, 303

Moisture Gauges & Meters, 334, 360

Mold, 107, 216, 229, 239, 250, 261-262, 304, 322-323

Mole, 151-152

Molucella (Bells of Ireland), 49

Molucella laevis, 41

Monarda, 122

Mosaic virus, 136, 260

Mosquito larvae, 119

Moss (es), 208, 271

Moth, 4, 45, 55, 113, 119, 151, 277, 311
 Angoumois grain, 131
 Banded sunflower, 310
 Casemaking clothesh, 131
 Indian meal, 131, 229
 Sunflower head, 310
 Sunflower bud, 306, 310
 Tobacco, 131
 Webbing clothes, 131

Mother's Day, 45, 55

Mulch, 6, 14, 59-65, 97-99, 107-111, 139, 249, 258-259, 271, 282-283, 302, 329, 333, 357-358
 Black plastic, 108
 Clear, 60, 108
 Embossed plastic, 60
 Inorganic, 99, 108
 Linear, low density, 60
 Organic, 107, 109
 Removal Equipment, 333, 358
 Woven polypropylene mat, 109

Mustard, 121, 143

Mycoplasm-like organism (See Phytoplasm)

Myrtle, 48, 218

Nasturtium, 144

National Pesticide Information Retrieval
 System, 311

Necrosis, 129
Neem, 126
Nematode, 118-119, 144, 272, 285, 287
  Parasitic, 121
  Root-knot, 273
Nicotene, 126
Nigella, 49, 53, 167
  damascena, 41, 143
Nitrogen, 58, 82-83, 88, 90, 92, 97, 248-249,
  257-258, 270, 283, 301, 308, 315, 320-321,
  328-329
No-decision systems, 4-5, 7, 10, 161, 164, 166,
  194
NOLO Bait, 119
Nosema locustae, 119
Nutrition, 81, 89-90, 111, 134, 138, 190, 312
Nutsedge, 108
Oak, 47, 52, 332
Oats, 49, 143
Obedient Plant, 44
Office Systems, 335, 374
Oklahoma State University, 1, 97
Onion, 45, 143, 263
Oregano, 53, 207
Organic, 32, 58, 78, 89-90, 99, 107, 109, 127,
  127, 135, 207, 255, 268, 280, 333, 355-357
  Matter content, 32
Organizations, 29, 333, 336
Ornamec, 258, 271
Ornamental corn, 207
Orthene, 127-128
Oryzalin, 258, 321
Osmocote, 87
Overhead watering, 72, 248, 272, 285, 301,
  320, 322
Oxidiazon, 302
Package (ing), 25-29
Paeonia, 44, 49, 57, 106, 275, 286
Painted daisy, 121
Painting, 78, 233-234, 306
Papaver somniferum, 49
Parasitic nematode, 121

Parasitic wasp, 121
Parasites, 114
Parasitoids, 117, 120-124
Parkers Variety, 57
Pathogens, 111, 117-119, 135-138, 250, 272,
  285
Pear, 248, 331
Penicillium rot, 261-262
Pennant, 258, 321
Penstemon, 189
Pentac, 128
Peony, 44, 49, 51-52, 56, 66, 91, 106, 167,
  192, 207, 231, 243-44, 276-278, 280-298,
  345, 350
  Bomb, 278
  Cultivars, 278-279
  Ringspot, 287
Peppergrass, 49
Perennial, 38, 42-48, 56-57, 90-91
Periwinkle, 143
Personal safety, 130
Peruvian lily, 167
Pesticide, 32, 78, 97, 100-104, 114, 126-131,
  149-150, 216, 311-312
  Emulsifiable concentrate, 129
  National Pesticide Information Retrieval
  System, 311
Pest control and management, 8, 70, 111, 125-
  126, 130, 132-133, 134, 316
  Vertebrate pest control, 8, 70, 146
  Integrated pest management, 97, 114, 358
pH, 77, 81, 83-84, 86-87, 89, 135, 189-190,
  220-221, 230, 237-238, 255, 268, 280, 301,
  307, 319
Phacelia, 122
Phlox, 106, 167, 189
  drummondii, 144
  paniculata, 44, 57
Phomopsis, 136
Phosphorus, 82-83, 88-89, 92, 97, 249, 309,
  321
Photosynthesis, 90, 163, 274

Phyllosticta, 286
  liatridis, 273
Physalis alkekengi, 41
Physan 20, 220-221
Physostegia, 189
  virginiana, 44, 57
Phytophthora, 136, 322-323
  cactorum, 286
Phytoplasm, 137
Phytoseiulus
  longipes, 121
  persimilis, 121
Phytotoxicity, 128-129
Piercing-sucking mouthparts insects, 115-116
Pincushion flower, 42, 45, 49-50, 106, 144, 167
Plant density, 66-67, 138, 251, 301, 324
Plant Marvel Laboratories Inc., 93
Planting, 3, 6, 55-69
  Date, 55-56, 269
  Spacing, 6, 65, 72, 208, 281, 322, 328
Platycodon grandiflorum, 45
Plume celosia, 39, 51
Poast, 105-107, 321
Pocket Gopher Control, 334, 368
Pods, 38, 49, 52, 207, 330
Point-source emitters, 74-75
Polianthes tuberosa, 46
Polyethylene tubing, 75
Polygonum
  aubertii, 122
  aviculare, 122
Polymer coating, 232, 325
Poppy, 45, 49
  California, 143
Poplar, 331
Populus, 218, 331
Port Orford cedar, 46, 226
Portulaca oleracea, 144
Postharvest, 3, 8, 40, 160, 188, 194-195, 217, 252, 263-265, 274-275, 316, 324, 345
Pot Marigold, 143

Potassium, 82-83, 88-89, 97, 249, 309, 321
  nitrate, 88, 93, 258, 320
  sorbate, 230
  sulfate, 88
Potpourri, 207, 345, 350
Powdery mildew, 44, 67, 140, 250, 272, 320, 322
Praying mantis, 120
Predatory flies, 121
Preparing the bed, 58
Pre San, 258, 321
Preserve (ing), 22, 48, 160, 207-209, 217
Preservatives, 169, 171, 190, 217, 234, 316, 324, 335, 370
  Glycerin, 217-230
  Glycol, 217-218, 221, 229-230
Pride n Joy, 50
Primary feeders, 310
Prive, 51, 122
Privet, 122
Pro-Gibb, 269
Problem recognition, 134
Produce markets, 26, 256, 336, 342, 346
Production bed, 3, 6, 13, 58, 84, 98-99, 110, 152, 162, 164, 179-180, 182, 248, 251, 320
Propagation, 136, 262, 270, 287, 332, 342, 344
Propylene glycol, 217, 230
Protozoa, 117
Pseudomonas, 135
Puccinia, 136
  helianthi, 315
  poarum, 273
Pumpkin, 52, 143
Purple cone flower, 43, 141-143, 167
Purslane, 144
Pussy willow, 332
Pustules, 250, 273
PVC plastic pipe, 78
Pyrethrin, 126, 312
Pyrus, 331
Pythium, 136, 139, 322
Quercus, 47, 218, 332

Raised-bed system, 59

Ranunculus, 106, 189

   repens, 122

Rasping-sucking mouthparts insects, 116, 284

Redbud, 46, 330

Reference Books, 333, 341

Refrigerated storage, 160, 168, 196-199, 201-204, 274

   Shelf systems for refrigerated storage, 199

Refrigeration, 196, 335, 344, 368

Reindeer moss, 208

Relative humidity, 201, 203-204, 212, 216, 226-227, 229, 250, 265, 308, 322

Repellent (s), 151, 156-158, 313, 334, 367

Restricted entry interval, 103

Retail florist, 12, 27, 55, 265, 315, 336-337

Rhamnus californica, 123

Rhizoctonia, 136, 139, 303, 322

   solani, 250, 262, 287

Rhizomes, 56, 100

Rhizopus, 313, 315

Rhus, 332

Ribes, 332

Rice harvester, 183

Rice weevil, 131

Roadside sales, 15-16

Roadside stands, 13-14, 166

Roadway accessibility, 33

Rocket candytuft, 41

Rodenticides, 153-154

Rogue, 134, 140, 142, 260-261, 287

Ronilan, 269

Root-knot nematode, 273

Rosa, 49

Rose, 39, 42, 49-50, 52, 90, 143, 151, 192, 208, 247-248, 267-268, 300-301, 303, 318-319, 338

   Chafers, 284

Rosemary, 52

Rotenone, 126-127, 312

Rototiller, 64, 100, 334, 363

   Multi row, 334, 363

Rear-tine Tillers/Walking Tractors, 334, 363

Rots, 65, 136, 261-262, 287, 303

Rotylenchus buxophilus, 287

Rough pigweed, 143

Roundworms, 118

Rudbeckia

   hirta, 106, 144

   nitida, 106

Rumex acetosella, 123

Rust, 40, 136, 171, 250, 260, 272, 313, 315

Ryania, 126

Sabadilla, 126

Safer grub killer, 119

Safer insecticidal soap, 126

Sage

   Azure, 144

   Mealycup, 45

   Russian, 53

   Velvet, 41

   White, 42

Salal, 47, 218

Sales, 12-18, 20-21, 25-28, 34

Salix, 47-48, 123

   torulosa, 332

   discolor, 332

Salvia, 53

   azurea, 144

   farinacea, (Blue Salvia), 45, 49

   leucantha, 41

Sand, 32, 77, 84, 92, 101, 108, 151, 231, 248, 255, 301, 321

Santolina chamaecyparissus, 123

Scab, 260

Scabiosa, 144, 167, 189

   atropurpurea, 42, 49

   caucasica, 45, 50, 106, 123

Scabious, 123

Scare devices, 156-158

Sclerotinia sclerotiorum, 273, 287, 314, 323

Sclerotium rolfsii, 303

Sea-holly, 44, 122, 167

Seaweed, 89

Secondary feeders, 311

Seed head (s), 2, 218, 312

Seed, sources, 352-354

Seeding & Planting Equipment, 334, 361

Senecio, 106

Sepal, 284, 291

Septoria, 136

   gladioli, 262

   liatridis, 273

   paeoniae, 286

Sesbania exaltata, 123

Sevin, 128, 312

Shasta daisy, 43, 105

Shock, 24

Sidedress application, 92

Silt, 77

Silver lace vine, 122

Silver thiosulfate, 188

Sleeving, 179, 192-193, 291

Slugs, 115, 128

Snapdragon, 38-39, 105, 167

Sneezewort, 121, 246, 248

Snowmound, 48

Sodium hypochlorite, 233

Soil

   Compaction, 109

   Fumigation, 62, 144

   Microbial activity, 86, 89, 109

   Moisture regulation, 108

   Preparation, 60

   Quality of, 32

   Test, 58, 81-84, 111, 135, 249, 309, 321, 329

Sol-u-bridge, 84, 96

Solidago, 45, 52, 57, 189

   canadensis, 123

Soluble salt, 32, 84-86, 89, 135, 308

Solution depth, 194

Sonia, 51

Southern blight, 303

Sorrel, 123

Spearmint, 122

Speedwell, 107

Spergula arvensis, 123

Spider mite (s), 113, 115, 121, 128, 250, 259, 303

Spinach, 144

Spinacia oleracea, 144

Spirea, 43, 332

   Blue, 39

   Bridal wreath, 48

   Red, 48

Spotting, 72, 129, 248, 301, 320

Sprekling virus, 260

Stage of maturity, 7, 71, 162, 166-167, 218, 248, 291, 296

Stair-step shelf system, 200

Stalk, 2, 295, 314-315

Star Valley Flowers, 1, 176

State Florist Associations, 333, 340

State Flower Growers Associations, 333, 338

Statice, 41, 44, 52-53, 106, 141-143, 167, 207, 213-214, 243, 299-304, 338, 346

   German statice, 106, 218

Steinernema

   carpocapsae, 119

   feltiae, 121

Stevens Labor Model, 3, 161, 164, 195

Stock, 34, 41, 55, 106, 140, 189, 260, 281, 287, 343, 346,

Storage

   Diseases, 176, 198, 202

   Organ, 56

   Pesticide containers, 130-131

   Refrigerated, 160, 168, 196-199, 201-204, 274

   System, 172, 175, 198

   Temperature, 7, 196, 198, 201-202

Strawflower, 51-53, 106, 143, 207

Stretch wheels, 63

Stylet, 115-116, 144

Subscription, 21

Subsoilers, 334, 364

Sugar (s), 169, 189-190

Sulfate of potash-mag, 88

Sumac, 51, 332

Summer phlox, 44

Sunflower, 40, 52, 64, 106, 143, 167, 243-244, 305-316

  Head moth, 310

  Bud moth, 310

  Head-clipping weevil, 310

  Maggot, 310

  Seed weevil, 310

  Stem weevil, 310

Superphosphate, 88, 97, 301

Suppliers of Fresh Flower Food & Preservatives, 335, 369

Suppliers of General Materials, 333, 349

Suppliers of Soluble Organic Fertilizers, 333, 355

Support system, 67-69, 257

Supra, 51, 312

Surfactant, 129, 220-221, 229-230, 235, 237-239, 319

Swag, 20, 24

Sweet Lissies, 40

Sweet pea, 167, 189

Sweet William, 38, 40, 56, 143

Sycamore, 52

Synthetic Organic & Biological Controls, 333, 355

Syringia, 48

Syrphid flies, 121, 123

Systemic absorption, 218, 227-228, 233

Systemic glycol, 221

Tagetes, 106

  erecta, 144

  patula, 144

Tamarisk, 123

Tamarix, 123

Tanacetum, 50

Tansy, 50, 52, 123

Taraxacum officinale, 123

Teknar, 119

Tensiometers, 111

The Scotts Company, 93

Thielaviopsis basicola, 287

Thrip (s), 113-116, 121, 128, 137, 140-141, 250, 259, 263, 272, 284, 302, 321-322

Thuricide, 119, 128

Thyme, 53, 347

Tickseed, 143

Tielaviopsis, 136

Tomato-spotted wilt virus, 116, 140-141, 323

Tool Carriers, 334, 364

Trachymene caerulea, 123

Transpiration, 196, 201, 225-227

Transplanter, 64, 360-361, 363, 367-368

Transplanting Equipment, 334, 365

Trapping, 147, 149, 151, 153, 158

Tree leaves, 52

Treflan, 105-107, 249, 258, 309

Trellis system, 69

Tribactur, 119

Trident II, 119

Trifluralin, 249, 309

Trifolium repens, 144

Tropaeolum majus, 144

Tropicana, 51

Tuberose, 46, 167

Tubers, 45, 136

University of Wisconsin, 136, 142

Urea, 86-88, 93

  Formaldehyde, 86

Vacuum breaker, 95

Valentine's Day, 55

Value-added, 22-23, 25, 48, 207, 324-326

Variability, product 5

Vectobac, 119

Vegetable (s), 2, 17, 59, 142, 188, 207, 220, 343, 347

Vegetative growth, 90-91, 319, 321, 328

Venturi bypass, 94

Veronica, 107, 189

Vertebrate pest control, 8, 70, 146

Verticillium, 136, 273, 287

Vines, 2, 48, 69, 332

Vineyards, 69

Virus, 115-117, 135-137, 140-141, 260, 285, 287, 323

   Mosaic, 136, 260

   Sprekling , 260

   Tomato spotted wilt, 116, 140-141, 323

Visual impact, 12, 17-18, 25, 212

Vitis, 48

Wall-mounted bucket separating unit, 173

Wasps, 120-122

Water quality and filtration, 77

Watering, 3, 6, 8, 65, 70-72, 81, 91, 94, 97, 111, 133, 144, 248, 250, 257, 270, 272, 282, 285, 301, 308, 320, 322, 328

   Labor, 6

Websites, 333, 348

Weed control, 8, 13, 59-60, 70, 99-101, 104, 107-112, 117, 133, 249, 258-259, 271, 283-284, 302, 309, 321, 329, 348, 366

Weeding, 3, 6, 99-100, 249, 258-259, 271, 283-284, 329

Wheat celosia, 39

White break, 260

White clover, 144

Whiteleaf, 122

Whole-firm approach, 8

Wholesale sales

   To retailers, 26

   To wholesalers, 27

Wholesalers, 12, 27-28, 166, 265, 337-338

Wild buckwheat, 122

Wild carrot, 122

Wild mustard, 121

Willow, 47-48, 123, 332

Wilts, 136, 273, 287, 314

Wind protection, 31, 33

Windbreak (s), 31, 33, 328, 334, 360

Wireworms, 259-260

Wisteria, 332

Witch Hazel, 331

Wood ashes, 89

Wood head (s), 292-293, 295

Woodchips, 207

Woody ornamental branches, 243, 327, 329

Woody stems, 46, 277

World wide web, 26

Woven polypropylene mat, 109

Wreath (s), 19-20, 22, 24, 48, 51, 207, 326

Xanthomonas, 135

Xeranthemum, 50

Yarrow, 48, 52, 56, 66, 105, 121, 167, 207, 243, 245-246, 248-250, 252, 346

   Fernleaf, 42

Yield (s), 91, 99, 146, 164, 204, 220, 228, 251, 274, 290, 295, 306, 315, 324

Z value, 222-223, 225, 229

Zea Mays, 50

Zehrer, John, 1, 176

Zinnia, 51-52, 64, 107, 167, 207, 231, 243, 317-326

   angustifolia, 318

   elegans, 42, 144, 318, 326

   haageana, 318

ABOUT THE AUTHOR

Alan Stevens is often described as a businessman who happens to work for a university. His twenty-six years of commercial experience from wholesale production to retail floristry provide a real-life perspective to his research and teaching activities. After receiving his Ph.D. from Texas A&M University in 1990, Dr. Stevens accepted a position with Kansas State University as the extension specialist for commercial floriculture and ornamental horticulture. He has written several award-winning cooperative extension publications on specialty cut flower production and is currently conducting research into glycerin preserving and color processing decorative plant materials.

Dr. Stevens is recognized as an expert in effective labor utilization and production systems development. He is an international consultant and travels extensively teaching owners and managers how "to work smarter and not harder." His copyrighted labor model is a widely used tool for managing labor in a broad spectrum of enterprises. Dr. Stevens has served two terms on the board of directors of the National Association of Specialty Cut Flower Growers, is currently the Executive Secretary of the Kansas Greenhouse Growers Association and serves as the Director for Development of the Eastern Kansas Horticulture/ Forestry Research and Education Center.